Passion, Poison, and Pretense:

The Murder of Hingham's Postmaster

D1315853

John F. Gallagher

John F. Gallagher (signature)

Riverhaven Books

Passion, Poison, and Pretense: The Murder of Hingham's Postmaster is historically based; some dialogue and scenes are fictional and are based on the author's research and professional experiences. All materials referenced may be found in the Notes and Bibliography sections at the end of this book.

Published in the United States by Riverhaven Books
www.Riverhavenbooks.com

ISBN: 978-1-951854-14-0

Printed in the United States of America
By Country Press, Lakeville, Massachusetts

Contents

Illustrations

Series of Biographical Sketches of One Thousand Representative Men Resident In the Commonwealth of Massachusetts, A.D. 1888-89. John C. Rand (Boston: First National Publishing Company, 1890))

Benjamin W. Harris (1823-1907) (Courtesy of Library of Congress)

First Universalist Meeting House, 1885 (Courtesy of Hingham Historical Society)

First Baptist Church, 1885 (Courtesy of Hingham Historical Society)

Receiving tomb, Hingham Centre Cemetery (Courtesy of the author)

Gravestone of Sophia Gardner, Hingham Centre Cemetery (Courtesy of the author)

"Meg Merillees" (Courtesy of Library of Congress)

Faben's Great Exhibition Advertisement, *Boston Herald*, March 31, 1857

Gardner "Holiday Gifts" Advertisement, *Hingham Journal*, 1856

John Todd Tailor Shop Advertisement, *Hingham Journal*, 1857

Advertisements, *Hingham Journal*, 1857; Hunt Druggist; Dr. Don Pedro Wilson Tooth Powder

Levi Hersey (1822-1900), husband of Abby Williams Gardner (Courtesy of M. J. Molinari, Granville, MA)

Frances "Fanny" Conant (1831-1875) (Courtesy of Library of Congress)

Reverend Isaac Henry Coe (1818-1911), prison chaplain (Courtesy of the State Library of Massachusetts)

Hingham Village, 1857

(Courtesy of Hingham Historical Society)

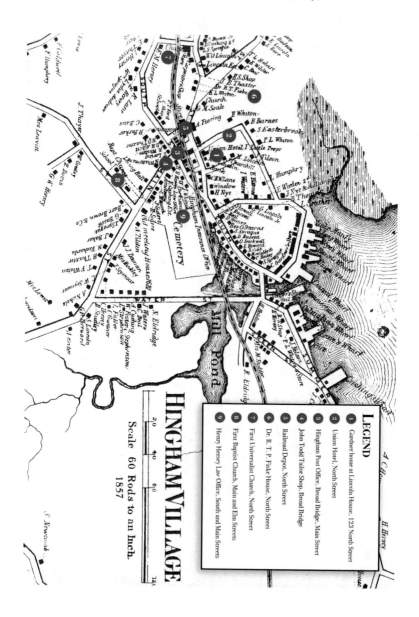

Scale 60 Rods to an Inch.

1857

HINGHAM VILLAGE

LEGEND

1   Gardner home at Lincoln House, 123 North Street

2   Union Hotel, North Street

3   Hingham Post Office, Broad Bridge, Main Street

4   John Todd Tailor Shop, Broad Bridge

5   Railroad Depot, North Street

6   Dr. R. T. P. Fiske House, North Street

7   First Universalist Church, North Street

8   First Baptist Church, Main and Elm Streets

9   Henry Hersey Law Office, South and Main Streets

Hingham Centre, 1857

(Courtesy of Hingham Historical Society)

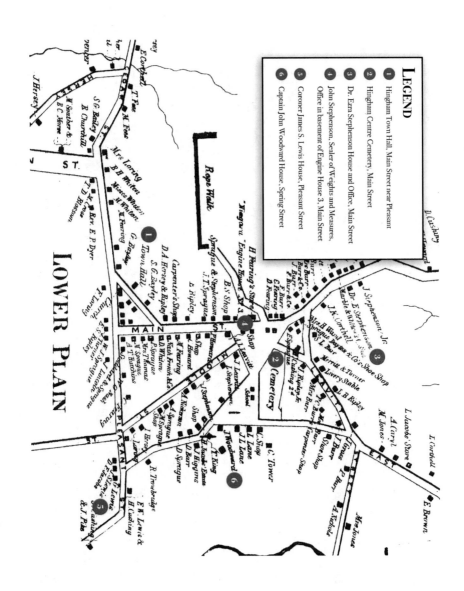

Chapter 1: An Unfortunate Mishap

Abby pleaded with her father to return home with her on the evening of January 27, 1857, but Hosea Gardner would not hear of it. There was too much work left to do before he closed up the post office and his shop in the north village of Hingham, Massachusetts. A blinding blizzard the week before had paralyzed the region and impassable snowdrifts ten to fifteen feet high had hindered the trains and coaches delivering mail. Days had passed before service was finally restored, and sacks of overdue letters and parcels lay strewn about in the cramped confines of Hosea's modest workspace.

"I can't delay this sorting any longer, Abby. I'm still far behind. It's best you return to your mother and brother before supper," he insisted.

"As you wish, Father," Abby acquiesced.

She was uneasy leaving her father alone, especially during the winter months. A light southeast breeze brought milder temperatures and moist air into the area during the day, but this gave her little consolation. The debilitating effects of a fever sore and bone disease in her father's early years had contracted the tendons of his right leg, causing a permanent, crooked deformity. The fever sore still plagued him and the cumbersome iron and rubber brace he wore hindered his mobility, especially in the snow and ice.

Gentle rain had begun to fall, so Abby stepped out of her shoes, into her boots, donned her bonnet and cloak, and pulled on her gloves.

"Be careful, Father," said Abby, retrieving her lantern and an umbrella from the stand at the doorway. "Do not tarry. I'll fret all evening awaiting your arrival home."

"Be careful yourself, Abby," Hosea replied. "I won't be long."

***

Abby's father, Hosea, had turned forty-seven the previous October. He was the eldest of six children born to Hosea, Sr. and Sophia Cole Gardner. His father died in 1840 at the age of fifty-three and left no real estate and few personal assets. His mother moved into the Hingham Centre home of his sister, Catherine, and her husband, John Wade, after his father's death.

Abby's mother, the former Abigail Marshall, was five years older than her father. Abigail was born in Islesboro, a small island off the coast of Maine in Penobscot Bay, and was raised by her parents as a Free Will Baptist. In search of a better life, she left her family farm as a young woman and ferried across the bay from Islesboro to Belfast, Maine, where she found work as a dressmaker in a tailor's shop.

When Captain Joseph Woodward entered the tailor shop on a spring day in 1829 and offered Abigail a position as a live-in domestic servant in his Hingham home, she accepted. Woodward, a master mariner and Islesboro native, had accumulated considerable wealth shipping goods and transporting passengers up and down the New England coast. He settled in Hingham in the early 1800s, married a local woman, and in 1820 built a large, Federal-style house in Hingham Centre for his wife and growing family. Abigail set sail for Hingham the next day aboard Woodward's schooner, *George*.

Abigail remained with the Woodward family until she married Hosea Gardner in 1833. She was six months pregnant on her wedding day and in May gave birth to a son, Andrew Marshall Gardner. He died four months later. Four more children were born to the couple over the next two decades, but only Abby and Marcus survived.

Abby's father had been a shoemaker and a public school teacher and had been active for many years in the towns' civic and political affairs. He had served as a Hingham selectman and assessor from 1848 until 1854, when he declined a nomination for another term to accept an appointment from President Franklin Pierce as Hingham's postmaster. He had always been a staunch temperance supporter, and when the Sons of Temperance Corner Stone Division was established in Hingham in 1846, he was among the first to be admitted. His efforts on behalf of the fraternal order did not go unnoticed, and members promptly elected him an officer the following year.

Hosea's first order of business as postmaster was to relocate the post office from North Street to a building on Broad Bridge where it would be more accessible to the village center and the train depot. Government regulations required him to keep the post office open from Monday through Saturday during "usual business hours." If mail arrived on a Sunday, he had to open the post office for one hour or more but "only after religious services had ended." He was also obliged to forward quarterly reports to the Postmaster General itemizing the types of mail sent and accepted, moneys received, and expenses paid. There was no delivery service, so everyone in town came by to collect or post letters and parcels. Her father would publish an item in the *Hingham Journal* to alert patrons if any mail remained unclaimed for ten days or more.

Hosea reserved a small area within the workplace for the sale of fancy goods, books, stationery, cigars, tobacco, and confections to supplement his $400 annual government salary. Abby assisted him with postal duties and retail sales, and in 1856, when the town connected and installed its first magnetic telegraph, her father entrusted her with full responsibility for its operation.

Abby lived with her parents and her brother, Marcus, in Hingham's North Village, the town's commercial center and the most populous of Hingham's three villages. Nearly half of the town's 4,300 inhabitants were living there in 1857. The Gardner family boarded in a rear extension of old militia captain Perez Lincoln's house on North Street, adjacent to Isaac Little's popular Union Hotel. One of Hingham's earliest settlers, Joseph Andrews, had built the Lincoln home in 1638, and it had served in the early years as a garrison to protect villagers from Indians, most notably during the Pequod and King Philip's Wars.

Abby's family had grown close to the Lincolns. When seventy-eight-year-old Captain Lincoln, infirmed and nearly blind, hanged himself in the shed behind the house the previous spring, the Gardners had consoled and comforted his widow, Deborah, and her daughters, Johanna and Lucinda, as if they were kin.

***

3

The bell atop the post office door jingled as Abby passed through and stepped outside. Across the street, an amber glow emanated from the windows of Elisha Cushing's book-binding shop and Henry Hersey's law office.

Just beyond on Main Street, a lone driver, "handling the ribbons" of his freight wagon, briskly approached the village from the south. He wheeled through the rain, slush, and mud past the First Baptist Church, Loring Hall, the "Old Ship Church," and Derby Academy. As he drew near, Abby could see it was Mr. Kenerson, the expressman. He tipped his cap and Abby waved. He slowed at the end of Broad Bridge, taking heed of the sign above the roadway – "Railroad Crossing. Look out for the engine while the bells ring." He crossed the tracks, turned left toward the depot, and disappeared from view.

Abby raised the front of her pleated hoopskirt and cloak and treaded carefully north along the icy brick sidewalk bordering the bridge. The scent of burning wood filled the air and tendrils of smoke curled lazily from chimneys as shopkeepers and villagers stoked their hearths. She saw Mr. Jones hanging his cured hams and sausages in the Hingham Market display window. His meats, fish, vegetables, and fruits were considered the finest in town. The whistle and bells of the South Shore Railroad's Boston-bound train cautioned moments later as it clacketed toward the station from Cohasset, an hour late for its scheduled 4:10 p.m. arrival. The locomotive's bright headlight illuminated the tracks and clouds of steam and lively sparks billowed from its brass nostril.

She reached the last building along the row of shops on the bridge. Everyone still called it Tilden's building even though Atherton Tilden had sold it in 1849 to the newly inaugurated South Shore Railroad. It was a two-and-one-half-story structure with two retail spaces on the first floor. Mr. Tilden leased one of the spaces and John Todd, the village tailor, leased the other. A "To Let" sign posted in Mr. Tilden's shop window announcing the closing of his hat and cap business saddened her.

Abby went next door and peered through Mr. Todd's window. She saw him altering a gentleman's suit in the soft glow of candlelight and camphene lamps. Collapsing her umbrella, she opened the shop door and entered.

"Good evening, Abby," Todd mumbled jovially, pins pressed between his lips. He removed them and offered Abby a seat. Bolts of woolen and cotton cloth, cashmeres, and doeskins lay spread on several tables. A heavy iron tailor's goose stood at the ready by the stove. Scarves, socks, gloves, shirts, collars, and suspenders were all on display as were several unfinished gowns, day dresses, men's suits, frock coats, capes, mantles, and cloaks.

"Thank you, Mr. Todd," Abby replied. "I'm sorry to trouble you, but do you intend to keep a late hour?"

"It seems I'm always here late at night, Abby, and trust I will do the same this evening. How can I help you?" the tailor asked.

"I'm concerned about Father. He insists on walking home alone in these treacherous conditions. He is overburdened with work, not only with the mail, but with his inventory. Might I impose upon you to keep an eye on him when he closes up and starts home?"

"By all means, Abby," Todd replied. "And if at all possible, I'll accompany him safely there."

"Thank you, Mr. Todd; you've always been so kind. I'll be along now. Please give my regards to Mrs. Todd. Good night."

Abby stepped from the tailor's shop and crossed the tracks. She crinkled her nose at the odor emanating from Town Brook as waste flowed easterly toward the Mill Pond through a culvert constructed by the railroad. Up ahead on North Street the ruddy, flickering radiance of candlelight and hearth danced in the windows of the old Thaxter mansion, where Mr. Leavitt lived with his family.

Abby turned east by Bampton's silk fringe and ladies' dress-trimmings manufactory in the Thaxter Building. Burr & Brown's cord and tassel dye house was beyond, its towering brick chimney belching black smoke into the darkening sky. She crossed North Street and

5

trudged by the Union Hotel where Peter Crowell was strewing rock salt on the main entrance walk and steps. He stopped momentarily and doffed his cap when she waved to him. She delighted in the lilt of his Irish brogue whenever they conversed.

Having reached the pathway alongside the Lincoln house leading to her home in the rear, she passed by the main house's sitting room window and discerned through the wavy, hand-blown glass the refracted images of Mrs. Lincoln and her two daughters, Lucinda and Johanna, wrapped in the firelight of their hearth.

Outside her door Abby stomped her boots on the mat, shook out and closed her umbrella, and extinguished her lantern before entering the house. She dropped her umbrella in the stand, removed her boots and outerwear, and carried them into the kitchen where she found her mother heating leftovers from the midday meal on the old cast-iron stove. Abby hung her clothes to dry near the hearth and warmed her hands and feet.

"Where is your father?" Abigail asked.

"He'll be along, Mother. He had some work to catch up on."

Her mother harrumphed.

Abby had grown increasingly anxious about the relationship between her parents. They had bickered constantly over the past several months, but they had taken great care to keep her and her brother Marcus from overhearing any of their more heated discussions. Recently a wall of silence had come between husband and wife, and a tense atmosphere had enveloped the home.

"Summon your brother and tell him supper is ready," Abigail instructed.

"Shouldn't we wait for Father?"

"Why?" Abigail replied. "Who knows when he'll return home?"

"Yes, Mother," Abby replied and went to the foot of the stairs leading to the bedrooms on the second floor.

"Marcus," Abby called, "we're ready to eat."

"I'll be right there, Abby," her twelve-year old brother said.

Abby waited until Marcus appeared. He hurried down the rickety stairs and accompanied her into the kitchen.

"How was school today, Marcus?" Abby asked.

"About the same as yesterday, Abby," Marcus replied. "I may be up half the night with the homework the schoolmaster assigned."

Mother, daughter, and son said a brief prayer before starting their meals. They ate in silence.

***

Hosea tidied up at about nine o'clock and scattered the last few embers remaining in the stove. He put on his black woolen cloak and his hat and gloves, locked the shop door, and started up Broad Bridge with his lantern in one hand and his cane in the other. The earlier rain had diminished into a fine mist, and most of the shops were in darkness. When he reached a point on the sidewalk just before Tilden's building, he stepped on an ice patch, lost his balance, and landed violently on his right side – his hat, cane, and lantern hurtling through the air.

John Todd heard a muffled cry for help. He opened his shop door, looked to his left, and gasped when he saw Hosea lying prone and helpless. He hastily threw on his coat and rushed to his friend's assistance. Captain James Soule was on the roadway up ahead and Todd summoned him with a wave.

"Are you alright, Hosea?" Todd asked.

"I'm in terrible pain, John," Hosea croaked. "I should have been more careful. Just give me a few moments."

"Of course, Hosea," Todd replied as his injured friend sat up.

"Here's your hat, Hosea," said Soule.

The two men waited for Hosea to recover.

"Can you make it back to your house with our help?" Todd asked.

"Yes, I'll be alright, John."

Soule picked up Hosea's cane and lantern and, with Todd, gently lifted the injured man by bracing his arms across their shoulders, and guided him home.

Soule rapped loudly on the Gardner door and Abigail answered.

7

"What has happened?" she cried.

"He took a nasty fall on the ice, Abigail," said Todd.

Abby and Marcus rushed to the door. Soule passed Hosea's cane and lantern to Marcus.

"Father, are you badly hurt? Oh, I feared this would happen," Abby sobbed. "I never should have left you!"

"Take off those wet clothes and lay him here on the sofa," Abigail instructed the two men. Todd removed Hosea's mud-spattered coat and hat and handed them to Abby. Hosea moaned and said he felt faint.

"Abby, is there any camphor and cologne here in the house?" Todd inquired.

The young woman left with the coat and hat and returned quickly with the strongly scented spirits and some cotton batting. Todd waved the oils to and fro beneath Hosea's nose and dabbed them on his forehead to revive him.

"Is this really necessary, Hosea?" Abigail chided, a cross look on her face. "It seems to me you're quite alright and will be up and out again in a day."

Soule and Todd looked at each other, bewildered. Abby and Marcus stood silently, their faces flush with embarrassment.

"John, I'd best send for a doctor," the sea captain said and left the house.

"Are you feeling any better, Hosea?" asked Todd.

"I'm still in unbearable pain, John. I'd be more comfortable without my boots. Would you mind?"

Todd bent to remove Hosea's right boot and Abigail said to her husband, "I should think you could take them off yourself and not trouble Mr. Todd."

Todd's eyes met Hosea's momentarily. He ignored Abigail's remark and slipped off the boots.

"From the way Mr. Todd took your boots off, I shouldn't suppose you were hurt much," Abigail scoffed with a haughty arch of an eyebrow.

She turned to Todd and said, "I can't see how Hosea could have hurt himself by merely slipping down. I've known people to fall twenty feet and not get hurt."

"I'll have to return to my shop, Abigail," Todd interjected, incredulous at her remark. "I left in haste and didn't lock the door." Turning to Hosea he said, "I'll be back as soon as I can."

Todd went back and retrieved a lighted lantern, locked the door to his shop, and as he descended the steps, Dr. Ezra Stephenson approached in his carriage. The fifty-one-year-old physician and Hingham native had attended local schools and Derby Academy. He was a skilled carpenter but had abandoned the trade to study medicine. He had received his medical degree from Harvard College in 1832 and opened his first practice in Barnstable on Cape Cod. He had remained there for six years before returning to his hometown to assume Dr. William Gordon's practice after his retirement.

Stephenson pulled up on his mare's reins when Todd hailed him with a wave.

"Doctor, your help is needed at Hosea Gardner's house. He has taken a bad fall."

"I heard, John. Captain Soule sent Mr. Little's Irishman, Peter, to tell me about the unfortunate accident."

"I just left Hosea's," Todd told Stephenson, "and I'd prefer not to return unless you need me. I stayed as long as I could bear it."

"What do you mean?" Stephenson asked.

"I'm appalled at the wife's treatment toward the poor man. He was in agony and she showed little sympathy for him."

"Just the same, I'd like for you to come along."

Todd acquiesced and boarded the carriage. The two men arrived at the Gardner home to find Hosea still lying on the sofa. Hosea's face was ashen and contorted with pain. The doctor performed a cursory examination and suggested moving the stricken man to his bedroom.

James Soule returned to the house and, with Todd and Stephenson, carried Hosea to an adjacent room and gently lowered

9

him onto the feather bedding.

"Are you doing any better, Hosea?" asked Soule.

Before her suffering husband could answer, Abigail replied, "You see he's well enough to take his boots off and you wouldn't suppose he was hurt much."

Soule's face darkened but he did not reply.

Dr. Stephenson cleared the room before he and Abigail removed Hosea's clothing and brace and dressed him in a nightshirt.

"What happened, Hosea?" the physician asked.

"I was walking along the bridge and slipped on the ice. My lame leg and hip took the worst of it," Hosea replied.

"Did you lose consciousness?"

"I believe so."

Stephenson examined Hosea's head and found no obvious trauma, but he couldn't rule out a concussion. There was tenderness and a contusion on the right side of Hosea's hip, but no broken or dislocated bones. He removed the dressing from the fever sore on Hosea's right leg and cleaned it with a soft cotton cloth and warm water before applying calomel and a fresh bandage.

"I'm going to administer some morphine for the pain, Hosea, and I'm prescribing camphor to hasten the bruise on your hip. This will increase blood flow around the injury. I expect you'll still be in some pain in the morning, but you haven't broken any bones. You'll recover. In the meantime, get plenty of rest."

"Thank you, Ezra," said Hosea as the physician collected his instruments and placed them inside his medical bag.

"I'll check back in the morning, Hosea," Stephenson said and quietly closed the door as he left the room.

Soule and Todd joined Hosea's family as they gathered around the doctor when he emerged.

"You'll have to keep an eye on him, Abigail. Call for me immediately if he shows signs of confusion or immobility in his arms and legs. Persistent vomiting and constant headache may also raise cause for concern," the physician said. "I'll return tomorrow. If his condition worsens in the meantime, don't hesitate to send for me."

Abigail saw Stephenson, Soule, and Todd to the door and Abby rushed to her father's bedroom, breathless and teary-eyed.

"I'm so sorry, Father," she sniveled and took Hosea's hand. "I never should have left you."

"There, there, Abby. It's not your fault. I was careless. I'll be fine once this pain subsides. I'll need you to take care of business at the office for a few days."

"Of course, Father. Can I get anything for you? You must be famished."

"No, I'm fine, Abby."

"Alright, Father. Now get some rest; and please don't let Mother anger you. You know how she can be."

Abby kissed her father and gently released his hand. She tiptoed from the room and closed the door.

Outside the house, Stephenson, Soule, and Todd drew together amid the soft glow of their lanterns. Todd expressed his disdain at Abigail's coldness toward her husband.

Stephenson knew the reason for Abigail's demeaning behavior but he wouldn't share it. Only ten days before, Hosea told him in confidence about the discord and deceit within the Gardner household. But he would not violate Hosea's trust.

"There's not much we can do about it," Stephenson said to Todd. "It's a family matter and best left alone. Hosea's daughter, Abby, will do everything she can to make sure her father is kept comfortable. Goodnight, gentlemen," said the doctor as he boarded his buggy and started for home.

***

When Hosea woke up on Wednesday morning, January 28, he was still in pain. He asked Abby to have Marcus run to his sister Catherine's home to inform his mother, Sophia, about his injury and ask if she would visit until he was back on his feet. Abigail overheard the conversation and entered the room.

11

"There is no need for your mother to come here, Hosea," Abigail said. "I can take care of you perfectly well."

"I know you can, Abigail, but you're busy enough just minding the household. Mother can help," said Hosea. "Send Marcus along, Abby."

Abigail glared at her husband and stormed out.

"Grandmother will be here within the hour," Marcus said to his father when he returned

"Thank you, Marcus; make sure the bed upstairs is prepared for her. I want you to go right to school as soon as she gets here," Hosea said.

Abby said goodbye to her father before she left the house for the post office.

"I hope you're feeling better when I return, Father," Abby said. "Is there anything in particular you need taken care of at the office and shop?"

"No, no, Abby," said Hosea. "I'm sure everything will be fine in your capable hands. I made great progress with the sorting yesterday. I expect you'll be busy with patrons who are eager to claim tardy mail and packages."

"Don't concern yourself, Father. Right now, it's more important for you to take heed of your health. I'll be fine."

***

Dr. Stephenson was tending to Hosea at his bedside when Sophia arrived. Marcus greeted his grandmother with an embrace at the front door.

"Let me take it for you, Grandmother," Marcus said as he reached for her overnight bag. "Father is in the front bedroom with Dr. Stephenson. Mother's in the kitchen. I'll bring your bag upstairs."

"Thank you, dear," the petite woman said as she hastened to Hosea's side.

"Oh, Hosea," Sophia lamented at the sight of her prostrated son. "Are you in much pain, dear?" she asked tenderly as she removed her heavy cloak. A bright glow emanated from the fireplace and warmed the room.

12

Hosea diminished the seriousness of his condition to allay his mother's fears.

"I'm fine, Mother. I took a minor fall last night and landed on my hip. It's somewhat painful, but the doctor has provided some relief."

"I'm treating him with chloroform liniment, Sophia," Dr. Stephenson said. "It should help ease the pain and hasten the healing. In the meantime, I'm prescribing two doses of [Epsom] salts, one teaspoonful each. The trauma to Hosea's hip may hinder his ability to purge his bowels, which I'll have to watch closely. The salts will promote evacuation and a drop of gin or brandy will help with digestion. Hosea should be back on his feet soon."

"Thank you, Ezra. I'll be staying for a few days to help Abigail keep Hosea comfortable."

Stephenson removed his pocket watch from his vest and, after a brief glance, hurriedly gathered his overcoat and medical bag.

"I have another appointment, Hosea. I'll come by again tomorrow."

Sophia pulled up a chair next to Hosea's bed. There she stayed throughout the day, applying the liniment and administering the salts. Although he vomited several times after taking the salts, by late afternoon, Hosea's condition had significantly improved.

Abigail came into the room early in the evening and Hosea asked her if he might have some gin.

"What about your pledge of abstinence?"

"Ezra said it may help, Abigail, and Hosea is permitted to use spirits as a medicinal remedy," Sophia said.

Abigail crossed her arms and scowled. "I'll get it for you, Hosea, but I don't want to hear any complaints if you start vomiting again," his wife chided.

"Perhaps I could have a bit of beef steak, too."

"I'll broil it up, Hosea," Sophia interjected.

"Thank you, Mother. The way I feel now, I shouldn't be surprised if I'm good as new in a few days."

"Hosea," his mother replied, "do not be hasty. It is best you wait until you're well rested. Abby is capable of seeing to your duties."

Hosea's optimism elated Sophia. She hurried into the kitchen, added some coal to the stove, and prepared the beef. Abigail removed a small flagon of gin and a glass from a cupboard. She added water and sugar and left the kitchen without a word.

Sophia put the beef on a plate when it was cooked and returned to Hosea's bedroom with a napkin and silverware. She found him sipping the gin Abigail had prepared.

Hosea pursed his lips.

"Where did you get this gin, Abigail? It has a queer taste," her husband said.

"I'm sure there's nothing wrong with it, Hosea. The medications you're taking are probably altering it," Abigail replied and left the room.

Sophia sliced the beef steak and fed Hosea small portions.

"Thank you, Mother. I can't recall my last meal."

Nearly finished, he held up a palm to his mother. The color drained from his face. He twisted sharply for the basin next to his bed and heaved.

"Oh, dear," Sophia exclaimed. She rose and set the plate and utensils on her chair and steadied the basin in Hosea's hands.

Abigail stormed into the room.

"This is just what I meant," she barked. "I warned you, Hosea."

She turned on her heel and left her mother-in-law to cope unassisted.

Sophia emptied the ewer on the washstand into a clean basin when Hosea quieted. She soaked his napkin in the cool water and folded it across his forehead. Sophia was entranced by the steady rise and fall of his chest as sleep overtook him. She dozed in a chair by the bed until a chill in the room woke her at about midnight. She added wood to the hearth, tucked the covers around her son, caressed his face, and wearily ascended the stairs to her bed.

***

14

On Thursday afternoon, January 29, Dr. Stephenson visited again and was pleased with Hosea's progress.

"The pain is much better, Ezra," Hosea said. "My hip is sore only when I move."

"I'm glad to hear of it, Hosea," said the physician as he laid aside the bedcovers and Hosea's nightshirt to examine the bruise.

"I'm still having some difficulty with nausea. When do you suspect this will subside?"

"Your stomach will settle, soon, Hosea. It is probably the salts. Have you had a bowel movement?" Stephenson asked.

"He has," grumbled Abigail, as she shifted impatiently at the foot of the bed.

"Very good," the doctor remarked, and turned to Hosea. "Let's halve the dosage of salts, but continue to drink fluids and, if possible, eat something light, Hosea. You should notice significant improvement by tomorrow morning. I'll come by at about nine to check on you."

Hosea rested for much of the day and by afternoon felt well enough to start the postmaster general's report. Early in the evening Abby returned from the post office and shop with the day's proceeds and together they balanced the respective accounts and completed most of the postal quarterly.

"You go on to bed now, Abby," her grandmother directed. "I'll stay here with your father."

"Alright, Grandmother," Abby replied. She kissed her father and grandmother goodnight and went up to her room.

***

By nine o'clock, Sophia had grown drowsy. She covered Hosea with an extra blanket before she withdrew to retire. She started up the stairs to her room when she heard Abigail in the kitchen.

"Goodnight, Abigail," said Sophia, poking her head through the kitchen doorway. "I'll be up early to look in on Hosea. If you need me for anything during the night, please wake me."

"He'll be fine, Sophia. I'll see to him," she replied.

Nearly an hour later, Abigail roused Sophia.

15

"He's talking crazy, Sophia. I think he's possessed by the 'Old Boy.' He says he's going to die."

Sophia tossed off her covers, alighted from the bed, stepped into her slippers, and wrapped a shawl around her shoulders. She followed Abigail by candlelight.

Sophia found her son complaining of agonizing stomach pain. She prepared a mustard poultice, lifted his nightshirt, and placed it across his abdomen. The heat seemed to provide Hosea with some relief.

Abigail withdrew from the room. It was more than an hour before she returned.

"How long do you expect to sit here, Sophia?" Abigail asked. "It's getting very late."

"I'm fine, Abigail."

"This is nonsense, Sophia. Go back to sleep. I am perfectly capable of taking care of him as a wife should."

"It's no trouble at all, Abigail. I'll stay with him."

Abigail glared at her and said, "You'll do it without a fire then; I do not intend to keep it burning. We have little firewood to spare."

Sophia watched in disbelief as Abigail extinguished the flames in the hearth and walked out in a huff. A poker scratched and scraped and fire hissed in the kitchen. Abigail stomped to the back chamber and slammed the door.

It was about three o'clock in the morning before Sophia left Hosea's bedside. He had drifted into slumber an hour before and seemed much more at ease. She tucked him in, kissed him tenderly on the forehead, and ascended the stairs to her room.

***

Sophia rose at six the next morning, Friday, January 30, and found her grandson feeding the fireplace in the kitchen.

"Good morning, Marcus. I hope you slept well," Sophia said.

"Good morning, Grandmother. I did, and I hope you did as well. I've started the fire in Father's room. He was sound asleep. I'll be leaving for school after breakfast; is there anything I can do for you before I go?"

16

"No, thank you, Marcus. I'll make myself some tea and toast after I've seen your father."

Abby and Abigail came into the kitchen. They all greeted one another and Abigail began preparing breakfast for her family.

Hosea was still sleeping when his mother entered his bedroom. Marcus's fire crackled and sparked on the grate as the flames consumed the seasoned cordwood.

Sophia waited quietly for Hosea to awaken. Suddenly he lurched, snatched the basin on his bedside table, and vomited. Abigail heard him from the kitchen and came into the room with Abby and Marcus.

"I have been suffering all night with stomach pain and retching," Hosea moaned. "I thought by now the effects of the salts would have dissipated."

Sophia took the basin and inspected the contents. The greenish matter was unlike anything she had ever seen.

"I don't like the looks of this, Hosea. I'll send for Dr. Stephenson immediately."

"It is indeed strange looking. It looks as if I've been eating spiders."

"Let me see it," said Abigail, wresting the basin from Sophia's hands and briefly examining the contents. She started for the door so she could dispose of this just as she had with the rest of her husband's repulsive bile.

"Abigail, save it for Dr. Stephenson to see," Hosea pleaded.

"I will do no such thing," Abigail declared. "I won't have this stinking stuff in my house."

"Abigail, please. It may allow Dr. Stephenson to better diagnose Hosea's condition," Sophia implored.

Despite Sophia's insistence and the children's pleadings for her to stop, Abigail rushed away with the basin and pitched the vomit into a slop pail at the back door. "If the doctor wants the disgusting filth so much, he can pick it up out of the water," Abigail scoffed at her children.

"Mother, I believe my wife has poisoned me," Hosea confided after Abigail had left the room. "Please be careful. I have no doubts she will try to poison us all. She says we are the greatest curses on earth."

"Surely you can't believe she would try to poison her own family, Hosea," Sophia said. "As much as I dislike her, I don't believe she is evil enough to do such a thing."

***

Dr. Stephenson reached the house as promised at nine o'clock and found Hosea retching. The physician was both perplexed and alarmed. Hosea complained of great thirst; his face was swollen and pinkish in color, his tongue a deep red and enlarged, his throat constricted.

"My stomach is burning up, Ezra," Hosea rasped. "It feels hot enough to make water hiss."

Stephenson turned to Abigail. "Have you been giving him the salts?"

"Of course," Abigail replied.

"Have they been effective?"

"It seems to me they operated sufficiently."

"That's not true, Abigail," Sophia said.

Abigail shot an angry look at Sophia and glowered at Hosea when he corroborated his mother's contradiction.

"Why have you deceived me, Abigail?" the doctor asked.

"I have not deceived you," Abigail fumed. "There was ample evidence of evacuation as far as I'm concerned," she protested, and stormed from the room.

"I cannot stress enough the importance of purging, Hosea. I'm going to give you some calomel. In one hour you're to take another dose with a teaspoonful of castor oil and lemon juice. Repeat every hour until you've had an operation but no more than three times," Stephenson directed.

"Ezra, I vomited earlier this morning," Hosea croaked. "It was green and not like anything I have ever seen. It looked as though I was spewing spiders. I wanted to show it to you but Abigail threw it out."

"We tried to stop her, the children and I, Ezra, but Abigail was determined to discard it," Sophia interjected.

"It was likely bile, Hosea, which indicates a possible bowel obstruction," Stephenson said.

Sophia stayed with her son for the rest of the day and most of the evening. His wife came into the room occasionally but said nothing. Hosea's brother, Alfred, came to visit but by then the concoction the doctor had recommended had proven effective after a second dose and Hosea had fallen asleep.

Chapter 2: An Inexplicable Death

Swirling snow and a brisk wind greeted Dr. Stephenson when he left his office in Hingham Centre early Saturday morning, January 31. Squinting through the flurry of flakes, he proceeded to the barn, removed his mare's heavy woolen blanket, and strapped on a feed bag of oats. He gave the horse some water before he hitched it to his buggy and set off for the Gardner house.

He found his patient in a perilous state. Hosea had satisfactorily purged himself but the burning heat of his stomach and the retching had continued. His heartbeat had slowed to an almost imperceptible pulse at the wrist, and he complained of a tingling sensation throughout his body.

Stephenson found this rapid decline in Hosea's condition and the appearance of new symptoms inexplicable. He was beside himself thinking he had missed something.

He discontinued the use of camphor and calomel and ordered the unrestricted use of brandy and beef tea, the application of mustard poultices to the stomach for pain, and frequent massage of Hosea's extremities to alleviate the peculiar prickling he was experiencing. Stephenson left the house gravely concerned about Hosea's survival.

When the physician returned in the afternoon, he found Hosea with no change in his heart rate. The retching and burning sensation in Hosea's stomach had continued unabated, the swelling of his face and tongue had increased, and his hands and feet were slightly blue. He had no recommendations for Sophia and Abigail other than to continue with the brandy and tea and the stimulation of Hosea's hands and feet.

***

Family friend Edwin Wilder visited after Stephenson's departure. Wilder, a twenty-eight-year-old house painter and glazier, had traveled from his home on Main Street where he lived with his family opposite the Second Parish Church in South Hingham. Abigail met him at the door and led him to the bedroom where Sophia was watching over Hosea as he slept.

"How is he keeping, Sophia?" Edwin whispered.

Wilder's voice awakened Hosea. He gave his friend a weak smile.

"It is good to see you, Edwin," Hosea said hoarsely.

"And you as well, Hosea," Wilder replied.

Sophia and Abigail left the room to give Wilder some time alone with Hosea. A moment later, Hosea dozed off. Wind and hail pattered the bedroom window as Wilder sat quietly on a small, slat-backed chair and watched his friend in slumber, his mouth slack.

Hosea reawakened presently and told Edwin he had enjoyed quite a nap. He drifted in and out of consciousness over the next hour, occasionally uttering unintelligible words and phrases. Edwin placed his hand on Hosea's forehead and knew at once his friend was burning up. He placed a cool, wet cloth across Hosea's brow.

"I don't understand this," Sophia whispered to Edwin when she reentered the room. "Only days ago it seemed he would recover. Now I fear the worst."

"I worry as well, Sophia. What does Dr. Stephenson say?"

"He is as bewildered as I, Edwin, and says he has done everything he can for Hosea."

"Is it possible Hosea has somehow ingested something to worsen his condition?"

Sophia shuddered as she contemplated Hosea's frightening words the day before about Abigail and poison. It couldn't be. Abigail would never do such a thing.

"I don't know how, Edwin," Sophia replied. "Abigail and I have been the only ones to administer the medications, and we have been with Hosea constantly. I've recently given him morphine as directed by Dr. Stephenson, but it was a small dose; certainly not enough to cause this dreadful change."

21

Wilder somberly shook his head and stood.

"I must return home now, Sophia, but I'll come back this evening. Is there anything I can do for you?"

"No, Edwin; there is no need. Thank you for coming."

Wilder withdrew and made his way to Otis Hersey's house. Otis was living nearby with his brother Franklin on North Street opposite the Hingham Insurance building.

"I just left Hosea, Otis. He's in a terrible way. I'm certain our friend won't be with us much longer," Wilder said to the forty-year-old silk and tassel maker.

"How can this be?" Hersey asked. "I heard he was making progress."

"Hosea's mother has been at his bedside since the mishap. She's puzzled by Hosea's rapid decline since he seemed much improved several days ago. I thought about poisoning and asked her what, if anything, had been given to Hosea to bring about the delirious state he was in. She said she had given him a small dose of morphine on Dr. Stephenson's orders, but it was so minimal it would not have caused the symptoms Hosea was displaying."

"It saddens me to hear this, Edwin," Hersey said.

"I'm going back to the house this evening to see if there is anything I can do to help the family, Otis."

"I'll join you there, Edwin, as soon as I've taken care of a few matters here."

Wilder returned to the Gardner home at about nine o'clock and found Hosea barely breathing. Otis Hersey arrived a half hour later and was met at the door by Lucinda Lincoln, who was there to help.

"Come in, Otis," Lucinda said. "The family is with Hosea in the front bedroom."

When Hersey entered the room, Hosea's mother, wife, and daughter were gathered around Hosea's bedside. They acknowledged him and thanked him for coming.

"Otis, may I have a word with you?" Wilder asked as he started from the room.

"I'm fetching Dr. Stephenson, Otis," Wilder said, buttoning his coat in the hallway. "I don't know what he'll be able to do for poor Hosea at this point, but at the very least he might make him more comfortable."

The hail had subsided and a steady rain had melted much of the earlier snow when Wilder came back with the doctor at about ten o'clock. Stephenson applied mustard poultices, and administered brandy and water and some drops of morphine, which he gave to Hosea every fifteen minutes.

"There is no need for you to remain," Stephenson told the family. "It's late and you all must be very tired. Please retire to your rooms. Edwin and Otis will keep watch with Hosea."

The family acquiesced and withdrew, but less than thirty minutes later, Abigail had returned.

"I can't sleep with his groaning," she muttered. "Besides, I think my place right now is with my husband."

"Very well, Abigail," said Stephenson. "I have another patient to see. I'll return as soon as I can. In the meantime, I've asked Edwin and Otis to continue with the brandy and water at fifteen-minute intervals."

Stephenson departed at eleven o'clock. Edwin took the tumbler of brandy and water from the stand beside the bed at the prescribed time, gently lifted Hosea's head from the pillow, and placed the tumbler to his lips. Hosea sipped feebly for a moment and Edwin set his head back down. He administered several drops of morphine. He repeated the dose fifteen minutes later, and again at the half-hour mark. At 11:45 p.m., he administered a third dose and almost immediately, Hosea began to retch.

Edwin turned to Abigail when Hosea settled and said, "I have not the heart to give the poor man another dose. He has suffered enough."

"Edwin, we must follow the doctor's orders," Abigail insisted.

"Abigail, I agree with Edwin," said Otis.

"Well, he's my husband. We'll give him another dose."

Soon the parlor clock struck midnight, heralding the advent of Sunday, February 1. Once more, Wilder pressed the tumbler to Hosea's lips but before the dying man could ingest the brandy, he bolted upright, eyes wide open, and vomited.

"Oh! Don't give him any more, Edwin," Abigail finally relented. "Let him die in peace."

Hosea quieted. It was still in the room, save the crackling fire and the clock's muted cadence. At thirty minutes past the hour, Hosea's face reddened and his breathing became shallower. Abigail rushed from the room and ascended the stairs to wake Abby and Hosea's mother but left Marcus undisturbed. Abby and Sophia sprang from their beds and hastened to Hosea's side. An hour later, the stricken man was dead.

Abby fell prostrate upon Hosea's lifeless form.

"Please, please Father, do not leave us," she wailed.

Pangs of guilt engulfed her. How could she ever forgive herself for letting her father walk home alone on the night he fell?

Abigail took her daughter by the arm and led her from the bed to the sofa in the parlor. Abby tried to free herself from her mother's grasp but Abigail would not let go.

"Stop sobbing, Abby. It is wrong to do so. It is the Lord's will and it is all for the best. You have always treated your father well and you have nothing to reflect upon. You must try to be resigned."

Hersey intervened, took Abby by the hand to the bed, and supported her as she gazed upon her father with love and tenderness. She bent and kissed his forehead, turned and embraced Sophia, and quietly withdrew from the room and ascended the stairs to her bed.

Hersey and Wilder remained with Abigail and Sophia. Hersey saw Abigail shed tears, but he did not believe her grief was sincere; he had witnessed her cold, indifferent behavior the entire night. Not once had she shown her departed husband a sign of tenderness. It was more important for her to stop the clocks in the bedroom and parlor. She superstitiously believed that if a clock stopped on its own with a corpse in the house, another family member would die within the year.

Sophia retired to her room upstairs. Abigail returned from the parlor and asked Wilder and Hersey for help with Hosea's funeral and burial arrangements.

"I'll find some decent clothes for him," Abigail said when the two men assented. She found a shirt and trousers in Hosea's chest, took them into the kitchen, and placed an iron on the fire. She returned to the death room with the freshly pressed clothing and gave them to Wilder.

"We'll need a clean white sheet, Abigail," he said.

Abigail returned a moment later and handed the sheet to Wilder.

"I must lie down," she said, and withdrew to her bed in the back chamber.

Wilder and Hersey removed Hosea's nightclothes and bathed him as best as they could. They dressed the corpse, wrapped it tightly in the sheet they had spread on the floor, and carried it to the parlor where they lowered it onto the sofa. Two hours had passed before Abigail returned to the parlor.

"Thank you both for your kindness. I imagine you're both quite hungry. I'll fix some breakfast."

Wilder and Hersey went back to the death room after they had eaten to dismantle the bed and dispense with the soiled feather mattress and bedcoverings. Abigail appeared at the doorway.

"Edwin, leave the bed as it is," Abigail protested.

"Certainly you don't want to keep this in the house?" Wilder asked.

Abigail paused momentarily.

"I suppose you're right, Edwin," she said and stepped to the bed's footboard.

Wilder thought he saw her take something from beneath the mattress. She held her tightly closed hand firmly against her side and hastened from the room.

"Did you see what she did, Otis?" Wilder asked.

"No, what happened, Edwin?" Hersey replied.

"I'm not positive, but Abigail may have taken something from the bed she didn't want us to see."

"What do you think it was?"

"I don't know, but it certainly seemed suspicious," said Wilder.

The two men rolled up the mattress and bed coverings and tied them with a soiled sheet they had ripped into strips. Wilder put them in his carriage for later disposal.

"Abigail, we will notify Mr. Newhall about Hosea's death and order a coffin. You can speak with him about funeral arrangements."

"Thank you, Edwin. I don't know how I can possibly pay for it."

"You needn't worry. The Sons of Temperance will assume the costs for the funeral and burial. Hosea is entitled to it as a chapter member."

"I wasn't aware. I'm relieved to hear this, Edwin."

Abigail thanked the two men once more and they departed.

***

Abby heard Mr. Wilder and Mr. Hersey bid her mother goodbye and leave through the front door. She went to Marcus's bed and gently stirred him awake. Marcus mumbled incoherently and pulled his covers over his head.

"Marcus, please," Abby persisted.

He threw his blanket aside and turned to her.

"What is it, Abby?"

When he saw his sister's tired, sorrowful expression he paled.

"Is Father alright?"

"Marcus, Father has left us. He is in God's hands now," Abby whispered softly.

Marcus's eyes welled up and he began to whimper. Abby embraced him and rocked him tenderly in her arms.

"We'll have to be strong for Mother and Grandmother now, Marcus. There will be a visitation here and a funeral at Father's

26

church in a few days. I'm going to need your help getting the house ready. I'll send a message to the school and ask them to excuse you."

"Where is Father now?"

"His body is at rest in the parlor."

"I want to see him!" Marcus exclaimed. He jumped from his bed and scampered down the stairs in his bedclothes.

Abby rushed after him. Marcus stood before his father's lifeless form reposing on the sofa. He inched forward and delicately lifted the shroud to expose his father's fixed, ashen countenance.

"He seems at peace, Abby," Marcus remarked solemnly, tears in his eyes.

"He is at peace now, Marcus. We will miss him dearly," Abby said as she pulled Marcus close.

Abby removed a pair of scissors from her housedress and bent close to her father's head.

"What are you doing, Abby?"

"I'm going to snip two locks of Father's hair."

"Are you sure it's alright?" asked Marcus, alarmed.

"Do not fret, dearest brother. These will be precious mementos of Father."

Abby cut the hair and placed the locks in separate paper folds. She handed one to Marcus.

"Keep this in a safe place, Marcus, and do not mention to Mother what I've done."

Abigail called from the kitchen.

"Abby, Marcus, come in here. We have much to do before the funeral. Both of you will need mourning clothes. See if you can borrow something appropriate from your friends or cousins. With your father's income now gone, we have little to spend on new clothing."

Abigail went to the back door of the house when the children left and retrieved the slop pail. She stepped into the shed behind the house, found a shovel, and tramped through the snow to the backyard. She quickly dug a hole, emptied and covered the contents of the pail, and returned the shovel. When she emerged from the shed, Dr. Stephenson was pulling his buggy up in front of the house. Undertaker Newhall arrived in his wagon moments later. She watched as the two men spoke briefly and greeted them as they came up the walk.

Joseph Newhall, a thirty-four-year-old carpenter, had been in business with his partner, Joseph Ripley, since 1845. Ripley & Newhall manufactured coffins, cabinets, and household furniture in their shop on South Street. In 1842, when he was in partnership with his brother, Nehemiah, Ripley had extended his business to include undertaker services.

Stephenson led Newhall to the parlor and Hosea's corpse while Abigail busied herself in the kitchen. The undertaker frowned when he saw the bend in Hosea's stiffened, deformed leg.

"Ezra, the leg is going to pose a problem," Newhall said. "The body will not fit into a standard coffin. I cannot design and build a custom box in time for the visitation tomorrow. Is there anything you can do to straighten the leg?" he asked.

"As much as I'd rather not do so, Joseph, I'm sure I can modify it surgically. Let me first inquire of Mrs. Gardner."

Stephenson stepped into the kitchen and found Abigail stoking the fire. He explained the circumstances and asked if she had any objection to his severing and straightening the leg.

"It certainly won't do him any harm now, Ezra."

"Very well, Abigail," said Stephenson, somewhat astonished by her callous response.

"I'll have to return to my office for my instruments and a table," Stephenson said to Newhall. "Can you meet me back here in an hour?"

"Certainly, Ezra," replied Newhall.

Stephenson retrieved his medical bag, surgical instruments,

dressings, and a portable table and found Newhall waiting outside the Gardner home when he got back. He set up the table in the room where Hosea had breathed his last and, with Newhall, carried the corpse from the parlor and laid it with care on the table. Stephenson parted the drapes for more light, closed the bedroom door, and proceeded to unravel the lower half of the shroud. Newhall removed the trousers.

"I'll need you to keep pressure on the leg for me, Joseph."

Once the leg was straightened, Newhall pulled on the trousers, Stephenson re-wrapped the shroud, and together they carried the corpse back to the parlor. Newhall's measurements assured him the body would accommodate a standard box.

"I'll be back this afternoon with the coffin and a bier, Doctor," Newhall said. "I'll ask Mrs. Gardner where she'd like to have the body laid out before I leave."

***

Abby busied herself preparing the house for the visitation to take place on Monday afternoon, February 2. Joanna and Lucinda Lincoln helped about the house with the cleaning, although Abby didn't think it necessary since her mother kept every room immaculate.

Abby and the Lincolns adorned interior windows and doorways, the parlor fireplace mantel, and the coffin bearing Hosea's corpse with black crape. Fresh pine boughs were cut and placed on the mantel and about the coffin to mask unpleasant odors. White cloths were draped over mirrors and picture glass and a black crape wreath with black ribbons was tacked to the front door's exterior.

"Why must we cover everything in black, Abby?" Marcus asked.

"It is a symbol of our mourning, Marcus, and a show of respect for Father. This is why we will wear black during the vigil and funeral. The wreath on the front door informs passersby of the presence of death and grief in our home."

"What about the white cloths covering the mirrors and picture glass?"

"Marcus, this may be difficult for you to understand," Abby answered gently. "Many believe the deceased's spirit will become trapped and haunt the house forever if it sees its reflection."

Marcus's eyes widened.

"But Abby, surely Father wouldn't frighten us."

"Of course not, Marcus," Abby said. "And if it was up to me, we wouldn't entertain such notions, but Mother insists on it."

"What will happen at the vigil and funeral, Abby?"

"Father's family and many of his friends will come to the house to pay their respects, Marcus. Grandmother and others will bring food and drink to the house for those who wish to spend some time with us during the visitation. The vigil will continue until the following morning, when we will bring Father to the Universalist Church for his funeral and the Centre Cemetery for his entombment."

"Why the Universalist Church, Abby? Father worshipped there, but Mother has always taken us to the Baptist Church."

"I know, Marcus. Mother intends to speak with Reverend Cargill about the arrangements. She's going to ask him if he will allow our pastor, Mr. Tilson, to participate during the service. Now please, do not worry. All will be well."

***

Flickering lamps and candles cast eerie shadows on the walls and ceiling as friends and relatives passed somberly by Hosea's coffin, offering condolences to Abigail, her children, and Hosea's mother.

Abby could not help but notice how indifferent her mother seemed. She watched as her mother greeted sympathizers with frivolity and good humor. Not once since her father died had Abby witnessed her mother express sorrow. Surely, Abby thought, the solemnity and finality of this occasion would arouse some sign of grief, but it was not to be.

Rev. Mr. John Cargill, Hosea's pastor from the First Universalist Meeting House on North Street, arrived at the house to pay his respects and led everyone present in prayers of supplication. When the brief service ended, Abigail guided the pastor into her kitchen.

"Mr. Cargill," Abigail began, "I am certain you and Hosea have discussed my preference to practice my faith as a Baptist. He has forbidden me to attend the church with our children and on several occasions has threatened me when I refused to abide by his wishes. I will respect Hosea's desire for a funeral at the church of his choice, but I must insist on the presence of my pastor, Rev. Mr. Jonathan Tilson, at the service. I have discussed this with Rev. Tilson and he has agreed to participate with your permission."

Cargill was struck by Abigail's business-like attitude and callousness during their conversation. He would not contest this strong-willed woman during this period of mourning and politely acceded to her demand.

"Mrs. Gardner, I welcome the participation of my friend, Rev. Mr. Tilson, at the service. I will call on him this evening," Cargill replied.

"Thank you, Mr. Cargill," said Abigail.

Among the many other mourners who visited the Gardner home was Dr. Don Pedro Wilson, a thirty-five-year-old dentist who practiced at the Union Hotel and in Boston. After offering his sympathies to Abigail and her family, he glanced up to see Dr. Stephenson enter the house. Wilson greeted him before he removed his overcoat and asked if he would step outside for a word.

"Ezra, I am troubled by a curious incident I witnessed on the morning Hosea died. I was in the hotel's outhouse behind the Gardner home and happened to hear a scratching sound. I looked out through the window and noticed Hosea's wife with a shovel digging a hole in the snow. She had a slop pail with her and emptied its contents into the hole and covered it. I thought it odd

31

she would discard the waste there rather than in the privy vault."

"It does seem a bit mysterious, Don Pedro," the physician replied.

"Well, there's more, Ezra. I happened to see my cats go near the slops and, a short time later, they died. Something in the slops, I suspect, killed them. I'm going to have a word with Mrs. Gardner. She should know better than to carelessly dispense with something harmful to the birds and animals."

"I'm sorry about your cats, Don Pedro. What did you do with them?"

"I put them in the vault. The ground was too hard to bury them."

The two men parted. Stephenson found Wilson's statements worrisome. The slops Abigail buried were likely from the pail containing the vomit Hosea's mother and children had insisted she save for his inspection. Perhaps Wilson was mistaken and there was another explanation, but it was too much of a coincidence. He wished Wilson had buried the cats rather than putting them in the privy where by now they would likely be corrupted and decomposed. A necropsy might have helped confirm the cause of death.

Stephenson went back inside and approached Hosea's mother to offer his condolences. Sophia leaned close, saw Abigail across the room engaged in conversation, and whispered, "Thank you, Ezra. Can you stop by my home after visitation? I'd like to discuss an urgent matter."

"Of course, Sophia," the physician replied.

Stephenson expressed his sympathies to Abigail and the rest of the Gardner family and departed. Later in the evening, he drew up to the Wade house on School Street in Hingham Centre where Sophia boarded with her daughter Catherine. Sophia invited him into her parlor and they sat by the fire.

"Ezra," Sophia began, "I have not slept since Hosea's death.

My mind is in great distress thinking about all I saw and heard while I nursed him. God forgive me, but I believe his death was by foul means perpetrated upon him by his wife. On the Friday before he died, Hosea said Abigail had poisoned him and warned she would do the same to me. I refused to believe Abigail would do such a thing and thought the medications had impaired Hosea's mind; but now, in retrospect, I believe she did poison him. I was deeply troubled by Abigail's lack of emotion at the wake and funeral. It was as if Hosea's passing had relieved her of some burden."

"Sophia," the physician said, "I, too, have suspicions, and I regret I did not conduct a post-mortem examination before this."

"Oh, Ezra," Sophia lamented, "I should have said something about this before, but I so much wanted to believe Hosea's death was brought about by the injury to his leg."

"It pains me to say this, Sophia, but I believe it is imperative that I perform an autopsy to confirm the cause of death."

Tears welled up in Sophia's eyes. She composed herself and after a few moments said, "I agree, Ezra. It distresses me, but you must do so."

"I will see to it, Sophia. I'll speak with Abby and Abigail and, after I've received their consent, I will proceed."

"Thank you, Ezra," Sophia said, "and I pray your examination will disprove the unspeakable thoughts coursing through my mind."

Stephenson bid Sophia goodnight and started for home. He recalled now with deep regret the distressing conversation he had had with Hosea at the post office a week and a half before Hosea had fallen on the bridge…

***

"Thank you for coming, my friend," Hosea had begun with sadness in his eyes. "I must speak with you about an extremely unpleasant matter. It concerns my wife. Please, sit down.

"I am in constant fear of Abigail and believe she wants to take

33

my life," Hosea said as he pulled up a chair for the physician. "I haven't slept for a long time and suspect I never will as long as I share a bed with her."

Stephenson was startled and asked, "What has she done or said to make you believe she has such intentions?"

"Ezra, time and again she has expressed her cruel opinion of me, calling me a nasty, worthless mass of corruption and telling me nothing would cure me but a ground sweat. If she had her way, she said, I should soon have one. She made the same remarks about my daughter, Abby."

Stephenson had found this incomprehensible: Abigail threatening her husband and daughter with a grave?

"Frankly, I'm surprised at this, Hosea. I had always believed you and Abigail enjoyed a stable relationship."

"No, Ezra; it is, alas, a bitter union. She has accused me of being impotent and has taken up with someone here in the village. I have spoken with this man, and I have advised him to refrain from keeping further company with my wife.

"I'm sure she wants me out of the way for this reason. In fact, I think she'd prefer to rid herself of the children, too. She has struck my son in the past and has generally been abusive toward both children."

Hosea was reluctant to identify the man, and Stephenson hadn't pressed.

"How can I help, Hosea?" Stephenson had asked.

"Will you speak with her? I think she has lost her mind."

"Alright, Hosea," Stephenson had said. "I'll have a discreet conversation with her and have an answer for you as soon as possible."

***

Stephenson tried to recollect when he had met with Abigail. He wasn't sure if it was the same day or the day after his conversation with Hosea. He remembered he had spoken with her at length and, in his professional opinion, she had shown no indication of insanity. Her only complaint was insomnia, and he had prescribed valerian.

He had returned to the post office the next day and disclosed his opinion to Hosea.

"There was nothing to indicate Abigail is mentally unstable, Hosea," the doctor had said. "If you still feel threatened, I'd suggest you leave her."

"As much as I'd like to, Ezra, I cannot, and it's because of the children. I cannot uproot them nor can I leave them for fear of what she might do to them. I'd never forgive myself for allowing such a thing to happen."

"Very well, Hosea," Stephenson recalled saying. "I respect your position, but if the threats continue, you must reconsider."

Stephenson remembered passing the Gardner home a week later and Abigail, who was out front, had called to him.

"Good day, Dr. Stephenson," Abigail had said. "Would you mind spending a few moments with me? I'm afraid the valerian has not helped."

The physician had followed Abigail into the house, removed his cap and outerwear, and sat at the kitchen table.

"Doctor," Abigail had said, "I must admit my insomnia cannot be relieved by medication. A heavy burden lies in my breast, and I cannot bear another day without speaking with someone about it. I beg you to hold our conversation in the strictest confidence."

"Of course, Abigail," Stephenson had replied.

"My husband is jealous of me and he is justified in feeling so. He is cross with me because he knows I love another man more than I love him. I lie awake at night thinking if I could have this other man by my side instead of my husband, I should be perfectly happy. Mr. Gardner is good for nothing as a man."

"This is most troubling, Abigail."

Abigail had nodded, tears filling her eyes.

Stephenson had then urged her to end the affair.

"Alas, if only it could be, but there is one complication. I am with child, and the child is not my husband's," Abigail had blurted.

This declaration had startled Stephenson, and he recollected asking Abigail several pointed medical questions and performing a very brief physical examination.

"In my professional opinion, Abigail, there are no symptoms to suggest you are with child. A more extensive physical examination is pointless."

"I'm certain of my condition, Doctor, and I will somehow find a way to cope," Abigail had asserted, dabbing at her eyes. "I suppose I must live on in my misery because the man I love has a wife and I have a husband."

"Who is this man with whom you have become involved?"

"I'd rather not say," Abigail had replied with downcast eyes.

Stephenson had changed the subject and had offered her a stronger medication.

"Thank you, Doctor, but I'm fearful anything I ingest might jeopardize this child and interfere with its birth. I would not have this child killed for the world."

***

On a crisp, bright Tuesday morning, February 3, pallbearers carried Hosea's coffin from the Gardner home to a waiting horse-drawn, black draped hearse. Abigail, Abby, and Marcus followed and took seats in a similarly adorned closed carriage. Passersby stopped and watched in silence as the cortege made its way through the village along North Street and past the depot to the Universalist meeting house. Friends, family, and neighbors wearing black mourning badges and cockades had filled the modest church to overflowing.

The church doors opened and the organist's plaintive reeds signaled the commencement of services. Everyone rose and Newhall entered with Hosea's coffin, wreaths and sprays of artificial flowers strewn atop it. The pallbearers lowered the coffin on a four-wheeled bier the church sexton had positioned beforehand and proceeded down the center aisle to the foot of the altar.

Rev. Cargill began the service with an opening prayer and readings from the Scriptures. Abigail sat stoically and Abby wept as each of the ministers delivered eulogies and offered consolation.

Mourners in carriages, wagons, and on foot followed the hearse on North Street and up Main to Hingham Centre Cemetery after the funeral. Caretakers had shoveled paths throughout the graveyard beforehand. The hearse proceeded through the northwest gate and passed headstones, obelisks, and box tombs before it reached four mound tombs, the first two owned by the Burr and Ripley families and the third and fourth used by the cemetery to store the dead until the frozen earth gave way to the spade and shovel in the spring. The hearse drew up to the third tomb. Newhall's assistants removed the heavy iron door, lifted the coffin from the hearse, placed it at the foot of the vault, and carefully arranged the wreaths and sprays alongside it. Reverends Cargill and Tilson led the assembly in final prayers and, when they concluded, Newhall's men guided Hosea's coffin through the damp, dark tomb's narrow opening and sealed it.

Dr. Stephenson rode to the post office an hour after the burial. He secured his horse and carriage to a hitching post out front and stepped inside to find Abby sorting mail for the newly appointed postmaster, Charles Siders. Siders, a forty-four-year-old Hingham ship broker had initially declined the post and had petitioned for Abby's appointment, but she did not meet the government's age requirements. He kept Abby in his employ as an assistant and had promised to hold the post for her until she reached age twenty-one in October.

Hingham businessman John Barnard acquired the space once occupied by Hosea and offered for sale the same articles of books, stationery, fancy goods, cigars, and tobacco. Barnard paid Abby a modest wage to assist him in the shop.

"Good morning, Charles. May I have a private word with Abby?"

"Good morning, Ezra," said Siders.

"Hello, Ezra," said Barnard.

"Of course you may," Siders answered. "John and I were about to step out for a few minutes anyway."

The two men threw on their coats and hats and left the shop, closing the door quietly behind them.

"How are you keeping, Abby?"

"I'm much better; thank you, Doctor. Staying busy helps me cope with Father's loss."

Abby's eyes were still puffy from hours of weeping.

"Abby, do you have a few moments for us to speak confidentially?"

"Of course, Doctor. Come with me into Mr. Siders's office."

Stephenson followed Abby into the same office where he had met Hosea more than two weeks before.

"Abby, I am deeply troubled by your father's death," Stephenson began. "There was no evidence during my initial treatment of his injury to suggest anything other than a full recovery. Unfortunately, there is only one way I can learn the true cause of his death. I must remove his body from the tomb and perform a post-mortem examination. I am truly sorry I hadn't considered this before."

"Oh, Dr. Stephenson, I am much confused and curious about Father's death as well."

Her eyes filled with tears. "It distresses me to disturb Father's resting place, but it would gratify me to know for sure. I can't bear to think he died from anything other than mortification of his leg, but an examination will bring my family and me peace of mind."

"Thank you for your understanding, Abby. I did not want to proceed without your consent. I have spoken with your grandmother, and she shares the same concerns," Stephenson replied. "I'm going to speak with your mother. Hopefully, she will be of the same mind."

"I don't know what to expect from Mother anymore, Doctor. Certainly everyone else in the family would agree an autopsy is prudent," Abby said.

Stephenson bid farewell and rode the short distance to the Lincoln house. He pulled his buggy up, tied his horse's reins to a post, and ambled up the path to the Gardner home in the rear. Abigail answered his knock on the door.

"Come in, Doctor," Abigail said as she widened the doorway. "What brings you here?"

Stephenson stepped in and got straight to the point.

"Abigail, I understand this is painful for you to consider, but I'm at a loss to determine what may have caused Hosea's death. I'd like to perform a post-mortem examination, but I'll need your consent before I do so," said Stephenson.

"I most certainly will not agree to such a thing!" Abigail hissed. "How can you come here and make such a cruel request?"

"I understand, Abigail, but I would be remiss if I did not make a determination. I regret I could not save Hosea, and I hope by examining his body I will be better prepared to identify similar symptoms in other patients who need my care."

"That's all well and good, Doctor, but I have always had a great dread and horror of such things and will not permit it," Abigail declared.

Stephenson would not yield, but the more he entreated her, the firmer she became in her objections.

"Very well," said an exasperated Stephenson at last. "I will do my best to honor your wishes, Abigail. Good day."

***

Stephenson dropped in on forty-nine-year-old druggist James L. Hunt at his apothecary on North Street to replenish his inventory of medications after his visit with Abigail.

"Good afternoon, Jim," Stephenson said, approaching the counter.

"Hello, Ezra. What can I do for you today?" Hunt replied.

Stephenson presented Hunt with a list.

"A shame about Hosea, Ezra," said Hunt as he perused the order. He looked up at the physician and paused momentarily before asking, "Is there anything to the rumor he was poisoned?"

"Why do you inquire, Jim?"

Stephenson was surprised Hosea's death had already become the topic of suspicious speculation in the village.

"Well, a peculiar thing happened but five days before Hosea fell on the bridge. His wife sent a young boy to my store for arsenic."

"What?" the physician exclaimed, stunned by this revelation.

"Yes, the young Dodge boy came and presented a note from Abigail asking for the poison. I packaged it carefully and sent him on his way. I was surprised she would send the boy out in the deep snow for it."

"Did the boy say why she needed it?"

"No, but I assumed it was for the same reason most everyone comes to me – a problem with rodents."

"Then what makes you think it was peculiar?"

"Well, the boy came back again and said Abigail had sent him to explain the poison was not for her but for an Irish woman at the cove. I couldn't understand why she would trouble the boy to trudge through the snow again to tell me."

"I know where you're going with this, Jim, and I hope I'm wrong. Do you still have the note the boy gave you?"

"No, I've disposed of it, Ezra."

"Jim, I'm not in a position to elaborate, but for now it is best we keep our conversation confidential."

"I understand, Ezra."

Stephenson completed his order, left Hunt's shop, and walked to the nearby Miller house where the Dodge boy lived with his aunt and uncle. He was met at the door by Dodge's aunt, Martha.

"Sorry to trouble you, Mrs. Miller. May I have a word with Charles?"

"What's this all about, Dr. Stephenson?"

"I'd like to ask about a recent errand he may have gone on."

"Charles, come down here," the aunt called. "Come inside, Doctor."

The eleven-year-old boy descended the stairs and greeted the physician.

"Hello, Charles," said Stephenson. "I have a question for you. Did you go on an errand for Mrs. Gardner recently?"

"Yes, it was about two weeks ago. I remember it was almost right after the storm. She asked me to take a note and some money to Mr. Hunt and return with what he gave me."

"Did you know what Mr. Hunt gave you?"

"No, I didn't, but I gave the packet to Mrs. Gardner and she gave me two cents."

"Did she ask you to do anything else?"

"Well, she asked me if I had told Mr. Hunt who the packet was for. I said I told him it was for her. She said, 'No, no, I got the packet for a Paddy woman who lives down by the cove. Go back to Mr. Hunt and tell him so.'"

"Did you go back to Mr. Hunt?"

"Yes, and I told him what Mrs. Gardner asked me to say."

"Alright, thank you, Charles."

The boy hurried back up the stairs to his room and his aunt turned to Stephenson.

"Is there anything wrong, Doctor? Is Charles in trouble?"

"On the contrary, Mrs. Miller," said Stephenson. "He has been very helpful. I can't get into any specifics, but if I need to speak with Charles again, I trust you won't object."

"Of course not, Dr. Stephenson. I'm somewhat confused and hope you'll soon explain."

"I promise you, Mrs. Miller, in due time the purpose of my visit will become quite clear. Good day."

Dark thoughts coursed through Stephenson's mind. He had

41

considered the possibility of poisoning on the Friday before Hosea died. He wished now he had recognized the symptoms before it was too late.

***

Stephenson answered a rap on the door of his Main Street home at dusk.

"Hello, Ezra. I hope I'm not intruding," said Reuben Reed, the thirty-one-year old husband of Hosea's sister, Alice.

"Not at all," said the doctor. "Please come inside."

Stephenson directed Reed to his office where the two men took seats.

"Doctor, I won't obfuscate. You've spoken with my mother-in-law and my wife and I, like her, fear foul play in Hosea's death. His wife is wretched and has caused Hosea nothing but grief for many years. Hosea has spoken to me in the past about threats his wife has made against him. He even mentioned poison. I regret I never said anything about this during Hosea's convalescence. My wife and I will not rest until we are certain this woman did not purposely rid herself of him."

"I can't say this is the first time I've heard these threats, Reuben, and I am as suspicious as you are. Hosea had also told me about his fears, and today I went to his wife and asked for permission to remove Hosea's body from the tomb and perform an autopsy. She refused."

"We're not interested in Abigail's opinion in the matter, Doctor. The rest of the family insists on an examination of the remains. I am prepared to remove the body in the morning with your assistance."

"I can't possibly do so, Reuben. It would be untoward and certainly illegal. Since Hosea's wife will not consent, the only way for the examination to proceed is through a coroner's lawful order. This will likely necessitate an inquest, and I intend to visit with Mr. Lewis this evening."

"Perhaps I should accompany you?"

42

"It's not necessary, Reuben."

"Very well, Doctor. Thank you very much and goodnight. I look forward to hearing from you."

Stephenson left for the nearby home of Justice of the Peace James Lewis on Pleasant Street after Reed's departure. Besides his duties as coroner, the fifty-eight-year-old cooper had held positions as Hingham town clerk, selectman, and school committee member.

Stephenson informed Lewis about the suspicious circumstances surrounding Hosea's death.

"I cannot confirm the cause of death without examining the body, James," said the physician. "I only wish I had arranged for the autopsy immediately after Hosea's death. I had fully expected him to recover, and when his condition worsened, I feared it was the salts I had ordered, or perhaps the calomel I had prescribed. The calomel, a combination of mercury and chloride, is a purgative and can be poisonous, but I don't believe he had ingested enough to cause death. Hosea's rapid decline, his statements to me about threats made by his wife, allegations made by his mother and brother-in-law, the deaths of Dr. Wilson's cats, the most recent revelation about Abigail's purchase of arsenic from Jim Hunt, and – with the exception of Hosea's wife – the family's insistence for an autopsy, now leads me to believe he may have died of arsenical poisoning. I implore you to open an investigation into his death without delay."

"An inquest is certainly in order, Ezra," Lewis said. "I will summon a jury to appear before me tomorrow afternoon at two o'clock. I'll need your testimony. I'll also have Hosea's mother give an account."

"Thank you, James."

"By the way, Ezra," Lewis said. "Did Newhall embalm the body before he delivered it to the tomb? I understand there is a growing trend among undertakers to preserve bodies with all manner of compounds, most notably arsenic."

43

"No, he did not. It certainly would have complicated the situation."

"Very well, Ezra. I'll see you tomorrow. Goodnight."

"Goodnight, James."

Chapter 3: An Inquest

On Wednesday morning, February 4, Coroner Lewis met with forty-seven-year-old housewright and town constable Gridley Hersey to relate the details of his conversation with Dr. Stephenson the night before and his decision to convene an inquest.

"Gridley, speak with Sophia Gardner and tell her I'll need her testimony at two this afternoon. She'll know what it's about. I also want you to instruct David and Martin Fearing, Peter and Joseph Sprague, George Bayley, and Demerick Marble to appear at Town Hall an hour before to serve as inquest jurors."

Built in 1845 and located on Main Street near Pleasant Street opposite the First Congregational Church, Hingham Town Hall was a light grey wooden structure, seventy by forty-two feet, with ten windows in the front, a transom over the front door, and a window in the back gable end. A large entryway led to a hall heated by two large fireplaces and adjoined by several committee rooms. A stairway separated by an iron banister led to a gallery on the second floor. There were four rows of seats in the gallery, and in the hall eighty-one settees, seven feet long, with a hat rack attached to each.

The inquest convened here at the appointed time and place, and the jurors were sworn in. Coroner Lewis appointed Martin Fearing as jury foreman. Abigail was not present, nor was she aware of the proceeding.

Coroner Lewis called the inquest to order and asked Dr. Stephenson to step forward and take the witness chair.

"Dr. Stephenson, before you sit, please raise your right hand. You solemnly swear the evidence which you shall give to this inquest, concerning the death of Hosea Gardner, shall be the truth, the whole truth, and nothing but the truth, so help you God?"

"I do," said Stephenson. He then related the circumstances surrounding his call to the Gardner home on the night Hosea had fallen, the subsequent treatment he had extended, and the steady decline in his patient's health.

"I knew not how to account for my patient's alarming symptoms. His spine and his brain were uninjured as far as I could judge. I prescribed demulcents to soothe his stomach, and cathartics to move his bowels.

"Between ten and twelve o'clock on Saturday evening, January thirty-first, I was again called to visit him. I found him insensible. The pulse at the wrist had ceased. The extremities were cold and death was evidently near at hand. I left. He died about one-thirty o'clock on Sunday morning, February first.

"When asked of what disease he died, I said I could not tell. The symptoms were new to me. They seemed to have no connection with the injury received by his fall. It is possible some existing latent disease in the stomach may have been forced into activity by the concussion produced by his falling. But wishing to be enlightened as to the cause of his death, I suggested to his daughter the propriety of a post-mortem examination, and she approved, in fact, desired it. But his widow, although she expressed an earnest desire to know the cause of her husband's death, utterly refused to consent to an examination of his body."

"Thank you, Dr. Stephenson. You may return to your seat in the gallery. The jury would now like to hear from Mrs. Sophia Gardner," said Lewis.

Sophia nodded to Dr. Stephenson as she proceeded to the witness chair.

Lewis administered the oath to Sophia and said, "Mrs. Gardner, thank you for coming. Please accept our condolences. Will you please relate for this inquest the circumstances attending Hosea's death?"

Sophia explained how Hosea had summoned her to his home to

nurse him after his fall. She went into great detail about Abigail's behavior during Hosea's convalescence and her refusal to save the queer looking vomit Hosea had expelled on Friday morning, January thirtieth.

"Was Hosea aware Abigail had discarded the vomit?"

"Yes, he was."

"How did he react?" Lewis inquired.

"When Abigail left the room with the basin, Hosea said he believed she had poisoned him and cautioned me, 'Take care, she will poison you, for she says we are the greatest curses on earth.' I said she would not poison me, and tried to divert his mind from the subject."

"What happened next, Mrs. Gardner?"

"On Saturday, the thirty-first, Mr. Edwin Wilder watched with my son. He said he thought my son must have taken something and asked me if he had taken morphine. I told him he had taken a very small quantity as medicine – nothing to hurt anybody."

"Mrs. Gardner, this inquest is of a mind to authorize a post-mortem examination of your son's remains. Do you have any objection to this?"

"I do not."

"Thank you, Mrs. Gardner. You are excused. At this time, I hereby authorize a disentombment and a post-mortem examination of Hosea J. Gardner's remains. This inquest is adjourned until such time as physicians have completed their analysis and reported their results."

Lewis and Stephenson conferred when the hall had cleared.

"I'm assuming you will perform the autopsy, Ezra."

"Yes, Joseph, but I'll call on Dr. Calvin Ellis, a pathologist at Massachusetts General Hospital, to assist me. He has extensive experience with post-mortem examinations. I'll also notify Dr. Charles Jackson, the state assayer, to analyze the viscera. I'll meet with Dr. Fiske at his office on North Street after I leave here to request his assistance, too. I'll tentatively schedule the autopsy for Friday to allow time for everyone to clear their calendars. I'll let you know when I've confirmed the details."

***

Undertaker Joseph Newhall and several assistants returned to Hingham Centre Cemetery in a wagon on Friday to remove and transport Hosea's corpse. A light rain had fallen and the air was thick and foggy. State assayer Dr. Jackson, Drs. Stephenson, Ellis, and Fiske, Coroner Lewis, the inquest jurors, and Hosea's brother-in-law, Reuben Reed, were present. A small group of curious passersby had gathered in the cemetery and were kept at a respectful distance by Constable Hersey.

Newhall's men pulled the wooden box out from the tomb's narrow opening and placed it on the snow. A sudden gust shook the overhanging tree branches and droplets spattered hats and coats and the coffin's top. A pair of chickadees chirped cheerfully from within the bare branches of a sleeping forsythia, oblivious to the grim, unfolding drama. Newhall pried open the sealed lid and set it aside. All reverently removed their hats and caps and surrounded the coffin to obstruct the view of onlookers.

"Jurors, please raise your right hands," said Lewis. "You solemnly swear you will diligently inquire, and true presentment make, in behalf of this Commonwealth, when, how, and by what means, the person, whose body lies here dead, came to his death; and you shall return a true inquest thereof, according to your knowledge, and such evidence as shall be laid before you, so help you God."

"I do," said the jurors in unison.

"All here, perhaps with the exception of Drs. Jackson and Ellis, knew Hosea Gardner during his lifetime," said Lewis. "Do you all agree, as you gaze upon the face in this coffin, it is in fact Hosea Gardner whose mortal remains lie within?"

The jurors nodded solemnly.

"Very well," Lewis said. "Mr. Newhall, please secure the

48

coffin and take it to Dr. Stephenson's office. The jurors are dismissed. Reuben, there is no need for you to accompany the body. I will ensure its safe return after the physicians have completed the post-mortem examination."

Newhall's men replaced the lid, hoisted the coffin onto the wagon, and took it to Stephenson's office three hundred yards away on Main Street. The body was removed from the coffin in the physician's examination room and placed on a portable "cooling" board, a table with cane latticework through which blood and fluids drained into a tray underneath. An ice block under the tray chilled the body and helped retard further decomposition.

Coroner Lewis spread wide the window drapes for light and cracked the windows to minimize the cadaver's putrescent odor. After Drs. Ellis and Fiske undressed the corpse, Ellis drained the blood vessels and began the examination with Stephenson's assistance. Fiske documented their observations and comments.

The physicians immediately noted the body was mostly pink in tone but the abdominal area displayed a greenish hue. Dr. Ellis used a scalpel to score the body's trunk from shoulder to shoulder above the sternum and from the sternum's upper margin along the midline to the umbilicus, exposing the abdominal cavity where he observed a small amount of serum. He and Ellis noted the stomach was a reddish color and was visibly inflamed. There was similar inflammation in the membranes supporting the intestines.

Stephenson bisected the sternum with a saw and separated the rib cage. The lungs showed no significant congestion and the heart contained some blood but was otherwise healthy in appearance.

Ellis made an incision from ear to ear at the back of the cadaver's skull and pulled back the scalp. Stephenson made two cuts in an elliptical pattern with a saw and removed a portion of the skull to expose the brain. Both men concluded the brain and membranes showed no abnormality.

Ellis opened the stomach and found some dark brown fluid.

The membrane lining was a pale green color and inflamed at the opening near the esophagus.

He closed the incision he had made in the stomach, tied it off high at the esophagus and low at the duodenum to preserve its contents, slit the connecting tissue, removed the organ, and weighed it on a clean scale. He reopened the stomach and deposited its contents into a sterilized glass vial which he marked and hermetically sealed. He sealed the empty organ in a separate sanitized bottle.

The small intestine was inflamed and contained a small amount of dark mucus. Thin fecal matter was found in the large intestine. Ellis preserved the intestines and their contents as he had with the stomach.

He examined the liver and kidneys and saw no abnormalities. He also examined the reproductive organs and ruled out impotence.

The last procedure was an inspection of the diseased right thigh. Stephenson had noted about two inches of dead bone when he altered the leg with Newhall.

"Some in the family have suggested Hosea may have died due to mortification of the leg, Calvin. I saw nothing to confirm the notion. I think it prudent for us both to examine it once more for the record," Stephenson said.

Ellis scored the leg along the prior incision and scrutinized the femur and connecting tissue.

"I agree with your opinion, Ezra," said Ellis. "Dr. Fiske, please take note. Dr. Stephenson and I have ruled out the diseased leg as a contributing factor in the death."

As soon as Stephenson had sutured all the incisions and re-dressed Hosea's corpse, Newhall's men returned it to the coffin and the receiving tomb.

Dr. Fiske completed his documentation and all three physicians attested to its accuracy with their signature. Dr. Ellis agreed to personally deliver the extracted viscera to state assayer Jackson for chemical analysis without delay.

***

50

Communicants attending services at the Universalist Meeting House two days later were astonished by Abigail's appearance with local expressman Eli Kenerson. A low murmur filled the church as the pair strolled down the center aisle and took seats on a bench near the front.

The church bell pealed and worshippers filed out when the services concluded. Three women huddled outside, watching incredulously as Abigail boarded her escort's wagon and the two departed.

"Can you believe this woman's gall?" asked one.

"It is shameful!" another exclaimed.

"Imagine them, sitting together as if a couple – her recently widowed and him a married man," said the first woman.

"Shush," said the third woman. "We don't know if there is anything going on between them. It's all rumor and innuendo."

"Oh, it's no secret here in town. They've have been carrying on for some time now," said the second woman. "Kenerson and his wife live in one side of old Mr. Hammond's house on North Street. The poor man is blind and Mrs. Kenerson sees to him. From what I understand, people have seen Abigail sneaking into the man's stable behind her house while he was there. But to think she would cavort with him so publicly when her husband died a week ago is simply disgraceful."

"How horrid!" the third woman cried. "Please stop; you should be ashamed. We have no proof there is anything intimate going on between them, and it's unfair to the man's poor wife."

"Speaking of the man's poor wife, I've heard Abigail has been sending her fancy dishes and confections. Someone said she laced the food with poison to do away with her and claim the husband," the second blurted.

"How ghastly!" the first exclaimed.

The three grew quiet.

"I don't understand why she's attending services here," the first woman resumed. "She's never stepped inside, except for Hosea's

51

funeral. It's my understanding she has always been in fellowship with the Baptist Church."

"Hosea once confided to me about the discord between him and his wife over their chosen places of worship. They had bickered on many occasions, mostly about their children and the church they would attend," the second confirmed. "As far as her fellowship with the Baptists, I've heard they have dispelled her from the congregation because of her adultery."

"I don't know about that," the first woman replied, "but a friend of hers told me they had quarreled on the Sunday before Hosea died. She said Hosea was in the habit of liberally abusing her when it came to their diverse opinions about the Sabbath and how it should be observed."

"It was about the post office. Hosea was obligated to open it on Sundays and she never accepted it," the second replied.

"I'll tell you how cold-hearted she is," said the second woman. "I understand she was quite ill some time ago and had sent for her sister to come from Down East to care for her. The sister was in feeble health at the time and her friends had urged her not to go. She came anyway and found Abigail much more comfortable than she had expected. The sister waited on Abigail until she herself had become so weakened she could not attend her any longer. And do you suppose Abigail reciprocated and saw to her sister? Oh, no. She sent the sister to the almshouse where the poor woman soon died."

"Can you imagine?" the first woman exclaimed. "After the kindness her sister had extended; how dreadful!"

The third woman had heard enough. "Well, as much as I'd like to continue with this idle gossip, ladies," she said sarcastically, "I must be along to prepare Sunday dinner. Good day."

"What is she getting so haughty about?" the first woman asked.

"Oh, don't pay any attention to her. She can be a bit snobbish at times."

The two friends laughed.

***

Coroner Lewis received a letter on February 10, four days after the autopsy, and hurried to Ezra Stephenson's office.

"Ezra, I have a grave report from Dr. Jackson," said Lewis and handed it to the physician.

Sir: I received by the hands of Dr. Calvin Ellis of Boston, the contents of the stomach and intestines of the late Henry (sic) Gardner, of Hingham, with the request to analyse (sic) them for poison. He also exhibited to me the stomach from the deceased person. I have made a thorough chemical examination of the contents of the bowels above mentioned, and have discovered a large quantity of arsenic in the fecal matter, obviously enough to have been the cause of death of the individual. In the course of a few days the precipitate will have subsided so as to enable me to determine the quantity of arsenic present, and I shall ascertain this point for the question is sometimes asked how much poison was present. I have fully proved the substance to be arsenic, by all the approved methods.

Charles T. Jackson, M. D., State Assayer, etc.

Stephenson removed his spectacles and looked up.

"This confirms what I had most feared, Joseph," he said sadly.

"I will have Constable Hersey place Mrs. Gardner under arrest. I intend to reconvene the inquest at four this afternoon and will need you for further testimony."

"Of course, Joseph; thank you," the doctor replied.

Lewis issued subpoenas for James Hunt, Charles Dodge, and Dr. Don Pedro Wilson, and instructed Constable Hersey to deliver them without delay. Hersey filed his signed returns of service at Lewis's office within the hour. Lewis handed him an arrest warrant for Abigail.

Hersey served Abigail at her home at three o'clock. Marcus was at school and Abby was busy at the post office.

"Mrs. Gardner, I am here with a warrant," Gridley announced as he entered the house and handed it to her.

"What have I done, Gridley?" Abigail cried. "How do you know he didn't poison himself? Who's to say his mother didn't do it?"

Hersey was taken aback at first by her questions but then realized inquest testimony and news about the autopsy had undoubtedly reached her ears. He made note of her unsolicited, incriminating remark.

"Stop and read it, Mrs. Gardner," Hersey demanded. "I don't know what the warrant contains."

"I can't read, Gridley," Abigail said and threw the document at him. He reacted quickly and smothered it on his chest.

"There's no need for you to be rude, Mrs. Gardner."

Gridley read the warrant to her.

"I absolutely deny the charges," she declared

"Well, you must come with me at any rate."

"Gridley, I cannot go. I have to attend to affairs here at home."

"I'm afraid they will have to wait."

"I'll need time to change," she grumbled.

"Fine, but please do not tarry."

Abigail went to her bedroom and dressed in her mourning clothes.

Gridley waited patiently but was anxious. "It's getting late. Are you ready to start?" the constable shouted.

Finally Abigail emerged from the bedroom and donned her bonnet and shawl. Gridley led her outside where she spoke briefly with Lucinda and Joanna Lincoln who were at their doorway intent on finding out why the constable's carriage was at the house.

"Joanna," Abigail said, "I am going with Mr. Hersey to the town hall. Will you please tell my children where I've gone when they return home?"

"Of course, Abigail," the forty-nine-year-old spinster replied. "Is everything all right?"

"Yes, yes, Joanna. I just need to straighten out some business."

"Shall I say when you'll be back?"

"I'm not certain, but I expect it will be before supper."

***

Gridley escorted Abigail into the hall and a seat at a table opposite Coroner Lewis at quarter to four. She was not represented by counsel. The inquest jury was seated to Lewis's left. Word about the inquest had spread far and wide and the hall was filled with Gardner family members, friends, townspeople, and reporters from Boston dailies and the *Hingham Journal*. Never in the memories of even the oldest of Hingham's residents had a murder taken place in their tranquil, harmonious community.

Lewis began in a voice trembling with emotion. "Mrs. Gardner, you are entitled to legal counsel before this proceeding begins. Do you have a lawyer to represent you?"

"I do not; nor do I need one," Abigail snapped. Although she was dressed in mourning, she was not wearing a veil and her scowl was there for all to see.

"Very well, Mrs. Gardner," answered Lewis. "We will proceed."

"Abigail Gardner, you are here to answer a complaint charging that you administered a quantity of arsenic in a mixture of gin and water to your husband with malice aforethought and with intent to kill and murder, and that the deceased came to his death from poison thus administered by your hand. Are you guilty or not guilty?"

"I am not guilty," Abigail replied. "I am perfectly innocent, and I say this before my Maker, and what such a story could be made from this I don't see. It is true I mixed some gin in sugar and water for my husband, but it is not true I ever mixed any arsenic, or ever bought a mite of arsenic in my life."

"Mrs. Gardner," Lewis said, "I caution you not to make statements without counsel. Your plea has been entered and we will begin this hearing with Dr. Ezra Stephenson's testimony."

Stephenson took a seat beside Lewis's table and, after being sworn, testified about his meeting with Hosea at the post office a week and a half before his fall and the concerns Hosea had raised during their conversation; his examination of Abigail for evidence of insanity at Hosea's request and his dismissal of such a condition; Abigail's accusation of Hosea's impotence and her admission of adultery; Hosea's fears of sleeping with Abigail in the house, and his concerns about her penchant for violence toward the children.

"Before God, I declare I am innocent, and what is stated is not true," Abigail vociferously interjected.

"Mrs. Gardner, I advise you once again to refrain from any further outbursts," Lewis admonished.

Abigail sneered.

Lewis turned to Stephenson and asked, "What did you advise Mr. Gardner to do about this situation?"

"I advised Mr. Gardner to leave her," the physician continued, "and given his statements said I should apprehend danger and if she entertained such feelings of animosity and bitterness it was the part of prudence to leave her."

"Whatever led you to think I ever intended to poison him?" Abigail erupted. Without waiting for a reply, she added, "That is not true. Before my God, it is not true. Well, I do think the language I have heard him use proved him an insane man. On Tuesday, I felt afraid he would really make way with himself. His razor was missing from the box in which he usually kept it, and we hunted everywhere for it. Abby found it at last in a box in the post office, where he had put it. I think he really intended to make way with himself. He often said he should not be here long to plague and worry us. But as for doing the act I never did it.

"Dr. Stephenson has told many untrue things. Dr. Stephenson was a great enemy to me and I always supposed he was. Mr. Gardner kept the post office open a good deal on Sunday and I spoke to him about it; told him it was not right, and asked him what the people would think of it; he replied, 'damn you, I'll knock you down if you give me any more of your sauce;' he said, 'damn you, it is none of your damned business.' He appeared very strange after and before he was hurt, and perhaps I could tell you many things which would appear as if he was insane. He said one morning, 'I am going to turn this house inside out.'"

When Abigail's tirade ended, Coroner Lewis asked the physician how long he had known Mr. and Mrs. Gardner.

"I've known them for many years, Justice Lewis."

"Have you ever witnessed anything to suggest either one or both of the Gardners were insane?" Lewis asked.

"I have not."

"Thank you, Doctor, you're excused. Please be available for further testimony tomorrow," said Lewis.

The coroner saw James Hunt seated in the hall.

"Mr. Hunt, please step forward and take the oath," Lewis said.

Hunt was sworn and took a seat in the chair vacated by Dr. Stephenson.

"Mr. Hunt, please explain what you know relative to the matter before this inquest," Coroner Lewis prompted.

"Yes, sir," the druggist replied. "This year, on or about January twenty-second, a boy entered my store and asked to purchase some poison for Mrs. Gardner. He had a note in his hand from her, which I read, and after he handed me the money he had in his possession, I gave him a packet of poison which I labelled with an engraved death's head and the word 'poison.' I told him to be careful with it."

"What happened next?" Lewis asked.

"About a half hour later this same boy came back to my shop at Mrs. Gardner's instruction and told me the poison he had purchased was not for Mrs. Gardner but for a Paddy woman. I thought it strange this young boy should be sent back to me to make such an explanation, especially since the snow was so deep."

57

Abigail leapt to her feet.

"I never wished the boy to say such a thing!" she cried, her voice quaking with indignation.

"Please sit down, Mrs. Gardner," Lewis said and told Hunt to continue.

"Are you sure it was Mrs. Gardner the boy referred to?" Lewis asked.

"Yes, I have since seen the boy and after questioning him about it," Hunt said, "he told me distinctly it was Mrs. Gardner who gave him the paper, and it was Mrs. Gardner who sent him back with the explanation."

"Oh, that," Abigail exclaimed, still standing. "I know all about it. I did send for it, but it was for a woman who lives at the cove, and suppose I did get arsenic, it does not follow I got it to poison Mr. Gardner with. As to proving anything you can't. You might as well try to prove he did it himself as to try to prove I did. Why I got this boy to go was because my boy was at school. She wished me to get it, and I got the Miller boy to go. She lived at the cove and so wanted me to go."

Coroner Lewis paused for a few moments expecting Abigail to go on, but she did not.

"Mr. Hunt, did you find out this boy's name?"

"Yes, his name is Charles Dodge," Hunt replied.

"Did you keep the note the Dodge boy presented to you?"

"I did not. I discarded it."

Lewis had no further questions for Hunt and excused him.

Lewis knew John and Martha Miller and saw them seated in the hall with their eleven-year-old nephew Charles Dodge. The Millers were Dodge's guardians and he lived with them and his cousins in a house near Abigail's. Lewis believed Abigail likely assumed Dodge was a Miller and hence her reference to the "Miller boy."

"Charles, come up here to the witness chair."

The boy was terrified. He turned to his aunt and uncle several times as he trudged to the front of the room.

"Charles," said Lewis as he presented a Bible, "by laying your hand here, you swear to tell the truth before God. Do you understand?"

"Yes," the boy answered.

"Do you swear to tell the truth?"

"Yes, sir," said Charles, his hand trembling on the Bible.

"Good, we will proceed," said Lewis. "Please tell the jury what you did for Mrs. Gardner on January twenty-second."

The boy repeated the story he had told Dr. Stephenson on the day Hosea was entombed.

"Charles, do you see Mrs. Gardner here in the hall today?" Lewis asked.

"Yes. She's seated at the table there," the boy said, pointing with a quivering finger.

"Thank you, Charles. You're excused," said the coroner.

Lewis later learned Abigail had asked Charles's cousin, fourteen-year-old Henry Miller, who lived with Charles in the same house, to run the errand to Hunt's. Miller had agreed, but later realized he could not go and had sent Charles in his place.

Coroner Lewis called the last witness. Dr. Don Pedro Wilson testified to seeing Abigail discard the slops in the yard.

"How far from her were you when you saw her?"

"I was only about twelve feet away."

"Did anything unusual happen after you saw her do this?"

"Yes, I saw my cats near the slops and, soon after, they both died. I dispensed with them in the hotel's privy vault."

"Do you see Mrs. Gardner here today?"

"I see her seated there," said Wilson, pointing in Abigail's direction.

"Alright, thank you, Doctor. You may take your seat in the hall. We'll adjourn at this time and continue the hearing at nine o'clock tomorrow morning. Mrs. Gardner will remain in Constable

Hersey's custody at her home overnight."

***

Dr. Ezra Stephenson's brother, John, a forty-seven-year-old blacksmith and scale and balance maker, had listened intently to the testimony. He and Ezra had spoken earlier about Hosea's suspicious demise, the inquest, and the post-mortem examination.

He hurried over to Dr. Wilson when the inquest adjourned.

"Don Pedro, do you have a moment?"

"Certainly, John; how are you?"

"These slops you alluded to. My brother Ezra mentioned them to me yesterday. Is there any chance they are still where Abigail left them?"

"I believe so. I went over to them a few days after I saw her with the shovel. It looked like someone has since scattered rock salt in the area. The snow is yellowish and the larger pieces of bread I had seen have disappeared, but most of the waste is still there," Wilson said.

"We ought to collect it. I'm sure the coroner will be interested in having it analyzed."

"I agree," the dentist replied.

"Let's meet at the Union Hotel tomorrow. I'll bring Hosea's brother-in-law, Reuben Reed, along. We can go out to the backyard and dig up whatever's left while Abigail's away and the inquest is in session," Stephenson said.

***

Marcus arrived home from school to find his house empty. He dropped his books on the kitchen table, went outside, and called for his mother. Hearing no answer, he went up to the Lincoln's door and knocked. Joanna Lincoln appeared at the doorway.

"Miss Lincoln, Mother is not at home. Do you know where she has gone?" Marcus asked.

"She left for the town hall with Constable Hersey at about four this afternoon, Marcus," Joanna replied. "She told me she hoped to return before supper."

"She didn't mention any business at the town hall when I left for school this morning. Do you know why she went there?"

"She didn't say, Marcus."

Marcus thanked his neighbor and sprinted for the post office.

"Abby," Marcus said. "Mother is not home. Miss Lincoln told me she has gone to the town hall with Constable Hersey. Did she say anything to you about it?"

Abby hesitated in answering. A villager had come into the post office earlier and told her about Constable Hersey and her mother's arrest. She didn't want to frighten her brother.

"I'm sure there is no need for worry, Marcus. Why don't you go back home and start on your school assignments? I should finish here soon and will start supper if Mother is not there upon my return."

***

Gridley pulled up to the Lincoln house with Abigail at twilight. Abby heard the pair talking as they approached and, with a quivering hand, opened the door. The commotion reached Marcus and he raced down the stairs from his room.

"Abby," said Abigail, "I don't want to discuss anything until I've had a moment to change and get settled. Mr. Hersey will be staying with us this evening. I'll sleep upstairs and he can make himself comfortable in the back chamber."

"Yes, Mother. I'll ready the room for him. I have food on the fire, too, Mr. Hersey, if you'd like to join us."

"Thank you, Abby," the constable replied.

The group ate in silence and, when they finished, Gridley took his mare to the Union Hotel stable to put it up for the night.

Abigail spoke with her children in Gridley's absence.

"Well, I hope you're happy, Abby! I've been arrested and now they've taken me before an inquest and accused me of poisoning your father; all because you agreed to his autopsy. I told you this would happen! It is an outrage," Abigail exclaimed.

"Oh, Mother, this is dreadful," Abby cried. "This is certainly not what I intended. Dr. Stephenson and Grandmother found the whole affair mysterious."

Marcus sat motionless, still fathoming his mother's words.

"Ah, yes, Dr. Stephenson. He was there at the hearing uttering the foulest, most fallacious accusations against me. I professed my innocence to the tribunal but they continued with the ridiculous charade. They had Mr. Hunt testify and the Dodge boy, and those two insinuated I sent for arsenic and used it to poison your father."

"Mother, what are we to do? Will you go to jail?" Marcus sobbed.

"Of course I won't, Marcus. Now stop your sniveling. Both of you prepare for bed. Gridley will take me back to Town Hall in the morning and I pray this disgraceful travesty will end."

***

"She appeared without counsel, and was apparently unmoved by the extraordinary charge preferred against her," said the *Boston Daily Advertiser* the next day. "Even up to the moment of her arrest she exhibited no signs indicative of an apprehension about the proceedings to be instituted against her, and only expressed stolid surprise at the horrid accusation…"

"Her phrenological developments are rather marked and prepossessing," the *Advertiser*'s correspondent added. "Her face impresses the stranger unfavorably, exhibiting cheekbones of remarkable prominence, sunken cheeks, and lack-luster grey eyes."

The reporter delved into Abigail's background, interviewing those in Hingham who knew anything about her. When he learned her origins were in Penobscot County, he telegraphed Maine newspapers seeking information and was rewarded with one particularly interesting tidbit of family lore.

"She is about forty years of age," he wrote. "Her maiden name was Marshall, and she came from Penobscot County, Maine. It is said she belongs to an energetic, spirited family, and according to one source, her grandmother once killed an Indian with a bread shovel on account of some depredation or other."

The *New York Herald* picked up the story on the wires. The *Herald* likened Abigail to the fictional character Meg Merillees, a half-mad Gypsy fortune teller portrayed by popular Boston-born dramatic actress Charlotte Cushman in a stage adaptation of Sir Walter Scott's "Guy Mannering."

***

Coroner Lewis visited twenty-seven-year-old Hingham attorney Henry Edson Hersey at his office at Main and South Streets after Gridley had departed with the prisoner.

"I'm sure by now you've heard about the inquest into postmaster Gardner's death," Lewis began.

"Yes, I have, Jim. I was saddened to hear about Hosea's death. I'd see him often at the post office. He was a kind man," Hersey replied.

"Earlier today I had Hosea's wife Abigail arrested and brought before the inquest. She was not represented by counsel and insisted she did not need one. She was unruly and on more than one occasion interrupted the witness testimony with what I'd consider to be incriminating statements. She finally held her tongue after several warnings from me. I believe it's unfair and unjust for her to place herself before the inquest jury tomorrow without legal representation. I have with me a transcript of the testimony and evidence presented today. It's unlikely she has funds to compensate you, but would you consider representing her at tomorrow's proceedings?"

"I have little experience in criminal matters, Jim," Hersey stated. "I've only recently been admitted to the bar and most of my practice thus far has limited me to civil matters."

"But you're an intelligent, Harvard-educated man, Henry. This might be the perfect opportunity for you to advocate in a different arena."

"Alright, Jim," said Hersey. "Perhaps you're right. I'll meet with Mrs. Gardner first thing in the morning."

"Thank you, Henry. I'll see you tomorrow. Good night."

***

A knock at the front door early the next morning alerted Gridley. He opened it to find Henry Hersey standing at the threshold.

"What brings you here at this time of the morning, Henry?" Gridley asked.

"Good morning, Gridley. I spoke with Jim Lewis late yesterday and he asked me to represent Mrs. Gardner today. I'd like to have a private word with her if you don't mind."

"Certainly, Henry; the family is up. Come this way."

Gridley led the lawyer into the kitchen.

"Mrs. Gardner, Mr. ·Hersey is here to see you. I'll be back shortly."

Gridley walked over to the hotel stable to retrieve his horse and carriage.

"What can I do for you, Mr. Hersey?" Abigail asked when Gridley departed.

"Mrs. Gardner, Coroner Lewis has asked me to represent you at the inquest."

"There's no need for your services, Mr. Hersey. I've done nothing wrong. Besides, I can't afford you."

"Mrs. Gardner, you're placing your life and your children's welfare in jeopardy if you proceed without legal counsel. Do not trouble yourself with the cost; I have agreed to represent you without a fee."

"I see. I appreciate your kindness, Mr. Hersey. It seems the whole town is against me."

Abby offered the lawyer some tea but he declined.

"Mother, I must leave now for the post office. I won't be able to attend the hearing," Abby said.

"Then off with you, Abby. I'll be back as soon as I can. Please see to your brother before you go."

"Yes, Mother," Abby said, and withdrew.

Attorney and client took seats in the parlor and went over the facts of the case. Gridley returned from the stable an hour later.

"Mrs. Gardner, the inquest will begin soon," the constable said.

"Alright, Gridley," said Abigail and waved him away.

Attorney Hersey placed his notes in his valise and stood.

"One last thing before I go, Mrs. Gardner. It is imperative for you to maintain your composure and suppress any outburst when witnesses are testifying. As your attorney I will provide you with the best representation I can, but anything you say during the hearing may incriminate you at future proceedings. If you have something important to say or have a question during the inquest, confer with me quietly and I will advise you."

Chapter 4: Damning Evidence

The town hall was filled to overflowing when Gridley pulled up with Abigail. More than one thousand men, women, children, and newspapermen had jostled for seats and places to stand, anxious to see the accused and hear the testimony. Hundreds more were spread across the lawn and on the stairway entrance, all engaged in animated conversation, counting on the throng huddled just inside the doorway to relay news as the drama played out. Several young men had climbed nearby trees hoping for a vantage point through the building's windows.

"I don't believe this, Gridley," said Abigail, tightly drawing her veil to hide her face. "News of this inquest must have spread through town like wildfire. How will I ever show my face again? And my children! Oh, my children! How will they ever bear the shame and embarrassment of this charade?" the widow cried.

Gridley sped quickly past the crowd assembled in front of the hall to the building's rear entrance, but several young boys saw him and raced toward the carriage.

"There she is! There's Mrs. Gardner," two young boys shouted when they saw Gridley pass by with his black-clad passenger. They gave chase and reached the carriage as the constable pulled to a stop. Gridley alighted and raised a hand to the small, excited group.

"You boys get back," he ordered. He helped Abigail down and led her away from the rapidly expanding horde as they jeered and taunted. A town official allowed the constable and his prisoner access then locked the door behind them. Gridley took Abigail to a room adjoining the main hall and waited to hear from Coroner Lewis.

Lewis was on the hall's raised platform making last minute preparations when Gridley arrived. He saw Dr. Stephenson seated in the front row and signaled to him. The two men spoke privately.

"You'll want to read this, Ezra," said Lewis, drawing a paper from his vest pocket. "I received this not an hour ago. It is postmarked from 32 Somerset Street, Boston."

Dear Sir,

I have at length completed the determination of the amount of arsenic in a given portion of the contents of the bowels of the late H. J. Gardner, and now wish to inform you I have found in five fluid ounces of the fecal matter from the intestines nearly seven grains of arsenous acid, or white arsenic. The exact weight of the arsenic obtained is 6.97 grains.

You will perceive that since four grains of arsenic is a poisonous dose, that even in a small part of the contents of Mr. Gardner's bowels I have found more than would be required to destroy life. He must have been heavily dosed with poison.

I made a mistake in writing the name of the deceased in my report to you, which please correct. Dr. Ellis supposed the name to be Henry J. Gardner, whereas in the newspapers I see it is Hosea J. Gardner. Please correct the report as the name should be written. If you have occasion to call us to Hingham before your Coroner's Jury please give us a day's notice of your intention so we may more conveniently leave home and our business.

I have been quite sick all day from the effects of the fumes of this analytic work and from the poisonous gases I have accidentally had to inhale during the work. It is rarely the case when a chemist has to analyse (sic) fecal matter from the large intestines and the work is so very disagreeable as to be avoided if possible.

Respectfully, your obedient servant,
C. T. Jackson, M. D., State Assayer

"The damaging evidence against Mrs. Gardner continues to multiply, James. Have you shown this to Henry Hersey?" Stephenson asked.

"I haven't, but I intend to do so at the afternoon recess. Drs. Ellis and Jackson are expected around three o'clock."

***

Gridley ushered Abigail to her designated seat in the hall. The audience pressed forward, craning their necks for a glimpse of her, but they were thwarted by her veil.

Lewis quieted the room with a bang of his gavel and a call to order.

Lewis summoned Hosea's mother to the witness chair. Every eye was focused on the petite, frail woman as she rose from the first settee. The coroner asked her to identify herself after she was sworn.

"My name is Sophia Gardner, mother of Hosea Gardner."

"Thank you, Mrs. Gardner. Please tell the inquest what you know about your son's death."

Sophia repeated the testimony she had given on the inquest's first day: Hosea's request for her care; her arrival at Hosea's home the day after his fall; his initial optimism for a prompt recovery and the steady decline of his health; Hosea's reaction to the odd tasting gin Abigail had prepared; the cold night she had spent in Hosea's room after Abigail had extinguished the fire; the curious appearance of the vomit he had expelled, and Abigail's refusal to save it for the doctor's inspection.

"Did Hosea say anything when his wife left the room with the basin?" asked the coroner.

"He said to me, 'Mother, I am poisoned, and she hates us both and will poison you, too.'"

Gasps and excited whispers rose in the hall at this revelation. Lewis rapped his gavel for order.

Abigail was barely able to restrain her fury. She glowered at Sophia.

68

Hersey placed a gentle hand on his client's arm to quell her emotions.

"Were you in the room when your son died, Mrs. Gardner?" Lewis asked.

"Yes."

"Was anyone else?"

"His wife and daughter were also in the room, as were Edwin Wilder and Otis Hersey."

"Did you have a conversation with Mr. Wilder before Hosea died?"

"Yes. Edwin asked if Hosea had taken any morphine or anything else to drug him. I answered I had given him morphine and soda, which the doctor had left for him. I told him it was a very small powder. I was supposed to give him a dose at five o'clock, but I had omitted it as he was so senseless."

"Thank you, Mrs. Gardner. Mr. Hersey, do you have any questions for the witness?"

"Mrs. Gardner, are you sure you saw your son's wife give him the gin?" asked Attorney Hersey.

"Yes, I am."

"Who sent for you?"

"I expect Hosea sent for me."

This was not the answer Hersey expected. Abigail had insisted she had sent for the mother.

"And what were you told was the reason for his request?"

"I was told he had fallen and hurt himself and wished me to stay with him. And after I got there, he requested me to stay."

"I have no other questions for Mrs. Gardner," Hersey said.

"Thank you, Mrs. Gardner," said Lewis. "You are excused. I have a few more questions for Dr. Stephenson. Would you please take the witness chair, Doctor?"

"Dr. Stephenson, please tell the inquest jury the details of Mr. Gardner's medical treatment after his injury."

Stephenson testified about his call to Hosea's house after his fall; the medical treatment he had provided; Hosea's rapid, inexplicable decline; Abigail's deceit when he asked if Hosea had had a bowel movement after taking the salts; her disposal of the vomit; her indifference when he and Newhall asked to straighten Hosea's leg; and his visit with Hosea's mother and daughter and their consent to a post-mortem examination.

"Did you make the same request of the widow, Doctor?" Lewis asked.

"Yes, and after speaking with her of the peculiarity of her husband's sickness and symptoms having been unaccountable, I said it would be a satisfaction to know the cause. She also said it would be a great satisfaction to her to know, though she believed it was from mortification of the leg. I told her the only way was to examine the body, and I asked for her consent."

"What was her answer to this request, Doctor?" Lewis asked.

"She said at once she could not consent to it. She said she always had a great dread and horror of such things. I told her the daughter requested it and the community required it, and I begged of her to allow me to solve the mystery. The more I entreated, the firmer she was, apparently, in her objections. I left, and this was the last interaction I had with her."

"Thank you, Doctor," said the coroner. "Do you have any questions, Mr. Hersey?"

"I have several," Abigail's attorney replied. He rose, stating, "You said you gave Mr. Gardner some quieting medicine. What was this medicine and who prepared it?"

"The quieting medicine I left was morphine, which I prepared myself and left with directions."

"Are you certain Mrs. Gardner told you the salts had operated?" Hersey asked.

"I am sure Mrs. Gardner, the wife, told me the salts had operated, and I am sure for several reasons," Stephenson said.

"Do you know who sent for you on Saturday night?"

"I'm not certain."

"Was it Mrs. Gardner, the wife?"

Stephenson thought for several moments and said, "I don't recollect being told it was Mrs. Gardner who sent for me."

Almost immediately after his answer he said, "I now recollect it was Mr. Wilder who requested the doctor."

"Did you consider Mrs. Gardner's objection to an autopsy as unusual?"

"It is not unusual for relatives to object to a post-mortem examination. Mrs. Gardner made great objection. She was willing to have a limb amputated, but she could not bear the idea of going further."

"I have no further questions," Hersey told Lewis.

"Thank you, Doctor. You are excused," said Coroner Lewis.

Lewis called James Hunt to the witness chair. After he was sworn, Hunt repeated the testimony he had given the day before. Attorney Hersey had only one question for the witness.

"Mr. Hunt, is there any reason you did not question eleven-year-old Charles Dodge more closely about the poison he had requested?"

"I didn't think it was necessary, sir," Hunt answered.

The coroner adjourned and instructed jurors and witnesses to return at 3:30 p.m.

Many in the audience remained in their seats and engaged in animated conversation.

"May I have a word, Henry?" Lewis asked Abigail's lawyer.

Hersey stepped into the anteroom and read Dr. Jackson's letter.

"It will be very difficult for Mrs. Gardner to overcome this evidence, James."

"I agree, Henry. I wanted you to see this before we resume. Drs. Ellis and Jackson will be here this afternoon to testify."

"Thank you, James."

71

Attorney Hersey went out to the hall and guided his client to an empty committee room. Gridley stood outside the closed door.

"Mrs. Gardner," Hersey began, "Dr. Jackson will testify when the inquest resumes. Mr. Lewis has received an official letter from Jackson relative to the examination of your husband's organs. Once again I advise you to maintain your composure and reticence."

"What does the letter say?"

"Dr. Jackson found arsenic in the specimens he received from the autopsy. He is prepared to testify that the amount of arsenic was enough to cause death."

"Ridiculous, Mr. Hersey. There is no way Hosea was given arsenic. These medical men and their scientific experiments; it's nothing more than hocus pocus."

"Be that as it may, Mrs. Gardner, Jackson's testimony will be damaging. Again, I caution you to remain reticent during the proceeding."

Abigail scoffed but agreed to hold her tongue.

"Gridley, would you mind taking us to the hotel for repast?" asked the young attorney when he and Abigail emerged.

"Not at all, Henry," the constable replied. "I could use a bite to eat myself."

Eager reporters besieged the trio when they exited the hall.

"Do you have anything to say, Mrs. Gardner?" one reporter shouted. "Why wouldn't you allow an autopsy?" bellowed another.

"Mrs. Gardner will have nothing to say, gentlemen," said Henry Hersey as Gridley cleared a path to his carriage.

Gridley conveyed his prisoner and her attorney along the muddied streets to the Union Hotel with the newsmen following close behind in their rented traps and buggies. He quickly escorted Henry and Abigail inside. They took seats in the hotel's dining room among twenty-five or so other patrons and ordered a light meal.

The reporters kept a conspicuous eye on Abigail from afar as she conversed with Gridley and Henry at the table. Unfazed by the stares and whispers of diners and the penetrating glare of the press, Abigail, according to one correspondent, ate "heartily" and appeared "as social and cheerful as usual."

***

An hour before Abigail's arrival at the hotel, Reuben Reed and John Stephenson had met in the lobby with Don Pedro Wilson. Reed had brought along a half-bushel copper vessel his wife used for washing. The three men proceeded to the Gardner's backyard and the spot where Wilson had seen Abigail discard the slops.

Stephenson had used a shovel to scoop up the bits of potato skins, tea leaves, and other material, and had emptied them into Reed's tub. He took the tub and its contents to Engine House Number 3 in Hingham Centre where he kept an office in the basement as the town's sealer of weights and measures. The container's contents would remain stored for nearly six months before Dr. Jackson would analyze them.

***

Drs. Ellis and Jackson arrived at the town hall from Boston during the recess. When the inquest recommenced at about 3:35 p.m., Coroner Lewis called Dr. Ellis to the witness chair. The bespectacled, mutton-chopped, thirty-year-old pathologist testified to his medical observations during Hosea's post-mortem examination and his delivery of the stomach and intestines he had removed from the cadaver to Dr. Jackson.

"Thank you, Dr. Ellis. Mr. Hersey, do you have any questions?"

"Yes, thank you, Mr. Lewis. Dr. Ellis, is it possible the organs would have presented the same appearance without the presence of poison?"

"Some of the appearances which I describe might have existed if no poison had been administered. I don't state them all as evidences of poison. It is not at all probable all could have existed without poison," Ellis answered.

"Was the disease of the bone indicated sufficient to cause death?"

"I would not undertake to say with these appearances a man must necessarily die."

Hersey hadn't heard Ellis's direct testimony as to how he knew the body he had examined was, in fact, Hosea Gardner's.

"How do you know whose body it was?"

"I happened to be present when the coroner's jury identified it."

"Thank you, Doctor. I have no further questions."

Lewis called Dr. Fiske to testify. Fiske stated he was present during the post-mortem examination and had taken notes during the procedure. He corroborated Dr. Ellis's testimony.

Lewis also called Dr. Stephenson again and he, too, corroborated Dr. Ellis's testimony and concurred with Dr. Fiske's statements under oath.

Dr. Jackson was the next witness. After he was sworn, he testified about his analysis of the viscera Dr. Calvin Ellis had delivered to him on the morning of February ninth.

"Dr. Ellis brought me two vials and one large-mouthed show bottle, as it is called. The two vials contained a dark, brown-colored fluid, which Dr. Ellis stated came from the deceased person's stomach. Dr. Ellis said this fluid was originally in one vial, but, this having broken in his pocket; he transferred it into two vials. The quantity of fluid in the vials was small; I think not more than three ounces. The show bottle contained about seven fluid ounces of fecal matter, mostly from the large intestines. Dr. Ellis also brought me the stomach to inspect, and we examined it together with a great deal of care.

"At the left extremity of the stomach, opposite the cardiac orifice, there were some spots of ecchymosis. Along the large curvature there were a few small and distinct ulcers, not larger than a peppercorn. We spread the stomach on our hands and I examined the surface using a microscope with a strong lens, at the window, in search of any particles of arsenic on the mucous membrane. I did not find any.

"I then undertook a chemical examination of the fluids using one of the vials I had received from Dr. Ellis for preliminary experiments. I did not find any poison in the fluid from the stomach in the portions I tested.

"I next turned my attention to the fecal matter from the intestines. I used two fluid ounces of it in my preliminary experiments and I found an abundance of arsenic."

Dr. Jackson removed a vial from his medical bag containing the arsenic he had found and displayed it to the coroner and the jury. Audible expressions of revulsion from the ladies present spread through the hall while the men pressed forward for a closer look at the specimen.

"After testing the arsenic and finding it to be such, I undertook to determine how much arsenic there was in the whole amount of fecal matter in my possession. From five fluid ounces of the fecal matter I observed ten and seven-tenths grains of sulphuret of arsenic, which is equivalent to six and ninety-seven one hundredths grains of arsenic."

Jackson removed another vial from his bag and showed it to contain the whole amount of sulphuret of arsenic obtained from the fecal matter.

"Portions of this were tested by reduction. The garlic odor of arsenic was revealed by the blow pipe, and a tube inserted revealed the arsenical mirror," Jackson explained. He went into great detail about other chemical and scientific experiments he had conducted to confirm the presence of arsenic in the fluids submitted to him by Dr. Ellis.

"The result of all these experiments is this – the contents of the bowels, by analytical examination, contained a sufficient quantity of arsenic to cause death in a human being. All the chemical processes are detailed in full in my notebook. As the poisonous matter was found in the intestines, the deceased must have lived long enough to have it pass through the stomach," Jackson concluded.

Attorney Hersey had no questions for the witness and Dr. Jackson was excused.

A *Boston Herald* reporter present during the proceedings watched Abigail with keen interest. He had expected an emotional reaction to the testimony from her but instead found a strong-willed, unflappable woman. He wrote, "Mrs. Gardner manifested the most stoical indifference to what was transpiring. Not a muscle of her face was moved; a naturally cold, determined, hard-featured, immovable countenance was always presented to the observer; she never suffered a feature to relax. I anticipated reasonably even a slight show of feeling, [during Dr. Jackson's electrifying testimony] but I was disappointed. I might as well have looked upon a granite statue."

Coroner Lewis was satisfied with the evidence presented and saw no need to call additional witnesses. He was not obliged to prove Abigail's guilt or innocence but merely establish she had more likely than not poisoned her husband.

Before adjourning, Lewis called Charles Augustus Dodge forward to be recognized for his appearance as a witness before the grand jury. Fearing the frightened boy would not return to testify, Lewis explained the penalties for failing to answer a grand jury subpoena as Charles wept.

Lewis asked Attorney Hersey if he intended to produce any witnesses or say anything before disposition. Hersey demurred and Lewis dismissed the jurors for deliberation. They returned quickly and foreman Martin Fearing handed Lewis the verdict.

Lewis unfolded the plain white paper and read the decision aloud: "That said Hosea J. Gardner died in his own dwelling on the first day of February instant, by a deadly poison called white arsenic, administered by his wife, Abigail Gardner, between the twenty-seventh and thirty-first days of January now last past."

Lewis signed the verdict and turned his attention to Abigail.

"Mrs. Gardner, I feel compelled, given the facts, to order your commitment to the jail in Plymouth to await further legal investigation in May next. The probabilities are so strong that you poisoned your husband I do not feel authorized to do otherwise. You are hereby held for trial without bail."

Spectators in the hall emitted a collective gasp.

"Mr. Lewis," Attorney Hersey, said, "my client wishes to settle some of her affairs before her commitment."

"Very well, Mr. Hersey. I will allow her to remain in Constable Hersey's custody overnight. He will remand her to Plymouth Jail in the morning."

Gridley took custody of Abigail after Lewis had adjourned and led her to the committee room for a word with her attorney. He closed the door and waited outside.

"What am I to do now, Mr. Hersey?" she shouted at the young lawyer.

"Mrs. Gardner, please calm down. Give me a moment and I'll explain."

"I won't calm down. This is outrageous. How dare they accuse me of such a despicable act?" she demanded, her voice quaking with indignation.

"Please, Mrs. Gardner."

***

James Lewis found Gridley waiting outside the committee room and spoke with him in a low voice.

"Gridley, this is a warrant to search the Gardner house, the shed, and the grounds," said Lewis, handing Hersey the document. "I want you to look for the paper fold of arsenic and any gin, brandy, castor oil, or other medications you may find."

Hersey put the warrant in his pocket.

"I'll stop by your home on the way to Plymouth tomorrow and

let you know what I've found, James."

Lewis departed and Gridley continued to wait outside the room. Abigail's shouting escalated and the constable intervened.

"Mrs. Gardner, it's time for us to leave."

"I have done nothing wrong, Gridley," she protested. "I will not be subjected to this treatment."

"Mrs. Gardner, you have no choice," the constable replied.

"I won't," said Abigail.

"Mrs. Gardner, if you don't quiet down and comply, I will be forced to place you in irons," Gridley said sternly.

Abigail finally relented and, with a huff, drew her veil.

Gridley took her by the arm and ushered her outside.

She scowled at the reporters clustered on the town hall steps.

"Leave me alone," she sneered. "I have nothing to say to you!"

"Step back," Gridley ordered the newsmen as he helped Abigail aboard. "And don't follow me."

Gridley gripped the reins, clicked to the mare, and they sped away.

***

Gridley extinguished his carriage lamp and reached under the seat for a lantern when he arrived at the Gardner home. He lit the wick, jumped out, and went to the other side to help his prisoner from the carriage. On the way up the path he told her about the search warrant.

"Is this really necessary, Gridley?" she fumed.

"The coroner has ordered me to do so and I am duty bound to obey him."

"Read it to me," Abby demanded.

The constable removed the document from his pocket and unfolded it. He raised his lantern for light and read aloud.

"You'll find no poison in my house, Gridley. Search all you want," said Abigail.

"When we get inside, I expect you and the children to remain in the kitchen until I've finished my investigation."

"Mr. Hersey will be staying another night," Abigail announced to Abby as she entered the house. "It seems Jim Lewis believes I've poisoned your father and I'll be going to jail in the morning."

Abby paled.

"Right now, Mr. Hersey wants to inspect the house. He wants us all in the kitchen."

Abby called to Marcus and he came down from his room.

Gridley removed his heavy overcoat, hung it on a nail, and warmed himself at the kitchen hearth for a few moments. Abigail and the children sat silently around the table and watched as the constable inspected drawers and cabinets, tin canisters and earthenware. He moved to the two bedrooms on the first floor. He found the front room where Hosea had died nearly empty. He moved to the parlor, found nothing, and ascended the stairs to search the bedrooms.

Gridley came back down to the kitchen.

"Well, Gridley?" Abigail sneered.

"You keep a remarkably neat house, Mrs. Gardner."

"Oh, how kind of you, Gridley," Abigail retorted with sarcasm. "Now tell me what you've found," she said, her voice rising.

"I've found nothing, Mrs. Gardner."

Abigail smirked. "I told you so, Gridley."

"I'll check the shed and the grounds in the morning, Mrs. Gardner. I'll only hurt myself looking around in the dark now."

"Suit yourself, Gridley. You're not going to find anything there either."

"I'll ready the room for you, Mr. Hersey," said Abby, "and I have food in the stove if you'd like to join us."

"You're very kind, Abby," the constable replied.

Marcus began to sob.

"Marcus, it will do neither me nor you any good to cry," Abigail scolded. "This foolishness will be over soon. I've done nothing wrong and intend to prove my innocence to the people in this town."

Abby stood in stunned silence.

They finished the meal quickly. Abby cleared the table and cleaned the dishes.

"Abby, I'll be leaving early with Gridley. You'll see to Marcus and tend to the house, of course. I don't want to come back here to find the place in shambles."

"Yes, Mother," Abby replied.

"Both of you to bed, now," said Abigail.

Neither Abby nor Marcus would sleep that night.

***

"…The brute-like actions and conversation of the woman, who committed this dreadful crime, testified to upon the trial, reveal a nature, the only impulses of which are those of the animal, and not of the human being," said the *Boston Evening Transcript* the next day. Her motive, the newspaper declared, was clear.

"Her intimate acquaintance with another man had turned every spark of affection which she ever had for her husband into the most bitter hate, and in order to be able better to gratify her illicit desires in respect to this other man, she took the life of her husband. The evidence of her guilt seems too conclusive to be overcome, and it is more than probable she will suffer the just penalty for her high crime."

"…The guilt of the woman, from the evidence, seems conclusive," the *Lowell Daily Citizen and News* chimed in. "Mrs. Gardner's neighbors represent her as a person of incredible heartlessness. While her husband lay dead in the house, and the funeral, her indifference and ill-nature was a matter of remark. In regard to the disposition of his property, by which her expectations in that respect were disappointed, she exhibited a peculiarly ill temper, and snappishly asked who that iron leg fell to (alluding to a mechanical contrivance used by the deceased lame man in walking)."

"The community is full of rumors concerning this strange

affair," the *Boston Traveler* declared, "one of which is, that for some time prior to the death of her husband, Mrs. Gardner had been in the habit of sending rare dishes and dainty sweetmeats to the wife of the man with whom she has been on such intimate terms, and it is darkly hinted that it was her intention to poison one other person – this man's wife – and then to marry him. The stable of this man is in the rear of her residence, and it is said she has been seen to frequent it on occasions when he was there."

Even the *National Police Gazette*, a sensationalist New York magazine concerned with all things criminal, publicized the case at newsstands throughout the country with excerpts of the inquest testimony from the *Boston Traveler* and the *Boston Journal*. The *Gazette*'s February 1857 edition published a sketch of Abigail.

***

Constable Hersey woke at sunrise to search the yard and shed. There were footprints in the snow leading from the hotel to a spot in the yard near the shoveled pathway. Someone had obviously dug up something there. He searched the shed and, satisfied there was no evidence within, went back into the house.

"Still nothing, Gridley?" asked Abigail.

"No, Mrs. Gardner."

"I told you so."

Hersey walked over to the hotel stable for his horse and carriage while Abigail packed a small bag with clothing and other personal effects before her trip to the jail. Gridley spoke quietly with Abby and Marcus in the kitchen while their mother was busy.

"Abby, I have a difficult request of you. I'd like to alert Sheriff Phillips at the Plymouth jail about my expected arrival time. Would you mind telegraphing him from the post office?"

"I'll be sure to do so this morning, Mr. Hersey."

"I'm sorry about everything. The events of the past week have been very painful for you both."

"Thank you. Yes, it has been very trying. Will you let me know how mother fared at the jail when you return?" Abby asked.

"Yes, of course, Abby."

Abigail appeared in the kitchen with her travel bag.

"Abby, you see to Marcus and make sure he gets to school. I don't want to be worrying about him while I'm away," Abigail said to her daughter.

Abby held Marcus close. "I will, Mother," said Abby, eyes glistening.

Marcus sobbed.

"Now don't you two make a fuss," Abigail said. "I'll be perfectly fine and will be home soon."

Gridley led Abigail outside to his carriage. Abigail thought she saw one of the Lincoln girls peeking through a window and when she turned to meet the woman's prying eyes, the drapes closed abruptly.

"I have to stop at Coroner Lewis's house first and return the search warrant, Mrs. Gardner."

Gridley pulled up at the coroner's Pleasant Street home and stepped inside.

"Did you find anything, Gridley?" Lewis asked.

"I'm afraid not, Jim."

"I'm not surprised," said Lewis. "She's had ample time to destroy or discard anything incriminating. Sign the return and I'll keep it with the inquest papers. How is Mrs. Gardner this morning?"

"She's unusually calm given her circumstances. I don't expect she'll be a problem."

"Alright, Gridley; I wish you well."

There was little conversation between prisoner and constable as they set off on the twenty-five-mile route to Plymouth; Abigail's lawyer had warned her not to speak with Hersey about the case.

On the town's outskirts, a man with a baker's cart was vending his wares alongside the roadway.

"Pull up alongside, Gridley," she demanded.

"I'll have one of your cakes, if you please," she said to the baker.

"What is your preference, madam? I have a wide assortment."

"Anything will do."

The baker carefully wrapped one of the confections and approached the carriage.

"Five cents madam, please," said the baker.

Abigail reached down and snatched the cake.

"I'm afraid I haven't any money at the moment, sir. Call at the post office in the north village and you'll be properly compensated. Go along now, Gridley."

Hersey clucked and his mare lurched forward. The baker stood dumbfounded, his mouth agape, as the carriage pulled away.

"I'd have thought a confection would be the last thing on your mind, Mrs. Gardner," the constable remarked.

"I imagine the warden will have little in the way of agreeable rations, Gridley. It's the least I can do for myself before I'm locked away in his horrid jail," Abigail replied.

They continued on in awkward silence through Scituate, Marshfield, Duxbury, and Kingston before reaching Plymouth Jail in Court Square. Hersey turned up South Russell Street and past the county courthouse to the old jail and the recently constructed house of correction. Fifty-seven-year-old Plymouth County Sheriff Daniel Phillips and Francis J. Goddard, Jail Keeper and Master of the House of Correction, notified by Abby's telegraph, greeted Hersey as he approached the jail's entrance at noontime. Forty-year-old Goddard took custody of Abigail and led her into his office where a guard entered her name, age, and the charge against her in a ledger.

A matron ushered Abigail to the jail's segregated women's unit.

"Do you expect me to bide my time in these deplorable conditions?" Abigail railed at the woman.

"I'm afraid we don't have anything more well-appointed," she replied.

There was a calico wrapper folded on a cot inside the cell.

"You are to change into prison apparel," the matron said, gesturing at the dress. "You can put your clothes and any rings, pins, and other jewelry in the bag you brought with you."

"How dare you? I am in mourning," Abigail huffed.

"I'm afraid you will have to abide by the rules. Every woman prisoner is required to wear the same type and color housedress – no exceptions."

"This is outrageous. At the very least I should be allowed to keep my jewelry. I want to look well when my friends call to see me."

"Jewelry is prohibited, Mrs. Gardner. You may keep your shawl. Now please undress."

Abigail changed into the wrapper and put her clothing, jewelry, and other personal effects in her bag.

"I'll make sure your bag is kept in a safe place, Mrs. Gardner, and I'll make your clothes available to you when it's necessary for you to appear in court."

Abigail glared defiantly at the matron.

"There better not be anything missing when I'm released from this godforsaken hovel," Abigail warned. "I'll see you released from your position!"

"Before I leave, Mrs. Gardner, I must remind you of certain rules you must obey while you are held here. I'll be back to explain them. In the meantime, there is no talking allowed in the cells, and violations will result in the suspension of certain privileges."

"We'll see about that," Abigail huffed.

***

Newspapers in major cities around the country continued to transmit and receive details of the Hingham murder by wire as the drama unfolded. Abigail's arrest and testimony from the inquest shared headlines in the *New York Herald*, the *New York Times*, the

Washington (D.C.) *Evening Star*, the Richmond (Virginia) *Daily Dispatch*, and the Honolulu *Polynesian* alongside articles on the slavery issue; the Dred Scott decision; newly elected President Buchanan's support of slavery in Kansas; states' rights; the Indian Wars in Florida and Utah, and the temperance movement. Locally, the *Boston Post, Boston Traveler, Boston Herald, Boston Daily Advertiser, Hingham Journal, Plymouth Rock,* and Plymouth's *Old Colony Memorial* competed for the attention of readers with extensive reporting.

A Plymouth *Old Colony Memorial* correspondent met with a confidential source from the jail soon after Abigail's incarceration.

"How is Mrs. Gardner faring through all this?"

"She's not what I'd describe as a model prisoner. She has no regard for authority and the matron cites her often for infractions," said the source. "She has no doubt she'll be acquitted. She insists her husband did away with himself."

Chapter 5: Hosea's Ghost

Coroner Lewis and Constable Hersey met with District Attorney James M. Keith at his office in the Plymouth County Courthouse several weeks after Abigail's arrest to discuss the Gardner case. Lewis handed the prosecutor the inquest transcript, as well as Dr. Ellis's autopsy report, Dr. Jackson's chemical analysis reports, and the arrest and search warrant returns.

"It looks as though nine individuals testified during the inquest, Mr. Lewis; am I correct?" Keith asked.

"Yes, there was testimony from five lay persons and four medical men, Mr. Keith. Dr. Stephenson attended Hosea Gardner up to the time of his death. Mr. Gardner's mother, Sophia Gardner, nursed her son in his illness," Lewis replied.

"Was the prisoner represented by counsel at the inquest?"

"On the first day, she was not." Lewis continued. "She made incriminating statements during the hearing and I cautioned her to remain silent but she ignored me. I contacted Hingham attorney Henry Hersey the same day and asked him to appear on the prisoner's behalf at the next session. He agreed to do so and represented the prisoner when the inquest continued."

"Is Attorney Hersey related to you, constable?" Keith inquired.

"Not immediately, Mr. Keith, but certainly distantly; all the Hingham Herseys are cousins by way of old William, the family patriarch," Gridley chuckled.

Keith smiled.

"I will need the names and addresses of everyone who testified, Mr. Lewis. I will obtain subpoenas for you, Constable Hersey, to deliver to each of them," Keith said. "As I interview these witnesses, I will determine the need for testimony from others who have knowledge of this case and I will forward additional subpoenas to your attention for service. I am especially interested in speaking with Mr. Gardner's two children."

"I will ensure prompt delivery, Mr. Keith," Hersey replied.

"Let's get on with your statements, gentlemen," said Keith.

The three men discussed the case at length until dusk. Before Lewis and Hersey departed, the district attorney met with Clerk of Court William Whitman and procured subpoenas for Drs. Stephenson and Fiske, Don Pedro Wilson, Sophia Gardner, James Hunt, and the Dodge and Miller cousins, and handed them over to Constable Hersey. Keith also obtained subpoenas for Drs. Ellis and Jackson and addressed them to the attention of the district attorney in Suffolk County for delivery in Boston.

***

Hosea died intestate and in debt. Abigail's incarceration left her indisposed to file for administration of Hosea's estate so the responsibility fell to Abby. Since she was under twenty-one-years of age, it was necessary for her to seek the assistance of Hosea's first cousin, Edward Porter, who owned a sail making business at the Hingham wharves with John Mayhew. Porter petitioned the Plymouth County Probate Court two weeks after Hosea's death for appointment as administrator of Hosea's estate on behalf of the Gardner family. The court approved Porter's petition and also appointed Hingham residents Edwin Wilder, Henry Siders, and Perez Jenkins (another Gardner cousin) to inventory and appraise Hosea's assets.

Hosea's limited means became quickly apparent. He possessed no real property. The contents of his home – his clothing, beds and bedding, chairs, a sofa, carpets, silver spoons, tables, looking glasses, clocks, and other articles of furniture comprised the bulk of his personal estate, along with a modest amount of cash and assets related to his business – books, stationery, confectionaries, perfumery, cigars, fancy articles, and fixtures in his store. These assets were appraised at nearly seven hundred dollars. Among the principal creditors were book publisher Brown, Bazin and Company; Dr. Ezra Stephenson; Hingham merchant Rufus Lane;

Hingham coal dealer Caleb B. Marsh; and Ripley and Newhall Company (for his coffin and burial).

On March 3, 1857, Judge Aaron Hobart, presiding justice of the probate court, after settlement of just payments and debts, "allowed unto Abigail Gardner, for necessaries, so much of her husband's personal estate in such articles as she may select in the inventory, as shall amount to the sum of two hundred dollars." Hobart, however, earmarked one hundred and twenty-five dollars of the allowance for the support of Abby and Marcus.

Abby and Marcus could no longer afford to board at the Lincoln house after their father's assets were liquidated. Abby's meager wages at the post office and Barnard's shop and the funds she and Marcus received from Hosea's estate barely met the cost of everyday life's essentials. Marcus found occasional work cutting wood or running errands, but he had not completed his schooling and Abby very much desired that he do so.

"Abby," Marcus pleaded, "where will we go?"

"There, there, Marcus. You needn't worry. Father's friend, Levi Hersey, has arranged lodging for me at Mrs. Davis's home on Main Street. I'll board there with her and her daughter, Ellen, who teaches at the school on Elm Street; and George Hunt, the baker on North Street at Hobart's Bridge, has offered to provide you room and board and work as an apprentice in his bakery."

"But, we'll be separated, Abby," Marcus cried with alarm.

"It's alright, Marcus," Abby said softly. "Mr. Hunt's proposal is a good opportunity for you to learn a trade. And he's promised me he'll still allow time for your studies. In the meantime, Mr. Siders has assured me he will pass the postmistress position to me when I'm old enough. Maybe then we can consider reuniting under the same roof. But you'll soon be a man, Marcus, and might want to consider your own path."

"What about Mother, Abby?" Marcus asked. "What is to become of her?"

"Marcus, we've discussed this at length. We do not know how mother will fare at trial. We can only hope her lawyers will do their very best."

Abby was deeply conflicted and would not share her innermost feelings with her younger brother. Uncertainty weighed on her mind about the cause of her father's death and the accusations made against her mother. She had witnessed the growing animosity between her parents, but she refused to believe her mother would deliberately poison her father. And she had heard the rumors swirling about town about her mother's alleged affair, had read the newspaper accounts of the testimony given at the inquest, and was keenly aware of the surreptitious glances people cast her way when they came into the post office on business or for a chat with Mr. Siders. She was embarrassed and ashamed at times. Her mother was a hard woman and she had often been the object of her wrath. But until it was proven her mother had murdered her father, she could not accept any of it.

Mr. Lewis spared her and Marcus from testifying at the inquest but she had no doubt the government would call upon them to testify at the trial. It terrified her. She did not know how they would cope with this dreadful ordeal.

***

On a late mid-March afternoon, a merchant and a banker from Hingham walked over from Boston's financial district to the Old Colony Railroad's busy terminal at Kneeland and South Streets. The brick edifice, built only ten years before, was considered the most completely equipped American station of its day and had a spacious waiting area with rows of benches, a gas lit smoking room, barber shop, telegraph office, newsstand, lavatory, bootblack, and check room.

The two men went in through the main entrance and weaved through a throng of lively passengers, trainmen, and baggage attendants on the sprawling concourse. They noted a young couple embracing, saying their goodbyes, and a policeman on one knee consoling a frantic child apparently separated from his parents. They proceeded to the ticket office where each purchased the fifteen-cent fare for the 5:50 p.m. South Shore train to Hingham depot, and strolled over to the newsstand to pick up the evening editions. Their train wasn't due to depart for another forty-five minutes, so they found comfortable seats in the quiet of the smoking room, shed their outerwear, and settled in with their dailies.

"There hasn't been much coverage on the Gardner case, lately," the banker commented as he reached into his vest pocket for his spectacles.

"I haven't read any news about it since her confinement in Plymouth Jail," the merchant replied. "I suspect we'll hear soon of her indictment."

"I've followed the case closely and can't imagine anything but a guilty finding from a rational jury."

"I agree," said the merchant, tamping tobacco into his pipe. "The testimony and evidence outlined in the *Hingham Journal* has certainly convinced me of her guilt and, I daresay, has convinced many others, including the editors."

"The court of public opinion makes it almost laughable to hold a trial at all."

The pair guffawed.

"There certainly has been no scarcity of criminal trials to read about lately," the merchant offered. "This evening's *Boston Traveler* has an article on the Reverend Isaac Kalloch scandal and the trial of James McGee, the Charlestown State Prison convict who murdered Deputy Warden Walker last December."

"A tragedy!" exclaimed the banker. "And two weeks after Walker's murder another inmate named Cater took Warden Tenney's life. I understand Cater will go to trial next week."

"The *Herald*'s giving them the same attention," the banker remarked. "Attorney General Clifford is prosecuting both McGee and Cater. I'm sure he'll be the lead prosecutor in the Gardner case, too," he added,

"Kalloch's case is no less a tragedy," the merchant observed. "Can you imagine? A Baptist clergyman and minister of the Tremont Temple Church accused of adultery? What is the world coming to?"

The banker turned to the classifieds.

"I don't believe this!" the banker exclaimed. "Look at this advertisement. *Faben's Great Exhibition of Wax Figures* is open for ten days at 85 Hanover Street, opposite Portland."

"That's in Scollay Square, isn't it?" asked the merchant.

"It is," the banker replied. "Faben is exhibiting a chamber of horrors. He's displaying life-size figures of Bond Street victim Dr. Burdell and his murderess, Mrs. Cunningham of New York City; McGee and Cater; and, our very own Mrs. Gardner of Hingham! Can you believe it? None of these people have been convicted and yet this Faben is capitalizing on these horrid cases, charging fifteen cents admission."

"Most likely a travelling showman, striving to attain P. T.'s wealth and fame," the merchant offered. "Barnum's museum of curiosities and wax figures in New York City has made him a rich man."

"Well, I for one will not patronize Faben's abomination," the banker declared.

"Nor will I," the merchant rejoined, "but I've no doubt Faben will find no lack of ghoulish gawkers at his door."

"How do you suppose he obtained their likenesses?"

"He has likely procured daguerreotypes of them; or maybe he dispatched sketch artists to their court appearances."

"Maybe their images aren't accurate at all and the whole thing is a hoax."

The two men laughed. The conductor's bellow for boarding carried from the concourse. They retrieved their coats and hats, folded their newspapers, and made their way across the concourse to the train shed and the waiting local.

***

An advertisement appeared in the *Boston Herald*'s morning edition two days later announcing the coming issue of a new weekly periodical entitled *Banner of Light*. The publication touted itself as a weekly journal of "Romance, Literature, and General Intelligence" – a "true family paper!" The *Banner* would feature a series of articles on the "Philosophy and Practical Teachings of Spiritualism" and a column entitled "The Messenger," with "several sterling communications from the world of spirits received through the mediumship of Mrs. J. H. Conant."

Frances "Fanny" Conant was among the most celebrated of mediums in mid-nineteenth century Boston. She had displayed the ability to communicate with the spiritual world at a young age and by age twenty-two she had received her first message as a public medium.

Born Frances Ann Crowell in New Hampshire, she moved to Lowell, Massachusetts, at age fifteen. She had married John H. Conant, a gas fitter, in 1850, and a year later the couple settled in Boston's North End.

The *Banner*'s premiere issue appeared on newsstands and at stores in Boston on April 11, 1857, at five cents a copy. Under "The Messenger" heading on pages six and seven, Mrs. Conant relayed two dozen messages from the departed to earthly friends and family. Among the spirits speaking through Conant was "H. J. Gardner, who died by poison recently."

> *Years ago I clasped one to my bosom whom I supposed would be true to me, to herself, to her children, and to her God. Dark is the page. She has proved unfaithful – she has proved a demon. She suffers – so do I – so do the children – so do the friends. I am here, I scarce know why; I was brought to you, for what purpose I know not. My name is*

Gardner; I lived in Hingham. I feel sad for those I have left behind – not for myself. My mother! My children! It is for them I am unhappy. She who was a part of myself has transgressed all human and divine laws.

I do not know when I returned to earth; it seems to be a mystery which is yet to be unraveled. I listened to the spiritual discussion when on earth, and read papers upon the subject which were left in my office, and gained some information in this way. But why I am brought to a medium who is a stranger, by spirits who are strangers to me, I am at a loss to account; but I suppose it is the will of God.

Oh, God! Forgive those who have sinned. This was my last prayer on earth – it is my first thought now. May they cease to do evil and learn to do well. May no more poisoned arrows be aimed at unconscious hearts. May the public deal in wisdom; may justice perform her mission; may charity also have an abiding place among the sterner members of the council. I see it, comprehend it, know the consequences, know the sin, and know also that stern iron will that urged the hand which sent me here. 'Tis for that I pray, that love may soften that adamantine heart, and make it all it should be in the sight of man and of God.

It comes to me that I have much to give you. For the present let us veil the past, and penetrate the future, courting blessings from thence. I am dead to the world, I live not in a visible form, yet I can return. I do return, and I shall continue to return, as I am to be an instrument through whom vengeance is to come, through whom peace is to come also; through whom pardon is to come to those who have sinned, who have desecrated the temple of the Lord God by murder.

I have friends. To them say my friendship will never

die, but continue to burn brighter and brighter, till I clasp them by the hand in the spiritual life.

I have children and a parent on earth. To them say that the love of a parent and of a child waxeth not old, neither decayeth it, with the body of dust.

I have enemies. To them I say, I sue for pardon for all wrong I may have done them, as together we must bow before the great intellectual throne of love, and together as forgiveness.

Many believed in Fanny's psychic abilities but still more doubted her powers were genuine. Among the Spiritualist movement skeptics were leaders of organized religion and public figures, including legendary showman P. T. Barnum, who considered mediumship a farce. In his 1866 book, "The Humbugs of the World: An Account of Humbugs, Delusions, Impositions, Quackeries, Deceits and Deceivers Generally, in all Ages," Barnum, a master of deception himself, cites mediumship in general and Fanny Conant and the *Banner of Light* in particular, saying:

"Having read obituary notices in the files of old newspapers and the published list of those recently killed in battle, the medium has data for any number of 'messages.' She [Conant] talks in the style she imagines the person whom she attempts to personate would use, being one of the doctrines of spiritualism that a person's character and feelings are not changed by death. To make the humbug more complete, she narrates imaginary incidents, asserting them to have occurred in the earth-experience of the spirit who purports to have possession of her at the same time she is speaking. Mediums in various parts of the country furnish her with the names of and facts relative to different deceased people of their acquaintance, and those names and facts are used by her in supplying the 'Message Department' of the '*Banner of Light*.'"

***

District Attorney James Keith convened a grand jury at the Plymouth County Courthouse on Wednesday, April 1, to secure an indictment against Abigail. He had summoned only those witnesses he believed necessary. Drs. Stephenson, Wilson, Ellis, and Jackson, Coroner Lewis, Sophia Gardner, and Charles Dodge testified. Jurors found sufficient probable cause to indict Abigail for murder and handed up a true bill.

The following Saturday deputy sheriffs marshalled Abigail from the jail to the courthouse for arraignment on the indictment before the Court of Common Pleas. The court entered Abigail's not guilty plea, set a May trial date, and ordered her held without bail.

The court appointed attorneys Charles G. Davis and Benjamin W. Harris to defend her. Davis, at thirty-seven-years old, had already gained prominence among his peers in the legal profession. Harris was three years younger than Davis and, along with his law practice, he represented parts of Plymouth County as a state senator.

***

Only days after Abigail's arraignment, the court postponed her trial until the September session and notified the prosecution and defense of the change. The delay exasperated Abigail but afforded her counsel much needed time to prepare for trial.

Abigail had grown accustomed to the jail's daily routine by this time. There was little work for her and other women prisoners; books and newspapers provided the only distraction. The jail cells were four and one-half feet by eight feet with walls eight feet high and were lighted by gas for two hours each day.

All of the female inmates, with the exception of Abigail, were serving time from one week to three months for minor offenses, including liquor law violations, bigamy, drunkenness, adultery, and assault. In several cases, the jail accommodated dependent, minor children of women who otherwise faced destitution outside the jail's confines. Watchmen provided lessons in reading, writing, and arithmetic, and religious services were conducted once a week.

Members of the state legislature, at the invitation of Plymouth selectmen, toured the historic town and its institutions two weeks after Abigail's indictment. Among the legislators were members of the Committee on Prisons and, along with other colleagues and Boston newspapermen, they visited the county jail and house of correction to inspect conditions and observe the treatment of prisoners.

The visitors encountered Abigail (dubbed the "Lucrezia Borgia of Hingham" by one reporter) in her cell during their tour of the jail and, with the turnkey's permission, engaged her in conversation. The lawmakers were fascinated with her calm, self-possessed demeanor despite the gravity of her situation. Abigail answered their questions freely and "with remarkable firmness."

"Gentlemen, I am innocent of the charge placed against me and regret my trial will not begin until September," a sanguine Abigail remarked as a *Boston Traveler* correspondent scribbled hastily in his notebook. "I can assure you I will be acquitted when the time comes."

"I admit my husband and I had our difficulties," she continued. "I am a victim of religious persecution. My husband forbade me from attending the Baptist church and on occasion threatened me if I did not sever my affiliation."

"How did your husband come to meet his death, Mrs. Gardner?" a solon boldly asked.

"There is no question in my mind. He took his own life," said Abigail.

***

Joseph Newhall departed for the post office from his cabinet shop on a pleasant spring morning to coordinate Hosea's interment with Abby who was alone inside when he entered. He removed his hat and rotated the brim in his hands.

"Good morning, Miss Gardner," said Newhall. "Do you have a moment?"

"Good morning to you, Mr. Newhall. How may I help you?" asked Abby.

"Miss Gardner, I'm sorry I must speak of this, but now is an appropriate time to inter your father's remains."

"Thank you, Mr. Newhall. I know how difficult it must be for you to come to me under the circumstances. I will inform Grandmother and other family members and I'll speak with Reverends Tilson and Cargill about a graveside service. I'd like to keep it a private affair."

"As you wish," said Newhall. "I'll wait to hear from you."

Abby confirmed the date and time with Newhall. He and his assistants removed Hosea's coffin from the receiving tomb at Centre Cemetery two days later. They carried it a few hundred feet to an open grave where Reverends Tilson and Cargill, Abby, Marcus, Hosea's mother, other family members, and several representatives from Hosea's temperance group were gathered. After the two clergymen conducted a brief prayer service, Newhall and his men committed Hosea's remains to the earth.

Abby had grown concerned with her grandmother's appearance as the services progressed.

"Are you not well, Grandmother?" Abby asked.

"I'm fine, Abby. There's no need for worry. I've felt weak lately, but I'm sure it will pass."

"Please, Grandmother," Abby replied, "if there is anything I can do, call on me."

"Thank you, Abby. You are such a devoted child. God bless you, my dear."

***

Attorneys Davis and Harris went over the inquest transcript and evidence at Davis's office frequently throughout the months of July and August. Their conversations with Abigail at the jail and a psychiatric examination they had arranged had persuaded them to abandon an insanity defense and attack the government's evidence head on.

"It will be important for us to emphasize the uncertainty of circumstantial evidence before the jury, Benjamin," Davis said.

"I agree, Charles. No one at the inquest ever testified to witnessing Mrs. Gardner administer poison or any other substance to her husband to cause his death. There were at least a half dozen people who had access to the victim during his illness. Any one of them could have done the deed."

"True; and we cannot rule out death by suicide or accident either. But perhaps we're getting ahead of ourselves. The government will first have to prove Mr. Gardner died as a result of poisoning. Dr. Jackson will be a critical witness for the government. We will have to discredit his analysis and findings with our own medical evidence," Harris remarked.

"We must also create doubt about the medicines and salts ingested by the man and the purity of these substances," said Davis.

"Not to mention the potentially lethal qualities of these compounds."

"We can expect the government to present the conversation Dr. Stephenson had with the deceased about Mrs. Gardner's alleged adulterous affair."

"Yes; and the government will also call the victim's mother. The victim allegedly told her his wife had poisoned him and would poison her, too."

"I don't understand why Mrs. Gardner would tell Dr. Stephenson about her intention to murder her husband. It makes no sense to me. Why would she? She would seal her own fate by making such a statement. Stephenson's credibility is a factor here."

"Maybe, but remember, she said her husband was jealous of her and he had cause. Perhaps he had grown tired of life and ended it in his own way. He was physically exhausted and his wife's admitted infidelity surely humiliated him," Harris asserted.

"We have much work left to do, Benjamin, and not much time with which to do it. Let's meet again tomorrow," Davis said.

***

District Attorney Keith left his home in Roxbury the week after

Abigail's arraignment to meet with the Commonwealth's forty-eight-year-old attorney general, John Clifford, at his state house office. A one-term Massachusetts governor, Clifford had achieved fame for his successful prosecution of Harvard professor John Webster in the sensational 1850 Parkman murder trial. The attorney general prosecuted all crimes punishable by death. The district attorney with jurisdiction over the county where the crime occurred assisted him.

Clifford greeted Keith warmly and, after brief pleasantries, they sat to discuss the Gardner murder.

"General," Keith began as he opened his leather satchel, "this case is entirely circumstantial in nature. No one actually witnessed the prisoner administer poison to her husband but, in my opinion, all other facts, when considered together, prove beyond a reasonable doubt there was no other who could have done so."

Keith laid out the case and submitted transcripts of the testimony given during the coroner's inquest and the grand jury proceedings. He discussed at length the results of the post-mortem examination, the chemical analysis of the organs, and the confirmed presence of arsenic; as well as Dr. Wilson's testimony and his eyewitness account of the prisoner burying the slop pail's contents beneath the snow in the yard behind the Gardner house and their recovery by Wilson and others.

"Where are the slops now, Jim?"

"The dentist believes they are in John Stephenson's possession. He was one of the men who collected them. I have not as yet spoken with Stephenson. I trust he still has the vessel. I'll make sure they are analyzed by Dr. Jackson as soon as possible."

Keith highlighted the statements of the druggist, Hunt, and the errand boy, Dodge, and the purchase and delivery of arsenic to the prisoner. He emphasized the inconsistent statements made by the prisoner at the inquest, the prisoner's inability to produce the mysterious Paddy woman, conversations made by both the prisoner and the victim to Dr. Stephenson concerning the prisoner's illicit affair and the threats she had made to the victim, and statements made by the victim to his mother about his fears of poisoning by the prisoner. He underscored the prisoner's cold, unfeeling behavior following her husband's death and interment, as well as her refusal to permit an autopsy and the indifference she displayed when she consented to the severing of her husband's deformed leg to accommodate the coffin's dimensions.

"Certainly, each fact, as it stands alone, does not prove her guilt," Clifford said to Keith. "But each of the facts together forms a chain of overwhelming circumstantial evidence. Mrs. Gardner certainly had the motive, means, and opportunity to poison her husband."

"Yes," said Keith. "Who else could have administered the poison? There were others who had access to Mr. Gardner during his illness, but none had a motive."

"What do we know about the man involved in this illicit relationship with the prisoner? Is there any truth to it? Does anyone know who he is and has anyone spoken to him?" Clifford asked.

"Our only basis for confirming the affair is through the prisoner's own admission to Dr. Stephenson. She wouldn't tell Stephenson who the man was. He is supposedly a married man named Kenerson who runs an express service in the town. He keeps his horses and rigs in a barn behind the Gardner house. People in town allege they saw the defendant frequently visiting the barn while Kenerson was there."

"Has anyone questioned this man?"

"I asked Constable Hersey to speak with him and Kenerson denies any involvement with the prisoner. He told Hersey he is happily married and was insulted by any suggestion of infidelity. It will be impossible for us to prove an adulterous affair without direct evidence."

"Then I suggest we proceed with the doctor's statement alone," Clifford said.

"I agree, General," Keith replied.

The two lawyers strategized on potential opening statements, closing arguments, and the order of witnesses. They agreed upon presenting the inquest coroner first. The remaining slate of witnesses was then established: the physicians and chemists; the druggist and the errand boy; the three men who recovered the slops from the snow; the tailor who discovered Hosea on the night of his fall; Edwin Wilder and Otis Hersey, who attended Hosea; Hosea's children, Abby and Marcus; the arresting constable; and, finally, Dr. Ezra Stephenson and the victim's mother, Sophia Gardner, to provide the most crucial evidence in the case. Clifford advised Keith to retain a civil engineer to draw up a plan of the Gardner house and surrounding grounds to use as a reference during trial.

"I'm confident we can present a strong case, Jim," Clifford continued. "My only concern is the widespread reluctance of jurors to convict anyone of a capital crime, let alone a woman. The county hasn't executed a woman since 1727; and it's been nearly sixty years since the Commonwealth has hanged one."

"I'm of the same mind. We'll have to use our challenges judiciously to purge the jury of death penalty opponents and empanel those who are prepared to weigh the facts with impartiality."

***

Sophia Gardner's health worsened as the days wore on. She feared she had unwittingly ingested some of the arsenic Abigail had given to her son and called on Dr. Stephenson.

Stephenson arrived at the Wade house immediately after receiving Sophia's request. During his examination he noted an accelerated pulse, redness and swelling about Sophia's face, and a smooth, shining appearance to her skin. She complained of thirst, headache, occasional vomiting, loss of appetite, and a burning pain in her limbs. On examining her hands and feet, the physician detected a thin, yellowish, serous fluid beneath the cuticles of her fingers and toes.

Now regrettably more familiar with the effects of arsenic,

101

Stephenson ruled out poisoning as the cause of Sophia's condition and instead diagnosed erysipelas, otherwise known as St. Anthony's fire, a skin infection fatal to feeble, aged patients. Its cause was still a great mystery to the medical profession and there was no known antidote. His only recourse was to treat Sophia with zinc oxide ointment, glycerin, and laudanum and water, and pray her condition would improve.

Stephenson advised Coroner James Lewis about Sophia's dire prognosis and he immediately contacted District Attorney Keith. Keith directed the coroner to depose her as soon as possible and Lewis did so the next day.

***

Correspondence between Keith and Attorney General Clifford continued throughout the month of August. Conflicts with their busy schedules hampered attempts to meet and further discuss the case. Keith forwarded a note to Clifford by messenger from his Boston office at 42 Court Street on August 20:

> *Dear Sir:*
>
> *I have completed the criminal business at Plymouth and find my civil suits will not be reached until next week. I shall therefore be in my office the remainder of this week and could consult with you there or at any other place you would designate. The trial is so near, no time should be lost in the preparation; and my time is so likely to be taken up by a large portion of next week I should much prefer to attend to it now if possible.*
>
> *Please let me know your arrangements as soon as possible and I will do all in my power to meet you at the earliest date.*
>
> *Truly yours,*
> *J. M. Keith*

Clifford offered to meet with the district attorney in Plymouth the following week but Keith could not agree on a date. He explained the circumstances in a note he sent to Clifford on August 21. He also informed Clifford about the activities of Attorney Charles Davis, Abigail's defense counsel, which included a trip to Abigail's home in Maine in search of family members and friends and a consultation with Dr. Isaac Ray, superintendent of the Butler Asylum for the Insane in Providence, Rhode Island, about a possible insanity defense.

Dear Sir:

Yours of the 20ᵗʰ is received. I am unable to state the days next week I shall be at Plymouth. I shall go down on Monday [August 24] *and then I shall have to wait my turn for a trial. I shall stop until I get a trial unless when I arrive, there is a strong probability that it will not be reached until the latter part of the week in which case I shall return and go down again later.*

Davis has been to Maine to hunt for evidence and talks of having Dr. Ray, as I understand, from Providence.

Would it not be well for you to see Drs. Jackson and Ellis at my office? I could procure their attendance if desired. In case you cannot come up tomorrow drop me a line stating where you will be and I will go where you send me as I am at your command.

Truly yours,
J. M. Keith

***

Clifford left New Bedford by train on Saturday morning, August 22, to meet Keith at his Boston office.

Keith removed several folders from his leather valise and from one removed Sophia Gardner's deposition.

"Mrs. Gardner is deathly ill, General, and I don't expect her to last through the week. I intend to visit her in Hingham again tomorrow, if possible," Keith began.

"This is an unfortunate turn of events, James."

Clifford scrutinized the deposition.

"I will have to make a strong argument at trial for the court to admit her deposition since it was taken in the absence of the defendant and her counsel."

"What about the transcript of her testimony at the inquest? The defendant was present with her attorney."

"I'm afraid not. The courts continue to prohibit prior recorded testimony as hearsay."

"But her testimony is critical. What are we to do?" Keith asked.

"There is a possibility," Clifford replied. "As you know, a dying declaration is one of the exceptions to the hearsay rule. We will have to show Hosea Gardner believed his death was imminent when he told his mother the defendant had poisoned him."

"And if the court disagrees?"

"Then we will have to rely on the testimony of others, particularly, Dr. Stephenson."

"Yes, General," said Keith. "I'll speak with Dr. Stephenson during my visit tomorrow to firm up his testimony. I'll also confirm the whereabouts of the copper vessel and slops; and I'll speak with Charles Dodge, the boy Mrs. Gardner sent to the druggist for the arsenic. Justice Lewis has told me the boy is terrified. I want to pin down his statements and assuage any fears he might have," Keith said. "His testimony is the strongest evidence we have linking the arsenic between Hunt and the defendant. I haven't had an opportunity to interview the Gardner children, either, and will speak with them if possible."

***

On Sunday morning, August 23, Ezra Stephenson greeted District Attorney Keith as he disembarked from his train at Hingham depot.

"Good morning, Mr. Keith. I'm afraid I have some sad news," Stephenson said, hat in hand. "Sophia Gardner died last night,"

"I'm sorry to hear this, Doctor. The poor woman has been through so much the past seven months."

"Yes, she has. I have no doubt arsenic had affected her health at some time. She firmly believed she had inadvertently ingested some of the toxin administered to her son, and I did observe some symptoms consistent with poisoning when I first treated her, but in my opinion she hadn't consumed enough to cause death. I am convinced Sophia's death was caused by a fatal skin condition known as St. Anthony's fire, but I will perform a post-mortem examination today to confirm my diagnosis."

"Thank you, Doctor," said Keith, "and if your examination should uncover any indication of poisoning in the viscera, I trust you'll contact me immediately?"

"I certainly will, Mr. Keith," Stephenson replied.

The two men found a quiet corner inside the station and spent an hour discussing the case.

"Can you tell me who has custody of the slops taken from behind the Gardner home, Doctor?" Keith asked when the discussion concluded.

"Yes, my brother, John, still has them in his possession under lock and key at his office in Hingham Centre."

"I see. Would you mind speaking with him? The trial is fast approaching and I'd like to have the slops and container analyzed as soon as possible."

"He has business in Boston tomorrow. I'm sure he would be more than happy to deliver them to Dr. Jackson."

"Thank you, Dr. Stephenson. It will be most helpful."

"I wish to speak with the Dodge boy, and I'd like to interview Miss Gardner and her brother and offer my condolences. Can you tell me how best to get to their homes?"

"I doubt you'll find the Gardners at home, Mr. Keith. I believe they are at the grandmother's house with family. As to the Dodge boy, he lives at Mrs. Miller's house, which is less than one hundred yards from here on North Street."

Stephenson accompanied the district attorney outside and

pointed to the residence. It was a beautiful day with a light, refreshing breeze from the harbor. Keith knocked on the door and was met by Mrs. Miller, the boy's aunt. She had met the prosecutor at the grand jury proceedings and was surprised to see him. He stated his purpose and she allowed him inside. He spent nearly an hour with the eleven-year-old and, at the end of their meeting, he concluded the boy would testify competently.

Keith next went across the street to the Gardner house. He found no one there so determined he would interview them before the trial commenced on the first day. He returned to the depot to wait for the next train to Braintree and his connection to Boston.

When he arrived at his Roxbury home in late afternoon, he sent a message to the attorney general. He brought Clifford up to date about his conversations with the witnesses, the contents of the slop pail in John Stephenson's possession, and confirmed the time and place they were to meet Drs. Ellis and Jackson.

Dear Sir:

I have just returned from Hingham where I learned that Mrs. Sophia Gardner died last night. I found the remains of the slop pail gathered up from the snow had been preserved and I had them conveyed to Dr. Jackson for analysis. I fear no good will result from the analysis however, for the remains had been kept in a copper vessel and Dr. Jackson says traces of arsenic are not infrequently found in copper.

I also saw the boy and found he told the same story, though he is extremely diffident and timid. I endeavored to gain his confidence and measurably succeeded. I found also he had some more idea of moral obligation than I had supposed so that he will be a competent witness.

Drs. Jackson and Ellis will meet us at the Samoset House [Plymouth hotel] *Monday evening, the 31st instant.*

Yours truly,
J. M. Keith

Within four days of Keith's letter to Clifford, Sophia's "rumored death by poison" appeared in Boston dailies and in the *Hingham Journal*, fueling public outrage and fervor for the conviction of her daughter-in-law. "Ever since the death of her son," said the *Journal*, "she [Sophia] had been failing, the symptoms of her complaints indicating she was suffering from slow poison, which it is believed she infused into her system while attending upon her son during his illness, in consequence of tasting the fatal draughts which were prepared for him by his wife."

Dr. Stephenson's post-mortem examination and an analysis of Sophia's viscera by the state assayer later validated Dr. Stephenson's diagnosis of erysipelas as the cause of death and conclusively disproved the presence of poison in her system.

A funeral was held in Hingham the day after the autopsy, and Sophia was laid to rest beside her husband, Hosea, Sr., at Hingham Centre Cemetery.

***

A *Boston Herald* reporter visited the Plymouth jail the day before Abigail's trial began. A guard led him to the jail's female ward, which she alone occupied. He wrote that the cell where she slept was "very neat and clean, and evidently well taken care of by its occupant."

The conversation began with small talk, Abigail noting the agreeableness of the weather. She refused to discuss her case and chose instead to speak about her dull existence within the prison's confining walls.

A mounting sense of apprehension seized the correspondent as his interaction with Abigail progressed. He detected "no softness in feature or expression, but a hard, masculine look which would deter a person from approaching her too familiarly, and make him cautious about offending her."

"Thank you for calling to see me," Abigail said at the visit's conclusion. "I look forward to visitors. I've been in jail for six months, but it seems like a year. I'm surprised more haven't called on the eve of my trial. I had expected to see some of my friends from Maine, but perhaps they haven't arrived as yet."

The jail's turnkey led the reporter from the ward and, locking the door he said, "She is the worst woman I have ever had to deal with."

"How so?" the reporter asked.

"Incidents of her volatile and disagreeable nature are too numerous to mention, but let me give you one example. It took place in the prison yard. She and other inmates were granted liberty from their cells to take advantage of the fresh air and sunshine on one particular afternoon. While strolling about, Mrs. Gardner seized a young female prisoner and threw her clothes over her head, exposing her underpinnings to a number of male convicts nearby. Mrs. Gardner sorely misjudged this dissolute inmate's temperament, however. The girl, who knew a little of the science of pugilism, resented the shame thus put upon her by knocking Mrs. Gardner prostrate with a well-directed blow over one of her eyes."

***

"Mrs. Gardner is a woman of about 50 years of age, of forbidding countenance, with an eye and general expression of features betokening evil things," wrote a *Boston Traveler* correspondent who visited Abigail later the same day. "She appears like a person possessing a guilty secret, and reveling in the enjoyment of the unenviable knowledge. To this time, she has admitted to no one her guilt, not even to her counsel. She stoutly maintains her innocence to those in whose hands her life is placed, though she converses freely with them as to all the incidents of the last sickness of Mr. Gardner. She is evidently a woman of large natural capability, but of little or no education, and without a particle of refinement, and an exceedingly poor development of moral qualities. Her conscience to the most casual observer would be pronounced infinitesimal. She jests, unreservedly, with the numbers visiting her, about the chances of her conviction or acquittal, and takes it for granted she 'never was born to be hanged.' When your correspondent saw her yesterday, her principal anxiety was about her appearance at the trial, in what costume she would make the most favorable impression to beholders.

"The line of defense is not fully determined. It must be insanity, insufficiency of evidence, or a want of irrefragable proof of guilt. Hardly anybody in Plymouth, however, anticipates a verdict of murder against the suspected woman."

Abigail Marshall Gardner, 1857
(Courtesy of *National Police Gazette*)

Broad Bridge, Main Street, Hingham, looking south toward Derby Academy -
wagon in front of post office; John Todd's shop in foreground left
(Courtesy of Hingham Historical Society)

Thaxter Mansion, North Street; sign on tree identifies Union Hotel
(Courtesy of Hingham Historical Society)

Lincoln House on North Street to right of Union Hotel
(Courtesy of Hingham Historical Society)

Union Hotel (now the site of Hingham Post Office), looking from Broad Bridge
and railroad tracks; Lincoln house to right of hotel; Thaxter Building, right
foreground (Courtesy of Hingham Historical Society)

Dr. Ezra Stephenson (1805-1874)
(Courtesy of Hingham Historical Society)

Dr. Robert T. P. Fiske (1799-1866)
(Courtesy of Hingham Historical Society)

Dr. Charles Thomas Jackson (1805-1880)
(From *Popular Science* Monthly, Volume 19, 1881)

Dr. Calvin B. Ellis (1826-1883)
(Courtesy of Francis A. Countway Library of Medicine, Boston)

Attorney General John H. Clifford
(1809-1876)
(From *New England Magazine*, Volume
25, No. 6, 1902)

District Attorney James Monroe Keith
(1819-1894) (from *The Independent
Corps of Cadets of Boston, Mass., at
Fort Warren, Boston Harbor, in 1862.*
Henry Watson Gore
(Boston: Press of Rockwell and
Churchill, 1888))

Stephen Henry Phillips (1823-1897)
(Courtesy of Peabody Essex Museum)

Charles Gideon Davis (1820-1903)
(From *One of a Thousand: a Series of
Biographical Sketches of One Thousand
Representative Men Resident In the
Commonwealth of Massachusetts,
A.D. 1888-89*)

Attorney Benjamin W. Harris (1823-1907)
(Courtesy of Library of Congress)

116

First Universalist Meeting House, 1885
(Courtesy of Hingham Historical Society)

First Baptist Church, Hingham, 1885
(Courtesy of Hingham Historical Society)

Receiving Tomb, Hingham Centre Cemetery
(Courtesy of the author)

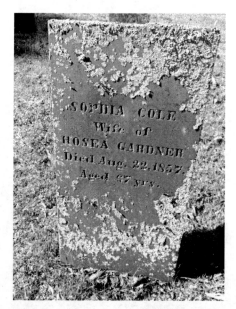

Gravestone of Sophia Gardner, Hingham Centre
Cemetery (Courtesy of the author)

"Meg Merillees"
(Courtesy of Library of Congress)

FABEN'S GREAT EXHIBITION

—or—

Wax Figures

ARE NOW EXHIBITING, FOR TEN DAYS,

—AT—

85 Hanover (opposite Portland) St.

A Full Representation of the Burdell
Murder! Life-Size Figures of

DR. BURDELL,   MRS. CUNNINGHAM and
J. J. ECKEL,   Daughters,
YOUNG SNODGRASS, MRS. GARDNER, Hingham
FARRELL the Witness, MR. & MRS. BRIGGS,
MAGEE and DECATUR, of Charlestown State Prison
and many others, all of which are pronounced by
judges to be perfect likenesses.
  Open day and evening.   Admittance, 15 cents.
    mh28   ..1w

Boston Herald, March 31, 1857, Mrs. Gardner Wax Figure

Holiday Gifts!

THE Holidays are at hand, and all those who are desirous of making glad the hearts of their young friends by some appropriate Gifts, are invited to call on the subscriber, who is prepared to show them the largest variety of Goods suitable for

PRESENTS!

EVER OFFERED IN HINGHAM,

consisting of

BOOKS, GAMES, TOYS,

TOILET AND FANCY ARTICLES,

All of which will be sold at

Astonishingly Low Prices.

H. J. GARDNER,

POST OFFICE BUILDING.

Hingham, Dec. 19, 1856. tf

Gardner Advertisement, *Hingham Journal*, 1856

FINE GOODS

For Spring & Summer Wear.

—ALSO—

READY-MADE CLOTHING.

JOHN TODD,

TILDEN'S BUILDING, has just received a large and elegant assortment of

Cloths, Cassimeres, Doeskins,
AND VESTINGS,

From fresh imported and domestic Goods, that will be manufactured into Garments made to order, in the best manner, and on as good terms as can be obtained in Boston or elsewhere.

The attention of the public is invited to his extensive assortment of

Ready-Made Clothing,

which is selected by himself with great care, and for superior workmanship and style is unsurpassed.

Also may be found at this establishment an elegant assortment of

FURNISHING GOODS,

Consisting of Undershirts, Drawers, Scarfs, Stocks, Gloves, Suspenders, Bosoms, Collars, Shirts, &c., &c.

Persons in want of anything in the above line, are invited to call, and they will find business done on a principle that will meet the reasonable expectations of all, and

PERFECT SATISFACTION GIVEN.

Having for a long time administered to the wants of the *outer* man, he hopes that the same liberal patronage which he has hitherto received may be tendered to him in future.

Hingham, March 20, 1857. tf

John Todd Tailor Shop
Advertisement,
Hingham Journal, 1857

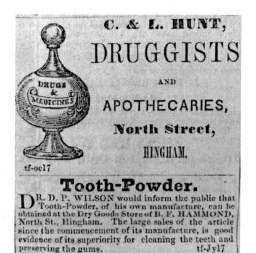

C. & L. HUNT,

DRUGGISTS

AND

APOTHECARIES,

North Street,

HINGHAM.

DRUGS & MEDICINES

tf-oc17

Tooth-Powder.

DR. D. P. WILSON would inform the public that Tooth-Powder, of his own manufacture, can be obtained at the Dry Goods Store of B. F. HAMMOND, North St., Hingham. The large sales of the article since the commencement of its manufacture, is good evidence of its superiority for cleaning the teeth and preserving the gums. tf-Jyl7

Advertisements, *Hingham Journal*, 1857;
Hunt Druggist; Dr. Don Pedro Wilson
Tooth Powder

Levi Hersey, husband of Abby Williams
Gardner (Courtesy of M. J. Molinari)

Reverend Isaac Henry Coe (1818-
1911), prison chaplain
(Courtesy of the State Library of
Massachusetts)

Frances Ann Conant, medium of
Hosea's spirit (Courtesy of Library
of Congress)

Chapter 6: The Trial

Abby and Marcus were up before dawn on Tuesday morning, September 1. They washed and dressed and had a light breakfast before their aunt and uncle, Alice and Reuben Reed, arrived at the house. They walked together across North Street to the depot to board the 6:40 a.m. Cohasset to Boston train bound for Braintree. It was a cloudless, balmy day with light, northeast breezes.

Abby cringed when she saw the number of people clustered about the depot's front entrance and beyond. A carnival atmosphere prevailed as those in line for tickets talked and laughed. The crowd swelled as carriages and buggies pulled up to the station and discharged harried passengers. It seemed the entire town had turned out for the trial.

"Uncle, I don't know if I can bear this," Abby said.

"It will be alright, Abby," Reuben assured her. "Go along inside while I wait in line."

"It's not necessary, Uncle. I purchased tickets yesterday while the station was quiet."

"Thank you for doing so, Abby," Reuben said with a breath of relief. "We may not have found a seat."

"I'm sure it won't be a problem, Uncle. The station master told me the railroad anticipated an overflow with the trial and added extra cars to the morning train."

A group of men and women at the station door ceased their conversation and stepped aside when they saw Abby and her family approaching. The clamor inside the station was deafening. Reuben opened the door, and Abby entered with Marcus and Alice. An awkward silence enveloped the overcrowded waiting area.

Abby saw Mr. Lewis, Mr. Hunt, Mr. and Mrs. Miller, their son, Henry, and their nephew, Charles Dodge, seated on a bench in a far corner. Abby looked in their direction and they all averted their eyes.

"May we go out on the platform, Uncle? I'd find it much more comfortable," Abby said.

"Yes, why don't we? It's a beautiful morning," Reuben replied.

Several men standing in front of the platform door doffed their hats and made way.

"Marcus, when the cars pull in, we will wait for the Millers and the two boys to board," Abby said outside. "I'd prefer to sit in another car to avoid any unpleasantness."

***

The train departed with its passengers from the Cohasset depot promptly at 6:35 a.m. for its twelve-mile, one-half hour journey to Braintree. It stopped at Nantasket and Hingham's Old Colony House and ten minutes later signaled its approach to Hingham village. The conductor, dressed in a double-breasted frock coat and straight visor cap, lowered the stairs on each of the cars as passengers emerged from the station and congregated on the platform. The Millers presented their tickets and, with Mr. Lewis and Mr. Hunt, took seats in the first car. Abby and Marcus stepped to the last car and waited for the conductor before they boarded with the Reeds.

They quickly found seats in the nearly empty coach. Workers had replaced the winter season wood stove with additional low-back seats in the center of the car. Dark, ornate wood decorated the interior. Two whale oil lamps attached to the walls provided light at night and mirrors installed at either end of the car allowed passengers to see themselves "as others saw them."

The train chugged away from Hingham, stopped in East Weymouth, North Weymouth, and Weymouth Landing, and continued on to East Braintree, where Abby disembarked with her family and other passengers to await the Plymouth-bound train from Boston. The Old Colony steam engine, with its bright yellow cars, pulled up to the platform on schedule. As soon as Abby and Marcus had found seats behind the Reeds, the train embarked for its hour-long journey to Plymouth, twenty-six miles away.

Two gaily dressed women boarded at the Hanson depot. They chatted and tittered as they made their way down the aisle and took seats opposite Abby and Marcus. Marcus amused himself watching them wind and tuck the steel bands of their hoopskirts for comfort.

Fifteen minutes after the train's departure, the loquacious pair quieted down. One of the women reached into her embroidered handbag and extracted a papier-mâché eyeglass case with a mother of pearl inlay. She curled a pair of blue-steeled wire spectacles from the case around her ears and unfolded a newspaper on her lap.

"Listen to this, Martha," the woman said moments later to her companion. She read aloud from the *Boston Traveler* morning edition.

"The trial of a female, on the charge of murder, is of rare occurrence in this country, and that alone is calculated to make this an occasion of unusual excitement and interest. Though instances of death where there were strong suspicions of the deliberate administration of poison, with murderous intent, are not unknown among us, yet we can remember no conviction upon a capital charge of this character, in this state, for the past quarter of a century."

"I've never been to a murder trial before," Mabel. "I can't wait to get a glimpse of the horrid Gardner woman. All the papers say she is guilty! I hope we can get seats in the courtroom."

"I'm anxious to hear about her steamy affair," Mabel replied. "Can you imagine? The press has claimed she cavorted with a married man in a barn behind her house!"

Marcus leaned close to his sister.

"Abby, those two women said something about Mother," he whispered.

"Don't pay any attention to them, Marcus. They obviously don't know who we are. If they did, they'd surely be more considerate."

Abby closed her eyes and a tear rolled down her cheek. *How will Marcus and I ever get through this day?*

She stared out at the bleak landscape as the train rocked to and fro along the narrow tracks. The obnoxious pair across the aisle prattled on with their foolishness until at last the reproachful stares of other passengers hushed them.

***

The Plymouth depot was bustling with activity when the train came to a halt at the platform. A conductor assisted Alice and Abby as they descended the car's rickety stairway. They were met with the smell of salt air and a flock of noisy gulls circling above. An ocean breeze carried the sound of clanging sails and pulleys on the fishing vessels and merchant ships moored at the waterfront.

Abby cringed when she emerged from the station and saw a newsboy on the corner waving the morning edition.

"Extra, extra," he shouted. "Read all about it. Mrs. Gardner on trial for poisoning her husband; trial here this morning in Plymouth; all the latest details!"

She took Marcus by the hand and hurried past with her aunt and uncle in tow. Nearly all the other passengers behind and in front of them clambered up Depot Avenue's steep incline. The stately Samoset House Hotel appeared at the crest. They turned south on Court Street and walked five blocks to Court Square. Passengers who had accompanied them from the station melded into an immense crowd, mainly women, already gathered at the courthouse steps.

"Come this way," her uncle said. "Constable Hersey told me to use the south side entrance."

A deputy sheriff was stationed at the South Russell Street door. Reuben showed him the subpoenas they had all received and he admitted them. A court officer escorted them to the district attorney's office, and Keith briefly interviewed Abby and Marcus.

"I don't know if I'll call you to testify today. It depends on how long it takes to empanel a jury. I can assure you your testimony will be heard by the end of tomorrow's session."

The court officer guided Abby and her family to the second

floor. He led Abby and Alice to a witness room designated for women and Reuben and Marcus to one set aside for men.

"I will return when the district attorney calls for your testimony," the officer said to all. "In the meantime, I advise you not to discuss the case. I will bring refreshments when the court recesses in the afternoon."

James Lewis and James Hunt were in the men's witness room and nodded to Reuben when he came in with Marcus. John Stephenson was there as well, and he and Reuben chatted amiably. The Miller and Dodge boys sat sullenly and said nothing. Abby and Alice Reed found themselves alone in the women's room. Mr. and Mrs. Miller had taken seats in the courtroom.

***

The courthouse door opened a half-hour before the trial was to begin and the crowd surged forward. Deputies and court officers jostled with men and women alike as they vied for admittance and one of the few remaining courtroom seats. Sheriff Phillips had reserved most of the seats in the gallery for the press and jury pool. Preference was given to the ladies. Disappointed spectators who were turned away, according to one correspondent, "[were] compelled to resort to the hotels, saloons, and shops, where an immense amount of smoking, drinking, eating and cursing, both loud and deep, [was] accomplished."

Attorney General Clifford and District Attorney Keith had already taken their places at the prosecution table. Attorneys Davis and Harris conversed quietly at the defense table, discussing last minute details as they awaited Abigail's arrival.

Shortly after ten o'clock a court officer guided Abigail to the right of the judge's elevated bench and into the prisoner's dock. She was dressed entirely in black and a sheer veil screened her face, much to the disappointment of spectators straining to see her.

Davis and Harris strode over to Abigail and conversed with her briefly. Davis placed his hand on hers in an obvious sign of assurance as she nodded at each of his comments.

"Court! All rise," Sheriff Phillips declared as he entered the courtroom through the door of the judges' chambers. Phillips stepped aside and Supreme Judicial Court Justices Metcalf, Merrick, and Bigelow emerged, ascended to the bench, and called the court to order.

Attorney General Clifford nodded deferentially to the magistrates. Metcalf had presided over the Webster murder trial prosecuted by Clifford in 1850 and Merrick, as opposing counsel, had represented Webster.

All remained standing as Plymouth's First Parish Church Pastor James Kendall opened the proceedings with a prayer. The prayer concluded and all but the attorney general took their seats.

"May it please Your Honors, the Grand Jury for the Plymouth County found and returned an indictment against Abigail Gardner, for the murder of her husband, Hosea J. Gardner. That indictment has been duly certified into this court. The prisoner, at a former day, was arraigned thereon, and pleaded not guilty. Counsel was assigned to aid her in her defense, and this day was appointed for her trial. The prisoner and her counsel are present in court; and I now move Your Honors, for the court to empanel a jury to try the issue."

Court clerk William H. Whitman, at Justice Metcalf's instruction, ordered Sheriff Phillips to summon the thirty-six Plymouth County men chosen at random for selection as jurors. Phillips signaled and two court officers ushered the jury pool into the courtroom through a doorway to the left of the bench. Whitman now addressed Abigail.

"Abigail Gardner, you are now set to the bar to be tried and these good men, whom I shall call, are to pass between the Commonwealth and you, upon your trial. If you would object to any of them, you will do so as they are called, and before they are sworn. You have a right to challenge twenty of the jurors peremptorily, and as many more as you have good cause for challenging."

Whitman called the list of prospective jurors one-by-one and after all answered to their names, they were sworn. Justice Metcalf summarily dismissed several for reasons of health and age. He discussed the statute pertaining to juror disqualification with those remaining.

"Gentlemen," Metcalf began, "the law prohibits the participation of a juror who harbors any prejudices or biases against the prisoner; who has already formed an opinion as to the guilt or innocence of the prisoner; or who has a relationship with the prisoner. You are to answer under oath whether you consider yourself as coming within the boundary of the disqualifying statute.

"You are also disqualified if you have any opinions on the subject of capital punishment as would preclude you from finding a verdict of guilty, under any circumstances, and you are to answer under oath, whether or not you entertain such prejudice."

Following challenges by the prosecution and the defense, and challenges by court on the questions of bias, opinion, relationship, and capital punishment, twelve men remained and were sworn. The court appointed Plymouth resident Thomas Loring as jury foreman.

Clerk Whitman once again addressed Abigail and directed her to stand. "Abigail Gardner, hold up your right hand."

Abigail complied and Whitman turned to the jurors. All stood.

"Gentlemen of the jury: hearken to an indictment found against the prisoner at the bar by the grand inquest for the body of this county."

Whitman read the indictment and at the conclusion said to the jurors, "To this indictment, gentlemen of the jury, the prisoner at the bar has pleaded not guilty, and for trial has put herself upon the county – which county you are. You are now sworn to try the issue. If she is guilty, you will say so; if she is not guilty, you will say so, and no more.

"Good men and true!" Whitman intoned. "Stand together and hearken to your evidence!"

Reporters in the courtroom were amazed by Abigail's coolness and indifference as she gazed upon the gallery, paying little heed to Whitman's oration.

The court announced a brief recess. Spectators waiting patiently on the courthouse steps were admitted to fill the seats vacated by the jury pool.

The court came in a half-hour later and Attorney Davis submitted a motion to have all witnesses, with the exception of medico-legal experts, removed from the courtroom and sequestered. The court agreed.

"The court will consider any breach of this sequestration contempt of court," Metcalf warned before officers escorted the few lay witnesses from the courtroom.

District Attorney Keith smoothed his hair and buttoned his jacket when the last witness filed out and rose to address the jury with his opening statement.

"May it please Your Honors, and you, Mr. Foreman and gentlemen of the jury: Many years have elapsed since a jury of the Old Colony was empaneled to try a prisoner for the highest crime known to the law; and we had all, doubtless, hoped, that in our day at least, no such event would have happened. But so it is, that in the discharge of the trust reposed in us as conservators of the public peace and guardians of the public safety, we are here, upon the threshold of our forefathers, called upon today to investigate the causes of the death of one of our fellow citizens, and the means by which, and the person by whom that death was accomplished.

"The prisoner at the bar stands charged with the willful murder of Hosea J. Gardner, her husband, and the father of her children. That principle of our nature, first inspired perhaps, by the omnipresent love of a devoted mother, which teaches us to look to woman for the most endearing traits that bind together the human family, will naturally excite your sympathy in behalf of the prisoner.

"But, gentlemen, crime has no sex, and the human and the divine laws, alike, justly hold all rational beings equally responsible for the consequences of their acts. And when we see the alarming frequency of death by poison, and the unlimited facilities placed in woman's hands for administering it, every day and almost every hour of our lives – in our food and in our drink, it would be the strangest folly and madness, even, influenced by any false chivalry toward her sex, to screen the female culprit from the just punishment which her crimes have merited. For however unnatural crime may seem in woman, and however true it may be that, in her highest culture, she approaches the angelic, history shows that in her depravity, she has often rivalled a fiend in acts of atrocity."

Abigail leaned forward and placed her hand on the dock's front rail, her face hard, visibly agitated by Keith's remarks.

"It is not my province to discuss the evidence in this case. That will devolve on abler hands, but rather to indicate such facts as the government expects to elicit in the progress of the trial."

Keith recited the government's understanding of the facts from the day of Hosea's injury until his death seven days later. He described the symptoms Hosea had displayed after ingesting a mixture of gin and water and other concoctions given him by his wife, the scientific detection of arsenic within the deceased's organs and the contents of a slop pail discarded by the defendant, and a local boy's errand to retrieve arsenic at the defendant's request only five days before her husband's fall.

The law did not oblige the government to prove motive in criminal cases, he said, "...but in this case, we think you will be satisfied by the evidence, that there was a motive arising out of the physical condition of the deceased, and that the prisoner desired his death for the purpose of removing an obstacle in the way of the gratification of her passions.

"The indictment contains three counts. The first charges that the prisoner administered arsenic to the deceased in gin; the second that she administered it to him in castor oil; and the third that she administered and caused to be administered to him, by some means and in some manner to the jury unknown."

The government was without important testimony from Hosea Gardner's mother due to her death before trial, the district attorney explained.

"But we think the evidence remaining as to the fact of poisoning, is conclusive to show it was caused by the prisoner."

Keith called for the Commonwealth's first witness, James Lewis, who was sworn after taking the stand and acknowledged he had convened an inquest jury on February 4 to inquire into Hosea Gardner's death. Lewis testified as to his knowledge about the deceased, the testimony at the inquest, and its outcome.

Lewis was excused after a brief cross-examination and the government called Dr. Ellis to the stand. After the physician was sworn, DA Keith asked him, as was customary, to state his name and occupation.

"I am Dr. Calvin B. Ellis, and I am a practicing physician in Boston. I am connected with the Massachusetts General Hospital."

"Last February, Doctor, did you have an occasion to examine the body of Mr. Hosea Gardner?" Keith asked.

Ellis testified for more than an hour about the autopsy and his delivery of Hosea's stomach and intestines to Dr. Charles Jackson. The district attorney paused to consult his notes and ensure he hadn't omitted any evidence he had hoped to introduce through Ellis. Justice Merrick looked up at the courtroom clock and interrupted.

"Mr. Keith, if you have no further questions we will recess and allow the defense to cross-examine the witness when we resume."

"Yes, thank you, Your Honor. I have concluded this witness's direct examination."

Ellis returned to the witness stand when the court reconvened at

2:45 p.m. and Defense Attorney Harris began his cross-examination.

Harris questioned the doctor about the organs he had collected in the hope of raising a doubt in the jury's mind as to possible contamination and a break in the chain of custody.

"Let's talk a bit about the glass jars you used to preserve the organs," Harris said. "Is it possible the jars themselves were contaminated before you placed the matter into them?"

"Not at all," Ellis replied. "I purchased the jars and ordered they be cleansed before anything was deposited."

"What happened to the jars after you placed the matter inside?"

"The jars remained with me in the room until I personally carried them to Dr. Jackson."

Harris asked the physician if morphine might have the same effect as arsenic on the stomach and other organs. Ellis admitted morphine was a narcotic poison but not an irritant and so could not have the same effect as arsenic. The court excused Ellis when the district attorney indicated he had no questions on redirect.

Dr. Jackson followed Ellis and, after being sworn, he testified as he had at the inquest seven months before. District Attorney Keith asked him more specifically about the amount of arsenic found in Hosea Gardner's body.

"The grand total of all the arsenic I found in the parts of Mr. Gardner's body submitted to me, was twelve and twenty-two one hundredths grains of the white oxide of arsenic, the arsenic commonly found in shops," Jackson stated.

"Can you tell the court how much arsenic is required to constitute a fatal dose in a human being?" the district attorney asked.

"Yes," Jackson answered. "Four grains of arsenic is generally a sufficient dose to kill a human being."

"If a man has ingested arsenic, how long can he expect to live?"

"A man poisoned by arsenic will live from twenty-four hours to three or four days. Sometimes he may live a fortnight, and then die from secondary effects."

DA Keith presented Reuben Reed's half-bushel copper vessel to the witness and asked him to identify it.

"This is the vessel brought to me by Mr. John Stephenson," said the physician.

"What did you find it to contain?" Keith asked.

"I found the vessel's contents to be potato skins, dried tea leaves, and other articles likely to be found in a household slop pail."

"And in what condition did you find the contents when they were delivered to you?"

"They were in liquid form."

"I show you this sealed bottle and ask you to identify the contents."

"This is the refuse I emptied from the copper vessel. After my analysis, I placed the material in the bottle and sealed it with my mark."

"What were the results of your analysis?"

"I found the contents to be rich in arsenic, and by the tests used I found the vomited matter among the slops to contain a very large quantity of the poison. I also tested the tub itself and found no arsenic."

"What was your reason for testing the tub?"

"Some pig copper contains arsenic in small quantities, but this did not. The only arsenic I found was in the vessel's contents."

The court admitted the copper vessel and the sealed bottle as evidence without objection from the defense.

"Did you recently have occasion to examine the contents of the deceased's organs?"

"I saw the stomach last Sunday. It was in a remarkable state of preservation. By my direction, it was put in a glass jar, marked, and tightly sealed."

DA Keith strode to the prosecution table and retrieved a glass jar containing the stomach in question.

"Do you recognize this jar and its contents, Doctor?"

"Yes, it is the same container and stomach I ordered sealed."

The sight of the organ aroused a collective groan from the women in the gallery.

"Is there anything remarkable about the condition of the stomach in this container?" Keith asked the witness.

"Yes, there is," Jackson replied. "If a stomach contains much arsenic, it will be long preserved. This stomach is remarkably fresh. It contains arsenic. A portion of the stomach has sufficiently decomposed to make the poison apparent to the eye."

The court admitted the organ as evidence and the court clerk marked it as an exhibit.

"What is your opinion as to the cause of Hosea J. Gardner's death?"

"I believe Hosea J. Gardner died from poison by arsenic," said Jackson.

"Thank you, Doctor. I have no other questions."

"Mr. Davis, Mr. Harris, do you have any questions for the witness?" Judge Metcalf inquired.

"Yes, Your Honor," Harris replied.

"Doctor Jackson, when was the last time you examined the stomach fluid?"

"I examined a part of it on August 26," Jackson replied.

"And from the time you first received the fluid vial from Dr. Ellis until the time you examined it in August, where was it kept?"

"It had been kept all the time in my office closet."

"Who has access to this closet?"

"No one but me," Jackson replied.

"Doctor, is it possible some other medication or substance given to Mr. Gardner during his illness may account for the presence of arsenic in his stomach and intestines?"

"Mr. Gardner received calomel during his treatment. Calomel contains mercury, and I found a slight trace of it in the fluid."

"Isn't mercury poisonous, Doctor?"

"Mercury in the form of corrosive sublimate and some other forms can be poisonous. The form of mercury in calomel is not poisonous," Jackson asserted.

Harris cross-examined Jackson for two hours, asking the same questions repeatedly to ensnare the physician in a contradiction. Attorney General Clifford twice objected to what he believed was already asked and answered but Harris continued. Jackson's tone became decidedly sharp as the examination neared an end. Harris finally relented after his questioning failed to shake Jackson's testimony.

The district attorney called Dr. Ellis back to the stand to satisfy chain of custody requirements relative to the stomach he had delivered to Dr. Jackson. Ellis was shown the glass jar containing the organ and he positively identified it as the same jar and the same viscera he had removed from Hosea Gardner and delivered to Dr. Jackson for analysis.

"Doctor Ellis, did you perform any other tests to establish the presence of arsenic before you delivered the stomach to Dr. Jackson?" Keith asked.

"I did. Frozen animal matters putrefy more readily than those which have not. Excessive heat also produces the same effect. Mr. Gardner's stomach had both been frozen and subjected to excessive heat. The stomach's present state," said Ellis as he held the jar aloft and examined it, "confirms the presence of arsenic as no decomposition has occurred."

Ellis's remark about there being no decomposition conflicted with Jackson's testimony of partial decomposition. However, the defense did not explore the contradiction.

The district attorney called pharmacist James Hunt to the stand. After being sworn, Hunt identified himself and testified about his interaction with Charles Dodge on January twenty-second and the boy's purchase of 180 grains of arsenic.

"Mr. Hunt, what does 180 grains represent?"

Hunt removed a small vial from his pocket. He had brought it to court at the district attorney's request.

"Mr. Davis," said Judge Merrick. "Before Mr. Keith pursues this line of questioning, do you have any objection?"

"No, Your Honor."

"Very well; you may proceed, Mr. Keith."

"Mr. Hunt, please display the vial to the jury."

Hunt held it aloft.

"How many grains of arsenic does the vial contain?"

"It contains 100 grains. Converted, it measures about six and one-half grams or two-tenths of an ounce.

"Thank you, Mr. Hunt."

"Did the boy tell you who the arsenic was for?" Keith asked.

"He did at his first visit, but he came back and said Mrs. Gardner wanted him to make it clear the arsenic was not for her but a Paddy woman who lived at the cove."

The defense asked Hunt several pointed questions but he remained steadfast in his testimony.

The district attorney called Henry Miller to testify about his conversation with the defendant and her request to have him go on an errand. Miller confirmed she had made the request and told the court he could not go when the time came and sent his cousin, Charles Dodge, in his place.

Defense Attorney Harris sought to place doubt in the jurors' minds about who actually asked Miller to do the errand.

"Henry, how often did you do errands for Mrs. Gardner?" asked Harris.

"I had never done an errand before for Mrs. Gardner, but I had often shoveled snow for her," the boy replied.

"What about Mr. Gardner?"

"I had done errands for Mr. Gardner and was carrying water for him when Mrs. Gardner asked me to go on the errand to Mr. Hunt's."

"Are you sure it was Mrs. Gardner and not her son Marcus who asked you to go on the errand?"

"It was not Marcus who asked me to go."

"What was the weather like on the day Mrs. Gardner made her request?"

"It was a pleasant day and there was snow upon the ground."

"Did you tell anyone besides Charles Dodge about the errand Mrs. Gardner asked you to do for her?"

"Yes, I told my mother about it on the day Mr. Gardner died."

"Thank you. I have nothing further for the witness, Your Honors," Harris said.

DA Keith rose and asked for his next witness, Charles Dodge.

"How old are you, Charles?"

"I'm eleven," the boy answered.

Keith examined the boy to establish his perception and ability to communicate and his understanding of truth and honesty.

"When I swear to tell the truth, and do not tell it, something would be done that would be worse for me," Charles said.

The court, satisfied the boy was a competent witness, directed he be sworn.

Keith led the boy through his testimony. He told of the errand he had done for Mrs. Gardner at Mr. Hunt's, the package labeled poison he had delivered to her, and her demand he return to Hunt's to tell the pharmacist the poison was not for her but a Paddy woman.

"Do you see Mrs. Gardner here in the courtroom today?" Keith asked.

"Yes," said Dodge, motioning toward Abigail.

"And this is the same woman who asked you to go to Mr. Hunt's and bring back a packet?"

"Yes, sir," Charles replied.

"Mr. Keith, it is getting late. We will adjourn until eight o'clock tomorrow morning," said Judge Metcalf.

A court officer appeared at the witness room door after the courtroom had emptied and stated, "The court has adjourned. You will have to return at the same time tomorrow."

Abby bowed her head and sighed. She had hoped to testify before day's end. Now she would have to face the same ordeal once more. She rose from the bench and, with her brother, aunt, and uncle, left the courthouse, walked to the depot, and took the cars back to Hingham.

***

Abby and Marcus used the same South Russell Street doorway when they arrived at the courthouse with their aunt and uncle for the trial's second day. Another large crowd had gathered on the courthouse steps and lawn.

District Attorney Keith spoke with them before they ascended the stairs to the witness room and gave his assurance they would be called to testify before day's end.

Inside the courtroom, attorneys for the prosecution and defense conferred quietly at their respective tables. When Abigail entered the courtroom in the custody of two deputies and took her seat inside the dock, Attorneys Davis and Harris spoke with her.

"How was your night, Abigail?" asked Davis.

"As good as could be expected, Mr. Davis. Do you suppose my two children will testify today?" Abigail asked through her sheer, drawn veil.

"It's likely, Abigail. It will be important for you to contain your emotions. The jurors will watch you closely for your reaction."

"I don't know what to expect from them. Neither Abby nor Marcus has visited nor corresponded with me since the inquest."

"I don't anticipate anything but truthful answers from them, Abigail. It must be very difficult for them to testify against you as witnesses for the prosecution."

"I don't know, Mr. Davis. They just as easily could have testified on my behalf. I have no doubt they have turned against me and I am infuriated."

***

The courtroom quickly filled with spectators. Excited ladies ushered by court officers to front seats in the gallery "scanned the prisoner and the gentlemen of the bar, whispering opinions to each other and twittering like a flock of bluebirds," a *Boston Herald* correspondent noted.

Justices Metcalf, Bigelow, and Merrick exited their chambers and smartly stepped to the bench at eight-thirty. A moment later the jurors filed in and took their seats in the box. Justice Metcalf nodded to the defense table.

"You may proceed, Mr. Harris."

"Thank you, Your Honors. The defense calls Charles Dodge."

The boy took the stand.

"Charles, I remind you, you are still under oath and have sworn to tell the truth. Do you understand?" Harris began on cross-examination.

"Yes."

"Please tell the court again where you spoke to Mrs. Gardner when she asked you to do the errand."

"I saw her in her house. I went at the back door."

"And did you go to the back door when you returned from Mr. Hunt's?"

"Yes. I met Mrs. Gardner there with the packet."

"What did you say when she asked you what you had told Mr. Hunt?"

"I said I told Mr. Hunt I wanted the poison for Mrs. Gardner. She said that was wrong."

"What happened next, Charles?" asked Harris.

"I offered to go back and tell Mr. Hunt. She said I could go back or not, just as I pleased."

"Then she didn't tell you to go back and tell Mr. Hunt a

different version?"

"No."

Attorney General Clifford and DA Keith shot each other an abrupt glance. This was not what the boy had told them before and during his earlier testimony.

Keith questioned the boy on redirect.

"Yesterday you said Mrs. Gardner told you the packet was for a Paddy woman. Correct?"

"She didn't say anything about a Paddy woman. I am sure of it."

"Didn't you testify yesterday that Mrs. Gardner sent you back to Mr. Hunt to explain who the packet was for?"

"No. I went back on my own accord and told Mr. Hunt it was for a Paddy woman."

"Did Mrs. Gardner say there was someone waiting in her house for the packet when you first went to her back door?"

"I didn't hear her say that, but she did tell me to hurry."

Keith turned from the witness, his hands clasped behind his back, his face a mask of anger and exasperation.

"Have you spoken with anyone about your testimony between last evening and this morning?"

"Mrs. Miller, my aunt, has told me what I must say in court against Mrs. Gardner."

Attorney General Clifford leapt to his feet. "Did not your mother or Mrs. Miller direct you when you came into court to tell the truth?"

Attorneys Harris and Davis immediately objected to the question and the court sustained it.

"Your Honors, the government moves to strike this child's testimony as immaterial," Clifford stated.

"Motion denied, Mr. Attorney General. The jury will determine the witness's veracity," Justice Metcalf ruled and, turning to the eleven-year-old boy, excused him.

A court officer shepherded Dodge from the courtroom and the

district attorney called Hingham selectman and civil engineer Charles W. Seymour to identify and testify to the accuracy of a plan of the Gardner premises he had prepared at the government's request in advance of the trial. Keith showed the plan to Harris and Davis who offered no objection to its introduction as evidence. Seymour examined the plan, identified it, and testified as to the relevance of the boundaries, reference points, and existing buildings depicted. The defense had no questions for the witness and the court admitted the plan as a government exhibit.

John Stephenson was the government's next witness. His sworn testimony began with an acknowledgement of his presence at the coroner's inquest.

"At the inquest, the coroner asked Mrs. Gardner to enter a plea to the charges against her. Can you tell the court what her response was to this request?" DA Keith asked.

"Mrs. Gardner replied she was not guilty. She said she was 'perfectly innocent before her Maker.'"

"Did she say anything during the inquest about the gin she had given to her husband?"

"When the complaint was read to her, she said she did mix some gin with water and loaf sugar but did not put into it any arsenic. She said she had never had arsenic in her house and when asked if she had ever bought any she denied it."

"Were you present at the inquest when Mr. Hunt testified?"

"I was."

"Do you recall him saying Mrs. Gardner had sent a boy for arsenic?"

"Yes, and when he said it, Mrs. Gardner interrupted him and said, 'Oh. I do remember. I did send for some for a woman down at the cove.' She then added, 'The reason I sent this Miller boy was because my boy was not at home.'"

"What else did she say?"

"She said many other things which I do not distinctly

remember. She said, 'Supposing I did purchase it. It does not follow that I gave it to Mr. Gardner. As to proving I gave it to him, you cannot do it.' I cannot remember the exact words which she used, but remember the substance."

Stephenson related the details of his visit to the Gardner's backyard with Reuben Reed and Dr. Don Pedro Wilson the day after the defendant was arrested. Stephenson said he and the two other men had retrieved the slops Dr. Wilson had seen the defendant deposit in the snow. He stated the refuse was placed in an empty copper vessel brought by Reed. The vessel and its contents remained in his custody until he brought it to Dr. Jackson for analysis.

Attorney Davis approached for cross-examination and asked Stephenson if he knew who had presided over the inquest he had spoken of earlier.

"The examination was before Coroner Lewis."

"And had Charles Dodge testified at this examination before or after Mrs. Gardner allegedly made the remarks concerning the woman at the cove?"

"He had not testified when she said it as best as I can recall."

"Did Henry Miller testify at the examination?"

"No."

"Did Mrs. Gardner identify this woman at the cove?"

"She said she didn't know the woman at the cove, but I think she did say something about a woman who was very old coming to her house."

"Did Mrs. Gardner have legal counsel representing her when she uttered her remarks at the examination?"

"No, she did not."

"Please tell the court exactly where you stored the copper vessel containing the discarded waste."

"I kept the vessel in a locked room in the basement under the engine house in Hingham Centre. I have an office there as the town's sealer of weights and measures."

Davis hoped to cast doubt about the integrity of this important evidence and draw jurors to the possibility of intentional or accidental tampering with his next question: "Who has access to this room?"

"I keep the key myself. No person had access to the room while the vessel was there unless they went in with me."

"Thank you, Mr. Stephenson. I have no further questions," Davis said and returned to his seat at the defense table.

Hosea Gardner's brother-in-law, Reuben Reed, took the stand for the government. Reed testified he was married to Hosea Gardner's sister, Alice. He corroborated Stephenson's testimony as to the retrieval of the slops and their placement in a copper vessel he had brought to collect them. He stated the vessel was normally used by his wife for washing. DA Keith showed Reed the Seymour map previously admitted as evidence, and Reed used it to identify the spot where he and Stephenson and Dr. Wilson had recovered the slops.

"How was this waste transferred to the copper vessel?"

"We took it up with a shovel and filled the vessel with the slops and the snow."

"Was there anything in the vessel before you filled it with the slops?"

"No, it was clean."

On cross-examination Attorney Davis asked Reed where he had obtained the vessel.

"I brought it from my house," Reed told Attorney Davis.

"Was this vessel used for anything other than washing, Mr. Reed?"

"No, sir," Reed replied.

DA Keith called Dr. Don Pedro Wilson when Reed was excused. Wilson testified as he had at the inquest to his presence in the outhouse behind the Gardner home on the morning Hosea died, his observation of the defendant burying the slops in the snow, and his later recovery of the slops with John Stephenson and Reuben

Reed. The government did not question him about the illness and death of his cats. Any testimony would be conjecture; there was no physical evidence connecting the deaths with the discarded slops.

Attorney Davis asked Wilson on cross-examination to describe where he saw Mrs. Gardner with the shovel.

"It was two or three feet from the path leading from the house to the shed."

Davis showed Wilson the Seymour diagram and asked him to indicate the spot. Wilson did so but with reservation.

"Mrs. Gardner was standing in a path. I do not know if it was the one specified upon this plan."

Judge Metcalf excused the dentist when the district attorney indicated he had no other questions for the witness and called for a brief recess.

Chapter 7: The Trial Continues

The government called John Todd to the witness stand when court resumed. Todd testified how he and Captain Soule had assisted Hosea after his fall on Broad Bridge on the night of January twenty-seventh.

"How far was Mr. Gardner's home from the site of his fall?" the district attorney inquired.

"About fifteen or twenty rods away," answered Todd.

"What happened when you arrived at his house?"

"We took him inside to the parlor. We saw Mrs. Gardner, Miss Gardner, and Marcus Gardner. Mr. Gardner complained of faintness and much suffering. We laid him upon the sofa, and I called for camphor and cologne. The daughter procured it and I applied some to his forehead."

"Did the defendant say anything while you were there?"

"Mrs. Gardner said she thought he wasn't hurt much and would probably be out the next day."

"What happened next?" the district attorney asked.

"I went out for two or three minutes then went over to my shop to lock the door which I had left open."

"Did you return to the Gardner home the same evening?"

"Yes, and when I arrived I found Mr. Gardner sitting up on the sofa. He asked me to take off his boots."

"Did the defendant say anything?"

"Mrs. Gardner said to Hosea, 'I should think you could take them off yourself and not trouble Mr. Todd.' I took the boots off and Mrs. Gardner said to her husband, 'From the way Mr. Todd took your boots off, I shouldn't suppose you were hurt much.' She said she didn't see how Mr. Gardner could have hurt himself by merely slipping down for she had known people to fall twenty feet and it did not hurt them. Mr. Soule then came in, he having been for the doctor. He asked Mr. Gardner how he felt and Mrs. Gardner replied, 'You see he's well enough to take his boots off and you wouldn't suppose he was hurt much.' I took the boots off very carefully, especially the one on the lame leg. The lame leg was the right one and he fell on the right side."

"Mr. Todd, do you know Captain Soule's present whereabouts?" Keith asked.

"Mr. Soule is at sea. He went last spring."

"Thank you, Mr. Todd. I have no other questions."

Attorney Harris approached the witness stand for cross-examination.

"Where was Mrs. Gardner when you arrived with Mr. Gardner?"

"Mrs. Gardner was standing in the middle of the parlor."

"Was she sitting upon the sofa in the room?"

"No."

"Do you recall if it was Mrs. Gardner who told you to place Mr. Gardner on the sofa?"

"I do not remember."

"Didn't Mrs. Gardner help you place him on the sofa?"

"No person did anything for Mr. Gardner, except us."

"Thank you, Mr. Todd. I am finished with this witness, Your Honors."

Attorney General Clifford now took up the examination for the prosecution and called Otis Hersey. Hersey was sworn and testified he had spent the evening on watch at the Gardner house with Sophia Gardner on the night her son died.

"When I went into the house Hosea seemed perfectly insensible," Hersey testified.

"Who was there when you entered?"

"Hosea's mother and his wife and Miss Gardner were in the room when I went in. Miss [Lucinda] Lincoln and Mr. Wilder were in the house. The family was very anxious for the doctor. Mr. Wilder sent for Dr. Stephenson and he came at about ten o'clock."

"Were you present when Dr. Stephenson examined Mr. Gardner?"

"Yes. As soon as he saw Mr. Gardner's condition, he ordered stimulants, internal and external, to be administered."

"What kind of stimulants?" Clifford asked.

"Mustard poultices, brandy and water, and some drops. The doctor ordered the brandy and drops to be given alternately every fifteen minutes."

"Do you know who mixed the brandy before it was given to Mr. Gardner?"

"No," Hersey replied.

"How long did the doctor remain at the house?"

"He stayed until quarter to eleven and he asked the family to retire. They did so. Miss Lincoln returned to her home and Mr. Wilder and I remained with Mr. Gardner. In less than half an hour I was surprised to see Hosea's wife come into the room. She said she could not sleep with his groaning. We gave him medicine until 11:45 p.m. At midnight we gave him brandy and water and it caused so much distress he sprang up and opened his eyes."

"Did the prisoner say anything?"

"Yes, Mrs. Gardner told us to continue giving him the brandy and water as the doctor had prescribed, but Wilder and I declined."

"How did she respond?"

"She displayed anxiety as she stood at the foot of the bed, then relented and said, 'Oh, don't give him any more brandy. Let him die in peace.'"

"What happened next?"

"About half past midnight Mr. Gardner's looks changed. Mr. Gardner's mother was then upstairs. I called the family and they came down. He continued to breathe very hard and groan. At half past one o'clock he breathed his last."

147

"What was the defendant's demeanor when Mr. Gardner died?"

"Mrs. Gardner appeared through the whole very calm and unconcerned."

"Did she cry at some point?"

"No."

"How did the others react?"

"Mr. Gardner's mother appeared very much grieved and the rest of the family were much affected," Hersey stated.

A *Boston Post* reporter, focusing intently on Mrs. Gardner for a reaction, saw her dab at her eyes with a wadded handkerchief – the first time he had seen her display even a hint of emotion during the trial.

Attorney Harris asked Hersey on cross-examination if the defendant was in the room when the drops of brandy and water were administered to Mr. Gardner.

"Yes, she was, and she was in the room when I observed how the drops distressed him."

"Mr. Hersey, you've stated the defendant appeared unconcerned when her husband passed. Are you sure she didn't evince some emotion?"

"She endeavored to shed some tears at one time."

"You're certain of this? She did not cry at any time?"

Hersey paused. "She did shed tears," he admitted.

"Why did you tell the court the defendant hadn't?"

"I said she did not because I thought they were crocodile tears."

"Do you bear a grudge or feel animosity toward Mrs. Gardner for any reason?" Harris asked.

"No," Hersey said firmly, "I am not sensible to a prejudice against Mrs. Gardner."

Hersey stepped down at the conclusion of his testimony and the government called Edwin Wilder to the stand.

Wilder testified about his visit to the Gardner home at nine o'clock on Saturday night.

"The family was very glad I had come. They thought Mr. Gardner was dying."

"Had you seen Mr. Gardner earlier in the day?" Attorney General Clifford asked.

"Yes, I saw him at about 3:15 p.m."

"How did he seem?"

"I found him then lying upon the bed and very low. He recognized me and appeared very glad to see me."

"Was anyone else in the room when you entered?"

"Yes, Mrs. Gardner, the mother, was present at the time."

"Please continue Mr. Wilder."

"Mr. Gardner was in a somewhat drowsy state and for a moment or two lost himself in sleep. Upon waking he thought he had enjoyed quite a nap."

"When you returned to the house at nine o'clock, what did you do?"

"I sent for Mr. Hersey and shortly after his arrival we sent for Dr. Stephenson."

"Did Dr. Stephenson respond to the house?"

"Yes, he arrived at about ten o'clock and stayed until about eleven. He left his directions with me. On a stand at the head of the bed were tumblers, one containing brandy and water. He ordered us to administer a dose every fifteen minutes alternately, with some other medicine which he had prepared.

"At 11:45 p.m., the brandy and water which I had administered distressed him considerably. At the time for the next dose I hesitated, but Mrs. Gardner, the wife, thought I had better give it to him. I did so; it distressed him a great deal. Mrs. Gardner then requested me not to give him any more but 'let him die in peace."

"What happened next?"

"At half past midnight we saw a great change in him and called the family. At half past one he died."

"Please continue," Clifford prompted.

"Hosea's wife left the matter of laying him out entirely with us. She brought the necessary articles and then retired to her chamber where she remained about two hours. When she came down she prepared breakfast for Otis and me."

"What happened next?"

"Otis and I started to take down Mr. Gardner's bed. Mrs. Gardner objected at first but then acquiesced. Before we started, I saw her take something from beneath one of the ticks, at the right-hand lower corner, and carry it to the kitchen. As she carried it out, she kept it by her side."

"Did you see what it was?"

"I did not," Wilder replied.

"Do you recall Mrs. Gardner's demeanor during her husband's final hours?"

"Yes, she was very cool and indifferent."

"And did the rest of the family exhibit the same emotions?"

"No, the daughter especially was very much affected. She went to Mr. Gardner's bed and begged her father not to die. Her mother blamed her for this and said, 'it was the Lord's will, and she must try to be reconciled.' She took her daughter from the bed and seated her on the sofa, saying 'she had always treated her father well, and had nothing to reflect on.' The daughter wished to stand by the bedside again and her mother objected. I led her to the bed and supported her until she saw fit to retire," Wilder testified.

"Was the boy, Marcus, at his father's bedside when he died?"

"No, he was not present."

"And Mr. Gardner's mother; was she present?"

"Yes, she was present and appeared considerably affected."

"One last question, Mr. Wilder," Clifford said. "Did you notice anything else before you left?"

"Yes, I saw a slop pail outside the back door. It was about two-thirds full and it contained bread, potato skins, tea leaves, and slops generally."

"Your witness, Mr. Harris," Clifford said.

"Mr. Wilder, you testified about the defendant removing something from the bed. Was this before or after she objected to having the bed taken down?" asked Harris.

"It was after."

"And are you sure about her removing something?"

"Well, I did not see Mrs. Gardner take anything from the bed; I thought she did from her movements."

Harris subjected Wilder to several more questions but failed to shake his testimony or elicit anything new.

The court excused Wilder and the government called Abby to the stand. A court officer stepped outside the courtroom and emerged moments later with her. He escorted her to the witness chair and she was sworn.

"The appearance of this witness excited deep interest and her position the warmest sympathy," a *Boston Post* reporter observed.

"Good afternoon, Miss Gardner," District Attorney Keith began.

Abby smiled nervously. Her apprehension and anguish were palpable.

"Please tell the court how you are related to Mr. Hosea Gardner."

"I was the daughter of the late Mr. Gardner."

"Were you at home when your father fell last January?"

"Yes, and I was there when Mr. John Todd and another gentleman whom I thought was Mr. James Soule assisted my father into the house."

"What condition was he in?"

"He appeared much injured and in great distress. His hip gave him much pain occasioned by the fall. It had been diseased for some time and he used a support for the limb made of India rubber and iron, applied from the hip downward."

Abby testified to Dr. Stephenson's arrival the same night and his treatment of her father's injury.

"How did your father feel the next morning?"

"He was not in as much pain."

"Did his mother come to your house?"

"Yes, at my father's request," Abby replied, "she came before noon on the same day."

"Did you also tend to your father during his incapacitation?"

"Since my father was unable, the care of the store, the post office, and the telegraph devolved upon me. During his illness they required my attention all day and until late in the evening."

"Were you able to spend any time at all with your father?"

"I saw Father every morning and night and sometimes in the evening," she recalled solemnly.

"When you saw him, did you administer any medicine to him?"

"I did not."

"How long did your grandmother stay at your father's side?"

"She remained until the Sunday following his decease."

"When did you first notice your father taking a turn for the worse?" Attorney Keith inquired.

"On Thursday morning he was not so well as the day before."

"Who was at his bedside?"

"My grandmother, mother, brother, and I were present."

"What happened while you were all there?"

Abby fidgeted in her chair and sighed. She glanced quickly at her mother.

"My father vomited. He said he wished to have what he had vomited saved until the doctor came. My mother insisted upon emptying it. I urged her to save it and all the rest wished it to be saved. She made some remarks which I do not remember and emptied it into a pail which stood outside the door. Father said something about it, but I do not think it was in mother's hearing."

"What did your father say?"

Attorney Davis objected before Abby could answer. The court must consider anything the father might have said while the defendant was absent as hearsay, he argued. Attorney General Clifford insisted the statements were admissible as a dying declaration, and as such, an exception to the hearsay rule. The court dismissed the government's theory.

The justices ruled that "There is no evidence before the court to indicate Mr. Gardner believed himself to be dying at the time he made the statement. The witness will not answer any questions about statements made by her father in the prisoner's absence."

The district attorney continued his direct examination.

"Did you say anything to your mother when she returned?"

"No, I went to the post office before she came back."

"Were you present when your father died?"

"Yes," Abby said.

Attorney Davis approached for cross-examination with the Seymour plan and asked her to indicate where her father died. She pointed to a room in the front of the house on the first floor.

"Was the room where your father died used as a bedroom?"

"Yes, my father and mother had used this first-floor front room where he died as a sleeping compartment all winter. They used it together up to the time of his illness. She then went to the back chamber and occupied it Friday, Saturday, and Sunday nights."

"Where do you sleep in the house?"

"My brother and I sleep in a room on the second floor directly above the chamber occupied by my father during his illness."

"Did your grandmother stay at your house on Thursday night?"

"Yes."

"Did she stay up with your father every night she was there?"

"I don't remember any night when my grandmother was up with my father. I think she was part of the night on Wednesday."

"Who sent for your grandmother?"

"Father did."

"Did your mother know he was sending for her?"

"Yes."

"Who brought your grandmother to the house?"

"Mr. Turner."

"Were you there when your mother and grandmother administered medicine to your father?"

"I did not see my mother or my grandmother administer anything."

"How was your mother feeling at this time?"

"My mother was in feeble health. Her health had been poor for several years. She had been under a physician's care in the fall."

"Do you know who her physician was?"

"Dr. Cutter of Boston," Abby said. "I have been with her to see him on two occasions. She took baths there."

Drs. E. G. and E. W. Cutter rented rooms on the upper story of 292 Washington Street, in Boston's Beacon Hill neighborhood. The rooms were equipped with electro-chemical baths developed by distinguished French chemist Professor Maurice Vergnes of New York. The Cutters visited New York for several weeks in 1855 to examine Vergnes's invention and witness its rehabilitating effects on patients suffering from "severe cases of paralysis, St. Vitus's Dance, inflammatory rheumatism, enlarged and stiff joins, neuralgia, and all diseases occasioned by the use of mercury or deleterious medicines." The two physicians, satisfied with the validity of Vergnes's claims, acquired the baths and introduced them to their patients.

"Have you always lived with your mother?"

"Always," Abby answered.

"And would you say she keeps a clean home?"

"She is neat in household affairs – remarkably neat."

"Miss Gardner, did your mother cry when your father died and shed tears at his funeral?"

Attorney General Clifford objected.

"Your Honors," Davis said, "I wish to show the defendant was a great talker and possessed a free and open nature entirely inconsistent with the qualities naturally to be attributed to a person who possessed the felonious characteristics of a poisoner. The defense wishes to learn the general conduct of Mrs. Gardner, to rebut the evidence given by the government which was presumption of her being a hard-hearted woman, and which had reference wholly to one particular period."

"The objection is sustained, Mr. Davis," Justice Merrick ruled. "First of all, the question of character has not been raised. Secondly, tears are not an evidence of grief, nor does grief always produce tears. I knew a man who lost thirteen friends in fifteen months without a tear, and still he himself went to the grave with sorrow soon after."

"Yes, Your Honor," Davis replied.

Turning back to Abby, Davis asked, "Miss Gardner, will you please tell the court the condition of your father's estate at the time of his decease?"

Clifford stood and objected once more.

"May it please the court," the attorney general said, "if the question is ruled as admissible, I insist the court should receive all conversations in regard to other matters as well as finances."

"Your Honors," Davis argued, "the defense claims the right to present any evidence which might show death was otherwise brought about. In Commonwealth v. Kinney, a capital trial, the defense was allowed to show the deceased was insolvent at the time of his death."

Wilder's account of the death scene and her daughter's testimony had overwhelmed Abigail. She sobbed continually, her shoulders quaking, tears flowing freely down her face.

"We are familiar with the case, Mr. Davis, and in fairness to the defendant the court will recess and have an answer to the matter at issue when court resumes at two-thirty."

With a bang of Metcalf's gavel, the three justices rose and retired to chambers. Spectators in the gallery smiled and nodded sympathetically at Abby as she walked past and left the courtroom.

Abby's aunt Alice was waiting for her when she returned to the witness room. Abby fell into her arms and wept inconsolably.

***

At precisely 2:30 p.m., the justices returned and called the court to order.

Attorney Davis withdrew his previous objections and stated he had no further questions for the witness. The court excused Abby and the government called her brother Marcus.

"Did anyone in the house ask you to fetch or administer any medications to your father?" DA Keith asked.

"I got some salts and liniment at the apothecary's during the week and gave them to Grandmother," the boy replied.

"Did you at any time administer any medicine to your father over the course of his illness?"

"No, sir."

The district attorney's final questions elicited Marcus's account of the strange vomit and his mother's disposal of it in the slop pail over everyone's objection.

Attorney Davis took up the cross-examination. "How do you know your mother discarded the vomit?"

"I saw her throw it into the slop pail. She said the doctor could see it there," Marcus answered.

"Do you remember your mother saying she didn't want such nasty stuff in the house?"

"I don't remember."

"Where was the slop pail kept?"

"We always kept it in the back entry."

"Can you tell us about the errand your mother asked you to go on the week before your father fell?"

"My mother asked me to do an errand, but I was going to school at the time and I went and told another boy, Henry Miller, to go for her."

Davis asked Marcus when, particularly, he had seen Miller, and

Marcus said it was after his midday meal, before the afternoon school session began.

"Where did you meet Miller?"

"I met him in the street."

"Are you sure it was Henry? Could it have been Charles Dodge?"

"I am not sure what boy it was I told."

"Who went to your house?"

"I did not see either of the boys go to the house."

"Thank you, Master Gardner. No further questions, Your Honors," Davis announced.

Marcus stepped from the stand and glanced at his mother. She smiled at him but he turned away, a pained expression on his face, and hurried from the courtroom.

DA Keith called thirty-one-year-old Isaiah Winslow Ayer, a former *Boston Traveler* newspaper editor and reporter who was now the paper's publisher. Ayer published a report in the *Traveler* about the Gardner inquest shortly after it concluded. Ayer stated he took down all of Abigail's speeches verbatim and corroborated the testimony of previous witnesses as to what Abigail had said at various times during the inquest.

The defense cross-examined Ayer but no testimony, either favorable or harmful, was elicited.

The district attorney called Dr. Ezra Stephenson to the stand. Stephenson said he had first attended the deceased on Tuesday evening, January 27, and had found him in excruciating pain. He went into detail about Hosea's condition at his first and subsequent visits and identified the prescriptions he had ordered and/or administered.

"Doctor, let's focus our attention on Friday morning. What condition was Mr. Gardner in?" DA Keith asked.

"I found Mr. Gardner to be vomiting and complaining of a severe burning pain at the pit of his stomach. He had a great thirst.

His tongue was red and swollen, his face was swollen, and there was a constriction of the fauces (the arched opening at the back of the mouth leading to the pharynx).

"Mr. Gardner told me he had vomited a great deal in the morning and had thrown up a peculiar substance which he had requested to be saved."

"Did he say what became of this peculiar substance?"

"He said his wife threw it away."

"Was there any other conversation on the same morning with Mr. Gardner?"

"Yes," the physician replied. "I asked him if the salts prescribed had operated. His wife said they had sufficiently. On Friday afternoon Mr. Gardner and the nurse mother told me the salts had not operated. His wife was present at the time and I asked her why I had been deceived. She told me it was operation enough.

"I thought if Mr. Gardner should have an action of the bowels it might relieve the vomiting. I put up five grains of submuriate hydrochloride, or calomel (a purgative), directed to be followed in one hour with a teaspoonful of castor oil and lemon juice (constipation relief), which was to be repeated every hour until an operation, or until he had taken it three times, making the proviso if the stomach would retain it."

"Did the prescription attain the result you had hoped to achieve?"

"Yes, on visiting Mr. Gardner on Saturday morning I learned he had retained the oil and it had produced a very powerful operation."

"Did Mr. Gardner's general condition appear improved?"

"I found him sunken and relieved of none of his uncomfortable sensations. One peculiar sensation, a tingling as if striking the elbow, required constant rubbing. I directed treatment – free use of brandy, beef tea, mustard application to the stomach, friction to the extremities."

"When did you see him next?"

"I called again in the afternoon and found things about as in the morning, except some slight action in the pulse. I directed a continuance of the stimulating course and left him. I saw him again in the evening between ten and eleven o'clock. He was pulseless, speechless, and dying. There was a curious pinkish hue of the face, and the tongue was evincing more stiffness or inability to move."

"What did you prescribe at this critical stage?"

"I still advised the free use of brandy and water."

DA Keith focused next on the conversation the physician had with the defendant about the undertaker's request to straighten her husband's deformed limb to accommodate the coffin's dimensions.

"Did you explain to the defendant the need for this procedure?"

"Yes, I did."

"And what was her response?"

"She had no objections. She said it could do him no harm. The limb was later severed and straightened with the assistance of another."

"When did you first endeavor to obtain the consent of Mr. Gardner's family for purposes of an autopsy?" Keith asked.

"On Tuesday morning following Mr. Gardner's funeral, I called at the post office and saw Mr. Gardner's daughter, Abby, and spoke to her of my doubts and lack of knowledge in the case. I said it would be gratifying to learn the cause of her father's death."

"What did she say?"

"She said it was in accordance with her feelings, and it would be gratifying to her to know the immediate cause."

"Who else did you speak with about this matter?"

"I left the post office and visited the prisoner, Mrs. Gardner, and after speaking of the peculiarity of her husband's sickness and symptoms having been unaccountable, I told her I thought it would be a satisfaction to know the cause. I also said her mother-in-law and daughter desired an examination."

"How did she react?"

"She also expressed it would be a great satisfaction to her to know, though she believed it was from mortification of the leg. I told her the only way to know for sure was to examine the body and I asked for her consent. She said at once she could not consent to it. She said she had always had a great dread and horror of such things. The more I entreated, the firmer she was in her objections."

"Did you speak to anyone else about an autopsy?"

"Yes. On Tuesday evening, Mr. Reed, the deceased's brother-in-law, called on me and requested I make an examination and proposed to accompany me to the receiving tomb."

"What was your answer?"

"I told him I could do no such thing in the manner proposed."

"But a post-mortem examination was performed, was it not?"

"Yes. Justice Lewis authorized the disentombment and autopsy."

"Were you present at the examination?"

"Yes. I assisted Dr. Ellis."

"What was your opinion as to the cause of death?"

"I came to the conclusion there was not sufficient lesion in any and all of the organs to cause death. In my opinion, the diseased leg did not cause death; there being no contusion sufficient to produce ecchymosis either externally or internally. I think Mr. Gardner's death was caused by the swallowing of arsenic."

It was eight p.m. by the courtroom clock.

"Mr. Keith," Justice Metcalf interjected, "this is a good time to adjourn. You may continue the doctor's direct examination when the court resumes at nine o'clock."

Chapter 8: A Plea of Innocence

Abby returned to the post office early Thursday morning, September 3, to catch up on her work.

"Good morning, Abby."

"Good morning, Mr. Siders. I hope my absence was not an inconvenience."

"It was no inconvenience at all, Abby. The mail is sorted and I have set aside the telegraph messages we received over the last two days."

"Thank you, Mr. Siders. I will start transcribing them right away."

Abby took her seat at the telegraph and spread the paper ribbons across her desk one at a time. The first message was from a *Hingham Journal* correspondent assigned to cover her mother's trial in Plymouth. Her alarm grew steadily as she deciphered and recorded each dot and dash imprinted on the paper. She had resisted reading anything about Mother's case after the inquest and had turned a deaf ear to the idle talk of those who had gathered on corners and in village shops to gossip about her father's death and mother's arrest. To this day they still whispered and stared. It was humiliating.

Marcus had had his share of difficulties, too. He had come home nearly every afternoon upset because his classmates and friends had assailed him with taunts and jeers about his mother. The mocking had diminished over the months, but Marcus had never recovered from the shame and embarrassment.

As she read Mr. Keith's opening statement and the witness testimony given while she was sequestered, a chill ran up her spine. Abby turned her back to Mr. Siders and wiped a tear from her face; she did not want him to see her upset. She regained her composure after a few moments and stoically resumed her work. When she finished, she delivered the transcriptions to Mr. Easterbrook, the *Journal*'s editor, at his office on South Street.

***

In Plymouth, the justices stepped to the bench at the appointed time for the third day of trial. Abigail, clad in the same black outfit she had worn since the trial began, watched the jury file in. The courtroom gallery was again filled to capacity, predominantly by women, many of whom had brought their crochet and knitting work with them. Day dresses of gingham, chambray, and calico with wide lace and crochet collars and pleated hoopskirts with flounces and fringe were on display in earthy hues of soft brown, olive, and amber.

Dr. Ezra Stephenson returned to the witness chair and the district attorney continued with his direct examination.

"Doctor," DA Keith began, "did you have occasion to speak with the defendant in the middle of January of this year?"

Attorney Harris bolted upright from his seat and objected to the line of questioning as immaterial to the charges against the defendant. He did not want the jury to hear anything about Abigail's alleged adultery.

"Your Honors," said Harris, "I know where the government is going with this and it seems to me any testimony introduced in regard to a different and distinct felony is incompetent to prove the crime of murder."

"Your Honors," Keith argued, "the government intends to introduce evidence which will prove, from the prisoner's own mouth, circumstances existing prior to Mr. Gardner's death which form a sufficient motive for the defendant to commit the crime of murder."

"The objection is overruled," Justice Metcalf stated. "You may proceed, Mr. Keith."

Keith nodded to Dr. Stephenson, and he testified about his meeting with Abigail on January sixteenth at her husband's request.

"Mrs. Gardner said she was restless at night and could not sleep. After making the usual examination, I prescribed fluid extract of valerian."

"Did you meet with the accused at a later date?"

"Yes. I had another interview with her on January twenty-third, at her request. I was passing her house when she called me in. She said she had not slept any better since taking the valerian. She said she didn't believe her troubles were to be relieved by medical treatment. The cause of her sleeplessness was of a domestic nature; her husband was jealous of her and he had some reasons for it, he knowing she loved another man more than she did him. She told me she laid awake nights thinking if she could have this other individual by her side instead of her husband she should be perfectly happy. She also said, using her own language, 'Mr. Gardner was good for nothing as a man; he did not ask to have intercourse with her oftener than once in four or six weeks, and it was then entirely unsatisfactory to her.' In reply to a statement made by me, 'It might be the case with any man,' she said she had had intercourse with the other individual, repeatedly, and with great pleasure."

Women in the gallery gasped and murmurs rippled through the courtroom until Sheriff Phillips brought it to a halt with a bang of his gavel.

"Did she have anything more to say?" Keith asked when the clamor subsided.

"She said she supposed she must live on in misery, as the man alluded to had a wife and she had a husband. She also said she believed she was with child, saying all the indications she was accustomed to formerly were present, enumerating some of the indications. I examined her slightly and told her I was uncertain but thought her age precluded the possibility of her being pregnant. She told me her age was about fifty years. She adhered to the opinion, stating her reasons, one of which was that her monthly turns ceased soon after having intercourse with the unknown party."

Another wave of whispers and titters rose in the gallery. A steely glare from the sheriff quelled the clamor.

"Did you make out a prescription for her?"

"I gave her some slight medicines. She said if I gave her anything, it should not be allowed to interfere with the child's birth – it was the child of another person, and not her husband, and she would not have it killed for the world."

"What else did she say, Doctor?"

"I do not recollect anything further."

"Thank you, Dr. Stephenson. Oh, one further question," Keith added before he turned from the witness, "do you know when Mrs. Sophia Gardner died?"

"Yes, she died about twelve days ago."

Keith asked Stephenson for the cause of Sophia's death but the defense objected. The court sustained the objection and would not allow the physician to answer.

"Thank you. No further questions, Your Honors," said Keith.

Attorney Davis began his cross-examination and asked the physician when he first suspected Hosea Gardner had ingested poison.

"I had the impression on the Saturday before Mr. Gardner's death that his sickness might be caused by poison. I first thought of poison on Friday, but more distinctly on Saturday."

"Did you treat him for poisoning?"

"I treated the symptoms for poison, but not specifically, as well as I knew how; the symptoms were not violent until Friday. Prior to this time, the symptoms were not inconsistent with any slight interruption of general health. All the symptoms between Thursday and Saturday night would be inconsistent with any other cause of death except by arsenic. I take all of the symptoms, the autopsy, and what was known after his death, in forming my opinion."

"Who did you instruct as to Mr. Gardner's care?" Davis asked.

"I gave most of my prescriptions and directions to his mother, who I understood was his nurse."

"And what did you prescribe?"

"I prescribed an injection of salts and oil, conditionally, or to be given if necessary."

"To whom did you give this prescription?"

"I cannot say to whom I gave this prescription."

"Do you know if an injection was given?"

"I don't believe it was given. I remember the mother saying the oil had operated profusely. I had instructed her not to give an injection unless the oil did not operate."

"Did the defendant ever identify this so-called 'other man' she was in love with?"

"I did not ascertain from her who the person was who had adulterous intercourse with her; she told me she would not tell me who he was for the world."

"Were there any symptoms to convince you Mrs. Gardner was with child when you examined her?"

"I was not satisfied she was with child. She said she had been pregnant from three to four months, the length of time she had the veil of secrecy."

"Are you sure you've told the court everything the defendant said to you during the examination?"

"I think I have given the entire language used by Mrs. Gardner during my visits to her."

"Had you ever examined Mr. Gardner for impotency?"

"At the post-mortem examination I looked for evidence of impotency but found none; arsenic has a peculiar effect upon the reproductive organs, but there were no indications in this case."

"When did you last speak with Mrs. Gardner?" Davis asked.

"The last conversation I ever had with her was in relation to the post-mortem examination."

Davis concluded his cross-examination and Attorney General Clifford, on re-direct, asked the doctor if he had determined the defendant's mental state during his examination on January 16.

"I concluded Mrs. Gardner was not insane."

"Dr. Stephenson, can you elaborate for the court how you determined Mrs. Gardner was not with child?" Clifford asked.

"I examined Mrs. Gardner's vagina through the abdominal walls and saw no evidence of such a condition. There might have been a slight enlargement of the uterus, but I cannot swear there was any," the physician replied.

The court excused Stephenson.

Abigail's penetrating glare followed him from the witness chair to his seat in the gallery.

The government called Constable Gridley Hersey, and he testified about his arrest of Mrs. Gardner in her home at three-thirty in the afternoon on February 10.

"What transpired during your conversation with the accused when you arrested her?" asked DA Keith.

"When I told her I had a warrant for her arrest, she seemed startled. She then said, 'Why, what have I done? I haven't done anything. How do you know but that he poisoned himself or that his mother did it?' I said, 'Stop, I don't know what the warrant contains. Let's see what it says.' I read it to her; she denied the charges. I told her she must go with me at any rate."

"How did she react?"

"She demurred somewhat. I told her she must put on her things and go with me to the town house as it was getting late. She repeated what she had before said and asked me how many persons would be there. I told her only a few. She again said she couldn't go but afterwards said she would if there was not going to be more than a dozen people there. She finally consented to go and went with me."

"Were you present at the inquest held on the day you arrested the accused?"

"Yes."

"Did Mrs. Gardner remain in your custody when the inquest concluded on the first day?"

"Yes, she did."

"Did she say anything to you?"

"I heard her statement in reply to Mr. Hunt's testimony and I had a conversation with her about it. She was speaking about how she could get clear. I told her the best way was for her to tell me where the Paddy woman could be found for I would look her up and she would be the best evidence she could have. She said she didn't know where she was. She said, 'She may be Down East by this time.'"

"Besides telling you she didn't know where this Paddy woman was, didn't the defendant tell you she did not know the woman's name?" Attorney Davis asked on cross-examination.

"She might have told me she didn't know the woman, but I am not confident."

"Did you conduct a search of the Gardner premises while the defendant was in your custody?" asked Davis.

"I did," Gridley replied. "I searched the house and the grounds."

"Did you find any arsenic?"

"I did not; nor did I find any medicines or intoxicating beverages."

The court excused Hersey after this brief questioning by the defense.

Attorney General Clifford rose and stated he had no questions on redirect. He did, however, offer for the court's consideration the sworn deposition Coroner Lewis had taken from Sophia Gardner prior to her death.

"Your Honors, I offer this affidavit as evidence of a 'dying declaration.' I feel it is my duty to offer this evidence but will not insist if the defendant's counsel objects," Clifford said.

"Your Honors," Attorney Davis replied, "I do not think the attorney general has a right to allow the jury to review this affidavit."

"The court agrees, Mr. Davis, and the affidavit is excluded," Justice Merrick ruled to Clifford's bitter disappointment.

"Your Honors, the government rests its case," said Clifford.

"Thank you, Mr. Clifford," said Merrick. "The defense may now offer its opening statement."

Junior counsel Harris rose from his seat and approached the jury.

"Gentlemen of the jury, this unhappy woman," Harris remarked as he gestured toward the dock, "sits here to be tried for murder and the government does not ask the conviction of any person unless their guilt is proved beyond a reasonable doubt. You must be clear it was not an unnatural death, an accidental death, or a suicide, before you can pass upon the question of murder. It is not her duty to prove either. She can only depend on you. Then you must feel sure she administered the poison, and was in a sound mind then, but we do not intend to plead insanity any further than what may be suggested by the course of the government in this particular. The case should rest alone on its merits."

Harris lectured the panel on the legal interpretation of the presumption of innocence and the burden the law placed on the government to prove the facts beyond a reasonable doubt. He cautioned the jury about circumstantial evidence. No one had seen the defendant administer the poison. The government's case was based solely on the assertions of arsenic being found in the deceased's body and the defendant having sent for arsenic, he said.

"Unless further proof is added to satisfy you the prisoner administered the poison, she is presumed innocent. The government must also prove beyond a reasonable doubt the death was caused by poison, and not by other causes. It must prove the party's guilt by a connected chain of circumstances. If a single link

168

in this chain is broken, it is sufficient to admit of a doubt, and the doubt must be given to the prisoner."

Reporters in the courtroom scribbled furiously in their notebooks to capture Harris's words.

"I have not yet heard a single fact elicited by the government to satisfactorily prove the prisoner's guilt. The fact she purchased arsenic is no proof of her guilt. Almost every family purchases this poison. The fact she threw away the matter vomited by her husband during his illness is no evidence of guilt. It is consistent to suppose she, being a remarkably neat woman, disliked having such filth in the house, and therefore put it outside the door. If she had known this matter contained poison administered by her, would she not have destroyed it entirely, and not have left it where it could be found at any time?" Harris reasoned.

Abigail held a handkerchief tightly in her hand and gently dabbed at her eyes, perhaps in recognition for the first time of the seriousness of her situation.

"That she objected to her husband's post-mortem examination is consistent with the idea she could not, as many cannot, endure the thought of having allowed the body to be mutilated by the surgeon. If it is believed she declared her unfaithfulness to her physician and it is assumed this declaration was true, it must be proved this was her motive for the commission of the crime, and it must be made to appear consistent with the supposition that any woman who commits the crime of adultery is led to the great crime of homicide. It is not right to infer such is the case; the fact must be made clear and incontrovertible. You, gentlemen, must presume the accused is innocent until the government has proved, beyond a reasonable doubt, she is guilty of the homicide of which she now stands charged."

Harris returned to the defense table and glanced briefly at his client. She nodded her approval. The court called for a brief recess.

***

The *Hingham Journal*'s correspondent hastened to the nearest telegraph office in Plymouth Center with Dr. Stephenson's sensational testimony and details of Harris's opening statement.

Abby was sorting mail at the post office when the telegraph signaled for her attention. She paled as she interpreted the reporter's words clicking across the wires. The newspapers had reported her mother's adultery before but never in such detail and it sickened her. How had she been blinded by her mother's deceit? And to think she would poison her father to be "perfectly happy" with another man. She'd never forgive her mother for her cruelty and betrayal.

***

When the trial recommenced, Attorney Davis called several government witnesses to clear up legal and evidentiary omissions and discrepancies. He then summoned Dr. Walter Channing, a former Harvard Medical School dean and a founder of the Society of the Abolition of Capital Punishment. After he was sworn, Channing established his credentials as a physician and professor of midwifery, medical jurisprudence, and women's diseases. Channing had testified as an expert witness at previous capital trials.

The seventy-one-year-old physician acknowledged his presence in the courtroom during Dr. Stephenson's testimony the day before. He also confirmed he had received a request from the defense to examine Abigail at the jail.

"I examined Mrs. Gardner this morning and found no signs of pregnancy," Channing testified. "I examined her externally and I am satisfied she is not enceinte."

"Doctor, you heard Dr. Stephenson's testimony concerning his conversation with the prisoner and her assertion of being enceinte. If what Dr. Stephenson alleges is true, have you formed any opinion as to the prisoner's condition at the time she made the statement?" Davis asked.

Attorney General Clifford jumped to his feet and objected before Channing could respond. The court ruled the question out.

Abigail, overcome with emotion, began to weep, concealing her face with her handkerchief and fan. The court ordered a five minute recess.

Dr. Channing returned to the witness chair when the trial resumed.

"Doctor, is it common among ignorant people to object to post-mortem examinations?" Attorney Davis asked to show Abigail's objection to the examination was not extraordinary.

"I object, Your Honors," Attorney General Clifford interjected. "Counsel's question was not one of those which came within any rule by which the court had limited such examinations."

"The court is in agreement with the attorney general," Justice Merrick ruled. "The witness will not answer the question. The prejudice is of common notoriety and counsel might so argue before the jury."

The defense rested its case and the attorney general indicated he had no questions. The court excused the witness.

"Mr. Davis, you may now present your closing argument to the jury," said Justice Metcalf.

"Thank you, Your Honor," Davis said. He rose from his seat and poured a glass of water from the ewer on the defense table. He took a sip, set the glass on the table, and stepped to the jury box.

"Gentlemen of the jury, it becomes my duty now to present as well as I might the evidence in behalf of the prisoner and the want of evidence on the part of the government, and to show you, as I believe I should, why you must return a verdict of not guilty.

"Prejudice and suspicion against the prisoner has become general, and you must make every allowance in your power for any bias or prejudice which might have crept into your minds. I beg you to remember it is through the gates of your verdict only that the executioner could enter. What higher consideration could you have than that your verdict might send a human being into eternity?

"Let me now discuss the merits of this case. In the first place, it must be apparent Mr. Gardner died of poison; second, that he did not die by his own hand or by accident; third, that the prisoner administered the poison or whether someone else did; and fourth, that the prisoner administered it feloniously or by accident.

"There is no evidence to conclude Mr. Gardner died of poison. And the appearance of the parts most likely to be affected was no such as would be likely to follow the inception of arsenic through the stomach. No arsenic was found in the stomach.

"The autopsy disclosed the presence of other diseases in Mr. Gardner, and from the result of the inspection of the intestines, and the autopsy, death was consistent with poisoning by arsenic, but the symptoms attending the death were not inconsistent with other causes. The government draws an inference of guilt from the two facts of the manner of death and the autopsy, which are entirely disconnected, and do not warrant the conclusion.

"There is no evidence as to the disposition of the body when entombed. How do we not know the arsenic found its way into the intestines by injection after death? Dr. Stephenson did not think Mr. Gardner was poisoned and did not prescribe for poison. The body is unaccounted for during a whole week, and the injection might have been accomplished by any enemy to Mrs. Gardner during this time.

"I do not throw any blame on Dr. Jackson, but I think the government wrong to entrust the whole matter of chemical analysis to one chemist. It was certainly very strange Dr. Jackson did not make a thorough examination of the liver and brain and settle this question, as to whether the arsenic was taken into the body before death or was injected subsequently.

"In the stomach, which Dr. Jackson says is affected first and most, there was no arsenic found. After the whole summer had passed, Dr. Jackson has looked into the stomach and says sulphuret of arsenic was discovered. We have Dr. Jackson's eye as the whole testimony showing there was any arsenic in the stomach.

"The next question is did Mr. Gardner commit suicide? There are some legal presumptions on this point. It is not common for wives to poison their husbands, and the greater the crime the greater the improbability of its commission. There is no evidence given to show Mr. Gardner and his wife did not live happily together. It is true she told Dr. Stephenson she did not love her husband. But when she said it, she evinced no determination of destroying his life. She must have been madder than all the madmen in all the hospitals in creation to tell him what she did, if she intended to poison her husband in a week.

"In consulting with her family physician, she confessed the deceased knew she no longer loved him, she had been faithless to him, and he was loathsome to her. He was himself afflicted with a severe and loathsome disease, resulting from a diseased bone, and this perhaps being a burden to himself and an eyesore in the sight of his wife, and being haunted by the pangs of jealousy, and well-founded jealousy, too, it is by no means strange for us to suppose the deceased died by his own hand. If she had been a woman without conscience, she would not have made such a confession.

"Did the deceased meet his death by accident? You heard Marcus Gardner testify he had purchased salts for his father; and the government made him a material witness. And is it not possible Mr. Hunt made a mistake and gave the boy arsenic instead of salts? Such a state of facts may appear ten years hence, as it is quite possible, after this prisoner has been hanged.

"Beyond all this the further and more important question comes up – if the deceased did die of poison, did Mrs. Gardner administer it? On this point the evidence is wholly circumstantial, and I would own necessarily so; and the government relies solely upon evidence showing the defendant had purchased arsenic. All the other facts in the case in relation to this point are entirely consistent with entire innocence; and I would ask it on this barren fact of the purchase, if any intelligent jury would say the crime had been committed and the accused is guilty.

"No secrecy was made about sending the boy for the arsenic – and she told him to be in a hurry. Why was she in a hurry? Did she mean to poison her husband the same day? She did not then give it to him, but if her idea was murder, she would have been likely to have done it then. In the first place, she asked her own son to go for the arsenic; he could not go. She asked the Miller boy; he could not go. Finally, Miller sent his cousin, Charles Dodge, to do the errand. All this does not look like secrecy, but just the reverse; and as to the story about her telling the boy to say it was for a Paddy woman, it has been shown it was a story made up by the boy himself by no instructions of the accused. The arsenic was bought in just as open and public a manner as if she had gone for it herself, and no sane woman with murder in her heart would have taken such means to assist her end. She was in the habit of going to Boston frequently, and it would have been there she would have bought the poison if concealment was an object, for had she bought it in Boston, the fact would probably never have been known."

Davis paused and his words hung in the air.

"So far as the rights of this case are concerned, it is the government's misfortune it could not produce the deceased mother. This should not be allowed to injure the defendant. It is the government's intent to feast you with horrors and make the circumstances of the post-mortem examination appear as awful as possible. One party who was present during all the days of the deceased's sickness is not here. Is my client to be hanged because this woman is dead? The prisoner is charged with administering arsenic in gin and water, or causing it to be mixed in castor oil, or giving him arsenic in some shape. The government not specifying the time at which Mr. Gardner drank the arsenic, it may be seen how important to the defense would be the cross-examination of Mrs. Gardner, the mother, who is now dead.

"Mrs. Gardner's question to Charles Dodge as to what he said to Mr. Hunt cannot have weight as evidence against her, for every father or mother who ever sent a child upon an errand could appreciate how natural the remark was. You must also attach importance to the prisoner's statement of never having bought any arsenic. Now a person might ask another if he ever bought a horse, and he would say he never did. But he might have purchased one sometime before for a man who had come to his house and requested him to do so. And attaching no importance to the fact at the time, it was natural for sale to escape his memory. The mode adopted by Mrs. Gardner in purchasing the arsenic was not unreasonable, furtive, or secret. She might have gone herself, and would have obtained it no more openly than she did by sending the boy.

"Witnesses have sworn the matter vomited from the stomach of Mr. Gardner was put by his wife in a slop pail. This is probably true. Then it is said the contents were afterwards thrown on the snow. Those actions are entirely consistent with innocence, and are rather proofs of innocence than of guilt. She did not hide the slops, or put them irretrievably out of the way, as she easily might have done, but kept them near the door for a long time, and finally threw them out on the white snow. Would not a guilty party have put it down a vault, gentlemen, or in a dozen other secret places nearby?" the lawyer asked.

Temperatures outside had reached the mid-eighties and not a hint of a breeze made its way through the open arched windows overlooking Plymouth Harbor. Davis mopped his brow with a handkerchief in the stifling courtroom and took another sip of water from the glass on his table. The court allowed the jurors to remove their coats and loosen their collars and ordered court officers to supply them with fans and water.

"What of her refusal to allow a post-mortem examination of her husband?" Davis asked when he resumed. "This is also entirely consistent with innocence, and the jury is not entitled to any influence, either good or bad, from this fact."

Davis next attacked the credibility of witnesses Edwin Wilder and Otis Hersey.

"The evidence in regard to the prisoner's taking something from the corner of the bed, after Mr. Gardner's death, is of no weight whatsoever. And besides, this testimony was made by a man deeply prejudiced. And so was the man who gave testimony in regard to 'crocodile tears.' I was shocked when I heard his testimony. Crocodile tears!" Davis exclaimed, his voice rising with emotion.

"If she, in that hour, whether she poisoned her husband or not, could not shed honest tears, she should be painted for the demon that stood beside mother Eve! We are not trying a human being, gentlemen, but a hyena! And she is not entitled to the rules of law. I beg you to give no weight to such testimony. You are not to believe the prisoner a person of hard feeling. No such facts have been proved. You are to deal gently with the erring, and give the prisoner the benefit of every circumstance in her favor.

"I have launched the lone life of the prisoner upon you, gentlemen of the jury – upon her country, which country you are. You do not belong to the court, nor to the prisoner, but each man to himself. You must each convict this prisoner before her life is taken. You must do it upon the evidence and not by jumping at conclusions. Unless you do so, you are murderers. You are to take her with you assuming that she is innocent, challenge every person, every fact and every idea that threatens to take her from you. If she is guilty, you must say so. If she is not guilty, for God's sake, say so."

Davis's argument now ended, the court recessed briefly and the jurors filed out. Ladies in the gallery pumped their lace and feather fans feverishly and took refreshment from water court officers had left on a table behind the gallery.

After the recess, Attorney General Clifford rose to deliver the government's closing argument.

"May it please Your Honors, and you, gentlemen of the jury; the present case is the most painful one that has ever come before me in my official capacity. But it is my duty, as it is yours, to look our official obligations in the face and go to the discharge of these duties with an earnest endeavor to perform them with fidelity and truth – without regard to the consequences."

Clifford appealed to the jury's sense of fairness and asked them, with "a calm and dispassionate view," to consider the evidence.

"I wish to remark here upon the weight to be given to circumstantial evidence, and of this class I would say that if it was never to be believed, then I must conclude that all security afforded by the laws must be abandoned. In the words of the Commonwealth's chief justice, the jury must give the same credence here to evidence, and give it the same weight as such knowledge is given on which discreet men act on matters most important to their concerns. This is all the weight I wish given to the evidence, but I will take occasion to say that this was a crime in regard to which no direct testimony could be reached. No one would see the cup offered to the lips of the one now dead, and circumstance must be heeded."

He attacked the defense theory that the government had not proved Hosea Gardner's death by poisoning, had not eliminated the possibility of accident or suicide as the manner of death, and had not disproven someone else could have administered the arsenic.

"In the first place, then, did the deceased die of poison? All the symptoms before death, and a most thorough examination shortly after death, showed that what was in his stomach must have been there before he died, and was afterwards most conclusively shown to be arsenic – a deadly poison – and the idea that it was injected after death is but simply preposterous. Had the counsel for the defense any idea that he could have affected Dr. Jackson's testimony, he would at once have called a host of medical talent to do it. He called no one. He had no hope of refuting the conclusive evidence.

"Second, was the death accidental or a suicide? If Mr. Gardner had been the means of his own death, he never would have entreated to have the vomited contents of his stomach examined by a physician. He never would have taken those medicines to check its action and to prolong the agony of his certain death for three horrible days. He would never have done this. You must reject this monstrous assumption and throw the supposition to the winds."

Clifford dismissed the theory of death by accident. The defense had not submitted evidence to support it. Was it possible? Yes, he submitted to the jury, "…but by no means even reasonably possible."

"The next question is, did the prisoner administer the poison herself, or did someone else? Who else could have done it?" Clifford railed. "No one save the mother whose child he was and she, the faithless wife, the accused, had admitted herself the mother had no opportunity to administer it. Who was it that wished the matter investigated? It was the mother who wished it – it was not the wife. A mother in love had watched the sickness of her son and a mother's weeping grief wished the cause divulged. An estranged wife and an accused criminal resisted the investigation to the end and with these facts before you, could you for a moment doubt which was the guilty party? I will not insult your good sense for an instant by supposing you entertained a doubt.

"Mrs. Gardner's counsel has said with thrilling emphasis that a human being who could commit this crime must be a moral monster – and he said it well. Gentlemen, I think she is. I think the epithet is richly deserved."

Spectators in the crowd noisily expressed their approval. Sheriff Phillips rapped his gavel and called for order.

"A murder – the administration of a few doses of arsenic," Clifford continued, "would perhaps be but a slight addition to her already vile and abandoned conduct, and the government has abundant reason to ask you to believe the statement. She bought the arsenic, she had it in the house, she had an opportunity to administer it, and I consider myself justified in saying that she had the disposition to do it. I consider it proved, that the matter thrown from her husband's stomach was the same as put in the pail and afterwards thrown on the snow, and found to be full of arsenic, and in view of all these things, I believe the guilt of the accused has been fully established.

"Of her motive, I will not speak. If under the evidence furnished by her confession, you, the jurors, as fathers and husbands, could not discern it, it would be idle for me to state it. It was grossly vile and with this allusion, I will let it pass."

Clifford thanked the jury and stepped to his seat at the prosecution table where the district attorney quietly congratulated him. He had spoken for nearly three hours.

Justice Merrick conferred briefly with Justices Bigelow and Metcalf.

"Gentlemen of the jury, the next step in this trial will be my charge and the commencement of your deliberations," said Merrick. "Would you prefer to have the case committed to you now or in the morning?"

Jury foreman Thomas Loring briefly consulted with his fellow jurors in a hushed tone.

"The jurors prefer to receive the case in the morning, Your Honor."

"Very well. Thank you, Mr. Foreman."

Justice Metcalf turned to the prisoner's dock.

"Mrs. Gardner, the court now offers you an opportunity to address the jury. The law gives you the right to be heard, but your remarks will not be considered legal evidence."

Abigail wiped a tear from her face. Turning to her attorneys, she looked for assurance. Attorney Davis went to the prisoner's dock, quietly engaged Abigail, and returned to the defense table.

"Your Honors, Mrs. Gardner has something to say, but she does not feel able to speak at this time," said Davis.

"Thank you, Mr. Davis. The court will allow the prisoner to speak in the morning. Court is adjourned."

Abigail spoke with her attorneys briefly after the jury filed out and the justices left the bench.

"It's 8:00 p.m. and it has been a long, trying day for you," said Davis. "Get some rest and we will speak again before court resumes in the morning."

A constable led Abigail from the dock and walked her out of the courthouse the few steps to the jail gates, across the yard, and up to her cell.

***

When court opened for the fourth day of trial on Friday morning, September 4, the courtroom was once again filled to capacity. Excitement filled the air in anticipation of the verdict and Abigail's address to the court. The court entered and Justice Metcalf signaled for the sheriff to bring the jury in.

Metcalf inquired if the prisoner was prepared to address the court.

Attorney Harris stood and said, "May it please Your Honors. I am instructed by the defendant, my client, to say that she is overpowered by her feelings. She is unable to express here this morning that of which her heart is full. She wishes me to say if I may be allowed."

"No sir!" Judge Metcalf thundered. "She may address the jury if she pleases. If she cannot for any reason, her counsel cannot for her; it is a personal privilege, sir."

Harris went over to the prisoner's dock and conferred softly with Abigail. She nodded to him, lifted her veil, and stood.

"I have much to say, but I do not know how to say it; I am here, feeble and low, but I have done nothing which should put me in this place. I feel I have been greatly injured and slandered by those who have prejudice against me; I know I am innocent and have no business to be here, but I am in a place where I cannot help myself, and I feel I have no one to say a word in my defense."

Overcome with emotion, Abigail bowed her head and pitifully sobbed for several moments before gathering her strength and continuing.

"I feel like one all alone in the world with no one to help me at all; I am so faint and weak I am hardly able to be here this morning; I thought last night I should be able to speak and to say considerable, but I am not. It is not because I am guilty that I can't say what I want to; I don't feel I have done anything which should put me here; I can declare before my Maker, and before you all, I am innocent of the charge which is made against me; I tell you here I am innocent, as I have done everywhere; someone has done the deed, and lays it to me, and I alone have to bear it; I feel like one dying by inches, and have felt so all the time."

Abigail paused once more, weeping and heaving. She gathered her composure eventually and continued.

"As true as you are a judge in this court," Abigail said, turning her gaze from the jury to Judge Merrick and the bench, "remember too that you have a judge in heaven who will judge you for what you do on the last day. Deal mercifully with me, and spare me for the sake of my children, they are as near and dear to me as my own life; they have been disgraced by what others have brought upon me. I have done nothing wrong myself; I know I have not done anything, therefore I feel I have been injured by the ill-feeling and prejudice of people against me, for which I am not to blame, sir."

Every eye in the courtroom was riveted upon Abigail's pathetic figure as she struggled with her emotions. Several ladies in the gallery dabbed at tears in commiseration but most in the courtroom, according to a *Plymouth Rock* correspondent, listened to Abigail's remarks "with more apparent curiosity than sympathy."

"I would that God would reveal from heaven by His pure spirit, to our minds and hearts, that I am innocent, and that you might know the guilty one."

Abigail sat momentarily but rose again and said, "I ask you to judge me rightly, and be careful that you do not condemn me not knowing what you do."

Abigail crumpled into her seat and bent forward, her face covered by her hands as she wept.

Justice Merrick delivered his charge to the jury and, upon its conclusion at 10:15 a.m., dismissed the jury for deliberation. Two deputies led the jurors from the courtroom through the west side door and along a corridor to the jury room where they gathered their belongings. They would begin their deliberations in more comfortable accommodations at Davis Hall, a red brick, three-story structure on Main Street, three hundred yards from the courthouse in Plymouth Center. Built in 1854 by Charles Davis, Abigail's attorney, there were shops on the first floor, offices on the second, and on the top floor, two spacious halls, all fitted with gas lighting.

Chapter 9: A Contentious Outcome

A somber atmosphere enveloped the jury room at Davis Hall as the twelve men reflected on the onerous burden placed upon them. An initial polling by secret ballot before they began deliberating revealed a split decision – six for conviction, six for acquittal. There was much work to be done.

They meticulously weighed the testimony, reviewed the physical evidence, and engaged in a spirited, contentious discussion until dusk, when the court ordered their transfer back to the courthouse jury room "in order that they should have no sleeping facilities," according to a *Weekly Messenger* correspondent. The court had apparently received word of makeshift beds being installed in the hall. As they exited onto the sidewalk outside Davis Hall, a crowd of people congregated on the courthouse lawn noticed them approaching and rushed inside the building, quickly filling the courtroom. They were disappointed when Sheriff Phillips informed them the jury had not reached a verdict. They were not deterred, however, and remained in their seats.

The jurors continued their deliberation in the second-floor jury room overlooking the jail yard and North Russell Street for the next two hours. At 6:00 p.m., Foreman Loring went to the door and spoke with the court officer stationed outside.

"Officer, the jury would like to address the court."

"Thank you, Mr. Foreman. I'll inform the sheriff."

Sheriff Phillips immediately alerted Clerk Whitman who in turn summoned the three justices, the prosecutors, defense counsel, and the jail.

As soon as Justice Merrick called the court to order, the jurors filed in and took their seats. Not one lifted his eyes to meet

Abigail's gaze as she sat dejected and frail in the prisoner's dock.

Clerk Whitman approached Jury Foreman Loring and received from him a piece of paper which the clerk handed to Justice Merrick.

"Mr. Foreman," said Merrick after glancing at the paper. "Has the jury reached a verdict in this matter?"

"We have not, Your Honor," Loring replied. "We are decidedly deadlocked and unable to reach a unanimous consensus."

Spectators in the audience let out a collective groan of disappointment.

"Thank you, Mr. Foreman. The jury has deliberated less than eight hours. The court asks you to return to the jury room for further consideration."

Abigail looked pleadingly toward her attorneys as the jurors left.

"Mrs. Gardner," said Attorney Davis, "we must remain optimistic. The jurors are divided, but how much so, we cannot know. We can only hope they are leaning toward acquittal."

"I understand, Mr. Davis, but what if they cannot decide? What then?" Abigail asked.

"We will address that issue when and if the time comes. For now, you must set aside your fears and rest."

"Easier said than done, Mr. Davis," retorted Abigail, realizing she would likely not learn her fate until the following morning.

Two deputies removed her from the dock and returned her to the jail.

The jurors labored well into the night and drew a second ballot at eleven-thirty. One juror who had voted to acquit on the first ballot had changed his verdict to guilty. The verdict now stood at seven for conviction and five for acquittal. A third and final ballot was tallied before dawn on Friday, September 4. The jurors had remained firm. Foreman Loring once more sent word to the court.

The jury filed into the courtroom at eight o'clock. Few spectators and reporters had remained overnight.

Court clerk Whitman once more addressed the jurors and asked if they had reached a verdict.

"We have not," jury foreman Loring said.

"Is there any probability you will?" Justice Merrick asked.

"There is not. I would remark to Your Honors that we have carefully considered the matter at issue between the Commonwealth and the prisoner, and are totally unable to agree. We therefore respectfully ask to be discharged."

"Let the papers be taken from the jury," Merrick instructed.

"Gentlemen of the jury," said Merrick, "you are hereby discharged. Thank you for your efforts on the Commonwealth's behalf."

Abigail showed little emotion as the jurors filed out.

Justice Merrick ordered her remanded to Plymouth Jail without bail until the government reached a decision on whether to try the case again.

"You mean I must stay in jail?" an incredulous Abigail said to her attorneys when the court had emptied.

"We will file an appeal for your release, Mrs. Gardner, but it is likely you will remain confined until the government decides whether it will retry you," Attorney Davis said.

"Why?" Abigail asked. "The jury couldn't convict me. How can they try me again?"

"Since the jury was deadlocked and unable to ascertain your guilt or innocence, the double jeopardy rule does not apply. The court has declared a mistrial. In other words, this trial never occurred and you may face a new trial on the same charge."

"How long will it take before the government makes a decision?"

"That I cannot answer, but it will be soon. The court will schedule a hearing and the government will announce its decision. A new trial likely will not take place until the court's next session in May," Davis answered.

"Nine months I must sit in that miserable cell. Why? I am innocent and yet I am being punished," Abigail railed.

"I understand, Mrs. Gardner, but this is our system of justice. The trial now past has exposed the government's strategy and the nature of their evidence. This will be beneficial going forward. Mr. Harris and I believe the most critical testimony presented by the government was given by the medical men and we intend to challenge their expertise and opinion when we next face the court."

"And if you fail and I am found guilty?"

"There are many different issues on which we can appeal, Mrs. Gardner. Insufficient and improperly admitted evidence and errors made by the court in its instructions to the jury are among them. Mr. Harris and I will review the case thoroughly. I assure you we will leave no stone unturned."

The deputies waiting patiently for the conference to end finally stepped in and removed Abigail from the dock. She sighed heavily as she stepped down.

Attorney General Clifford and District Attorney Keith were perplexed by the jury's indecision. They knew they had presented a very strong case.

"It seems to me," Clifford said to his colleague, "five of the jurors, even after having denied any reservations during empanelment about finding a death verdict if the facts were proven, had reconsidered. Or, perhaps, they had perjured themselves at the outset about their impartiality and had never intended to find the defendant guilty."

"I don't know," Clifford continued. "It is always difficult for the government to empanel a death-qualified jury given the restricted number of challenges it is allowed. I have seen this reluctance to condemn a prisoner to death on many occasions, and I believe it will continue until the law is changed, Jim. The legislature, as we speak, is reviewing the law of murder, and I am encouraged by the positive conversation among our lawmakers about a change in its definition."

"How quickly do you suppose such a change will happen?" Keith asked.

"It is in committee now," said Clifford. Senator Caleb Cushing has recommended dividing the crime of murder into degrees. A conviction of first-degree murder will result in a death sentence. A second-degree murder conviction will call for a sentence of life imprisonment. And it will be up to the jury to determine which degree is appropriate."

"But if the accused is given the benefit of the doubt, won't there be more people likely to commit murder, knowing they may avoid the death penalty with a second-degree verdict?"

"It is true that jurors may more quickly find a prisoner guilty in the second-degree to avoid responsibility for sentencing him or her to death. The government's only recourse should a pattern develop is to, perhaps, abolish the death penalty altogether," Clifford opined. "As for an increase in murder, I don't agree."

"Aside from the issue of capital punishment as a factor in the jury's indecision in our case, it is also apparent the absence of testimony by the victim's deceased mother was critical," said Keith.

"Yes," replied Clifford. "I had hoped the court would accept her deposition, but the rule of law on hearsay evidence is clear. I'm certain if the mother had testified in this case, she may have swayed the five jurors who opposed conviction. The victim's statement to her about his wife poisoning him would have had a significant impact.

"I believe the Dodge boy's inconsistent testimony was not helpful, either," Clifford said. "Obviously he had been influenced by someone to change his story. It may have been a mistake to put someone so young on the witness stand, but it was the only way we could connect the prisoner directly to the arsenic."

"I agree. He was our most important link in the chain."

"At any rate, it is my intention to retry the prisoner. I have no doubt she murdered her husband. Even without the mother's testimony, the evidence is overwhelming. I don't know if any jury will sentence this woman to death, but perhaps the legislature will have enacted the new law on murder before the court schedules her trial," said Clifford.

***

Word quickly spread from the courtroom to the streets and throughout the town and county of Plymouth. Abby was in disbelief and gripped with fear when she received the news by telegraph. What would happen next? The idea that the court would free her mother from jail and send her home was too frightening to consider.

"Abby, it's unlikely the court will release your mother," said Coroner Lewis when Abby met with him to share her concerns. "The government will petition the court for a new trial, and your mother will remain in custody until a decision has been made."

"I don't see how the jurors could possibly have failed to convict my mother, Mr. Lewis. How do they account for that?" Abby asked.

"It's my understanding the majority of jurors did see it that way. As for those who did not, I suspect it was less a matter of overwhelming proof than it was a struggle with their consciences. Taking the life and liberty of a fellow human being is a burden not to be taken lightly, so, in a way, I can understand their ambivalence to convict."

"Yes, I can understand that, too. It must be the most difficult decision anyone could ever make. Yet each man at empanelment swore to set aside his views on capital punishment and not allow them to interfere with his judgement."

"It's true, Abby, but when the time comes, and a man must make a final decision the weight of his responsibility may overshadow all other considerations."

***

The *Plymouth Rock* correspondent covering the trial met with Moses Bates, the newspaper's editor, at his office.

"No question in my mind the holdouts on this jury were too timid to send Mrs. Gardner to the gallows, Mr. Bates."

"It may well-nigh shake the opinions of the people as regards the right of trial by jury," Bates replied. "Don't misunderstand me. I'd never say anything to prejudice the rights of a person charged with a crime, and I believe every person is innocent until proved guilty. What I am referring to is the falsely so-called 'philanthropy' which influences jurors against finding a guilty verdict because they happen to doubt the propriety, or justice, of the penalty which the law attaches to the commission of crime."

"Mrs. Gardner's trial was an anomaly in this county," the correspondent said. "It's the first time a woman has been tried here for her life, and it is perhaps natural that a great degree of sympathy should be felt in her favor."

"But there are other facts which jurors should also consider when they take the oath to decide by the law and the evidence," Bates said. "Murders by poison have become alarmingly frequent of late, and the public, as well as prisoners, demands some protection at the hands of juries. I believe the government proved beyond a reasonable doubt that Mrs. Gardner purchased enough arsenic to kill forty men, and with that arsenic in her possession she voluntarily called in her physician and told him that she was an adulteress and that her husband was disagreeable to her. Within five days from that time, her husband is found with arsenic in his stomach. The government proved it was the cause of his death. While no attempt is made to show that any other person either administered the fatal draft or had any motive for doing so, Mrs. Gardner has maintained a sullen silence in regard to who or what she purchased the poison for, and still five jurors are found whose squeamishness will not allow them to find a woman guilty, though the evidence can be reconciled with no other theory which it were possible to set up."

"I have no doubt that in many instances decisions of this kind come from a conscientious belief that capital punishment should in no case be inflicted," said the correspondent, "but as far as I'm concerned such influence is nothing more nor less than perjury on the part of the juror who meets the interrogatories of the court with the assurance that his opposition to capital punishment will in no respect affect the verdict he will render."

"I agree," said Bates. "Do we know if the attorney general intends to try Mrs. Gardner again?"

"It's a matter of conjecture; some say she will not be tried again but will be discharged from jail after serving a year or two. I don't believe it's true."

"Another trial is likely in my opinion, although I can't say with how much success," the editor replied.

"In one respect I'd be satisfied to let Mrs. Gardner go untried," said the correspondent. "During her whole trial the court house was thronged with females, many of them carrying their dinners or having them sent to them, and not only old maids and mothers, but young ladies of tender age were present during the recital of the trial's most disgusting scenes and while testimony was rehearsed which is unfit for publication. Not only did they retain their places in the courtroom, but, judging from appearances, made the disgusting testimony the subject of remark among themselves. I hope I never again witness such a scene in that or any other courtroom."

"If the females of this town and county have so little self-respect that they are willing to make themselves the subject of contemptuous ridicule among a crowd of strangers who are unaccustomed to such scenes elsewhere, then the authorities should interfere," Bates said. "And if Mrs. Gardner is to be tried again, I trust every female will be excluded from the courtroom. I know it was the sheriff's wish to exclude them in the trial that has passed.

"Our conversation will be at the center of an editorial I intend to publish next week. These issues are too important to ignore and certainly warrant the public's attention; and in the interest of fairness and transparency, we will deliver a copy to every juror," Bates concluded.

***

Juror Roland Copeland of East Bridgewater received the *Rock*'s September 10 edition and took immediate and strenuous exception to Bates's opinion.

"I cannot believe this editor's audacity, Elizabeth," Copeland said to his wife. "He says if a juror admits his opposition to capital punishment during empanelment and assures the court his views will not influence his impartiality either way – now listen to this, 'is nothing more nor less than perjury.' How easy it is for him to criticize from his lofty perch. How dare he?"

"You have every right to be upset, dear. How difficult would it have been for him or someone on his staff to ask you and other jurors for a comment? It would only seem fair. Perhaps you should write Mr. Bates with a response," Elizabeth said.

"I intend to do just that, my dear," Copeland said, slamming the paper on the kitchen table. "I'll put my thoughts to paper and send the letter to Bates before day's end."

Two weeks after Copeland had written him, Bates replied publicly rather than by personal letter. In the *Rock*'s September 24 edition, Bates did not retract any part of his September 10 editorial, nor did he apologize for his opinion. Instead, he printed Copeland's letter in its entirety to allow readers to "draw their own conclusions as to whether the *Rock* should reverse any of its expressed opinions…"

> *Now sir, as I was the only man upon that panel opposed to capital punishment (so far as I know), certainly the only one who expressed such opposition in reply to interrogatories by the court; and as you have sent me your editorial, I feel called upon to reply, albeit five of the jury are included in the acrimonious criticism in which you*

191

indulge. My view of capital punishment as stated to the court is that it is wrong and inexpedient. But I can act impartially nevertheless.

And now, sir, having performed conscientiously, and to the best of my ability, what I conceived to be my duty as a juror, in the trial of Mrs. Gardner, why do you say that five jurors including myself are found whose squeamishness will not allow them to find a woman "guilty?" I must say for myself, that the charge is entirely gratuitous and unfounded. The others, who thought with myself [sic] that there was want of sufficiency in the proof of guilt, can speak for themselves. You think "the late trial may well-nigh shake the opinions of the people in their safety for the public as regards the right of trial by jury." Now if anything is to endanger the public safety in this regard, it is, I submit, such treatment of jurors, by the press, as the jurors just discharged have received at your hands. But I do not see why such a calamity as that of which you speak, should happen on account of the disagreement of the jury in a given case, when at the same time the people of all parties and classes, are divided in like manner as was the jury, which it is very evident is the case, although men would bring in "guilty" in private, when as jurors they would not so decide; would say "guilty" upon evidence not given under oath, when as jurors they would not; still without the restraint of responsibility, all men are by no means ready to say the proof is sufficient. The same reason, sir, is not alike conclusive upon your mind and mine, hence we may honestly differ upon a given subject.

You say "if the females of this town, and county have so little self-respect, etc.," then "the authorities should interfere, and if Mrs. Gardner is to be tried again, we trust every female will be excluded from the courtroom, as we know it was the wish of the sheriff that they should be in the trial that is past." I do not know what authority the authorities have to exclude the public, including the female portion, or to exclude them alone, from attendance on such a trial. It is their sacred right, and I think it will be a long time (however much yourself and the sheriff may desire it) before the public will justify the exclusion of females should they desire to attend, while one of their number is on trial for her life. Exclude them! Distrusting their sense of propriety! What tyranny would that not be? And who shall say that a fallen and unfortunate woman shall be deprived, in her trial hour, of the humane and pitying presence of her sex? Who, demanding justice, desire to know that justice may be done? And if their purity and virtue will not preserve their self-respect let that perish, but let liberty survive. And if any wish to leave on account of the presence of the other sex, it is to be hoped their right to do so, with as little interruption as may be, will not be impaired in the least degree.

***

As Abigail languished in her jail cell and the capital punishment debate raged on, Attorney General John Clifford prepared for a new trial. Public and political discourse on the fairness and necessity of the death penalty had fueled efforts for reform for nearly thirty years.

The debate centered on murder's common law definition. Harvard professor John Webster was found guilty in 1850 of the murder of George Parkman in Harvard's medical school laboratory. Common law defined murder as the killing of a human being with malice aforethought. The absence of malice distinguished manslaughter from murder. The punishment for murder under common law was death; manslaughter was punishable by life imprisonment.

In his appeal to Governor George Briggs and the Committee of Pardons, Webster contended he had acted impulsively and with passion when he struck Parkman the fatal blow. He sought the commutation of his sentence to life imprisonment, arguing his actions lacked the critical elements of premeditation and malice and more aptly suited the elements of manslaughter. Webster's appeal failed and he was publicly hanged on August 30, 1850, in Boston's Leverett Street Jail.

***

On October 16, 1857, the *Hingham Journal* announced and applauded Attorney General Clifford's decision to try the Gardner murder case a second time. The *Journal*'s editors believed the facts presented at trial had overwhelmingly proven Abigail's guilt.

"How any other result was reached, it is impossible for us to conceive; and nothing can be more certain, that nothing short of a conviction in her case will satisfy the judgment, and the moral sense of right and justice of this whole community. Not that there is anybody here that wants or desires that she should be hanged. But they do want and claim that justice shall be done, though the heavens fall. It is exceedingly probable that were she convicted, the entire community would unite as one man in a petition to have her sentence commuted to imprisonment for life."

In clear support of the September 10 *Plymouth Rock* editorial the *Journal* added, "…And when another jury is empaneled to try her [Mrs. Gardner] case according to law and evidence, we hope no man will be allowed to sit in the jury box who has any conscientious scruples in regard to the rectitude and justice of capital punishment, or who would hesitate to find a verdict against the prisoner on that ground."

Abigail was not without her supporters, however. The following week, the *Journal* published a rebuttal from a concerned citizen identifying himself only as "N.G."

Messrs. Blossom and Easterbrook: It appears by your

last issue that this lady is again to be put on trial upon the charge of murder. Upon what grounds a new trial is to be again gone through with, we are not informed, unless it is to suit a certain class who appear to be clamorous for her conviction. Mrs. Gardner had been confined in prison something over six months before her trial, giving the government ample opportunity to be prepared for the prosecution. The trial is past and the result we all know. Does the government complain now of any unfairness, or has there any new evidence appeared? Nothing of the kind.

The prosecution was carried on with all the zeal and ability of which it was capable. Why, then, should she be subject to another harassing trial? I do not propose to give even an opinion of her innocence or guilt. It is not every guilty person who is convicted. Some who are not guilty are convicted. We, the government, chose our own method of convicting a person charged with a crime. After choosing our own weapons, it seems the height of folly to complain if we do not obtain a victory.

I deem it an act of great injustice to censure a jury of impartial men under oath to bring in a verdict according to the law and evidence, because their verdict does not tally with our notion of the case. If their views of capital punishment prevented their giving a verdict otherwise, they perjured themselves. Before such insinuations are thrown before the public, we should be sure the charge could be well sustained.

I do not propose to discuss the character of Mrs. Gardner here, but really I am surprised at some remarks in your paper of last week. "To loose such a hardened and desperate character as Mrs. Gardner." Nowhere is an attempt to forestall the public feeling in regard to Mrs. Gardner's character. This is uncandid and unfair, especially where a trial is pending. She has not been proved yet to be a "desperate character;" and we have yet to learn that she has been so considered by her neighbors or friends. The fact of her being a member of a respectable church in this town at the time of her arrest shows her to be, at least, in reputation, respectable.

If Mrs. Gardner is to have another trial, it should be had without delay. It is neither honorable nor right to keep a person in long imprisonment, and after all perhaps fail to sustain the charge. And who is to suffer the loss, for perhaps a year's imprisonment, in case a jury will not convict her? We know what has been the result of such things, and protest even against another trial unless good reason can be shown for it. But if another trial must be had, it should be without delay, and with a view to inflicting as little punishment as possible in case the charge is not sustained.

"One of the People," challenged the opinion voiced by "N.G." with a letter published by the *Journal* the following week.

Messrs. Editors: The communication in your last, from "N.G.," I have read with mingled feelings of pity and indignation. I think that both the judgment and heart of the writer must be at fault. The term used by him at the commencement of his epistle – "this lady" – is enough, I think, to cause a rise of indignation in the bosom of every virtuous female. We know of no female friend as related in heathen mythology, to whom the term "lady" might not be applied with as much propriety. Where is her high, moral worth, or her virtuous accomplishments? I, for one, think that even the term female, as applied to her, is sufficiently humiliating to the sex. We might enlarge upon this gross misnomer, but forbear at this time.

"N.G." asks, "Does the government complain now of any unfairness?" I think it does, with good and sufficient reason. Those jurors solemnly swore to try the case at issue, according to law and evidence, unbiased by the law of capital punishment. Now, if I am rightly informed, one of those jurors has since asserted, that had it not been for that law, they should have readily agreed upon a verdict. Now, if this is correct, have we not reason to complain? I, for one, am compelled to believe that some of those jurors went into that panel with a fixed determination not to convict. Therefore, I deny the assertion of "N.G." when he says, "Nothing of the kind."

"N.G." says "he is really surprised at some remarks in your paper, 'To loose such a hardened and desperate character as Mrs. G.'" Now, in all candor and fairness, I would ask what milder term those of us who know her could apply, overwhelmed as we are by the positive assurance that she fatally poisoned her husband; and also with the strong presumption that she caused the death of his mother by lingering poison? And we are sustained in this assurance and presumption by the remark of the deceased husband to his mother, "Abigail has poisoned me, and she will poison you." Therefore, we of the community think it sufficiently proved that she is a hardened and desperate character.

"N.G." next refers to the circumstance of her being a member of a respectable church at the time of her arrest, shows her to be, at least, in reputation, "respectable." That she was a "member of a respectable church," we admit; but we have been credibly informed that the church were, previous to the death of her husband, meditating measures for dealing with her for her immoral and unchristian walk. "N.G." has probably forgotten (or he never knew) that

Judas Iscariot was a member of a respectable church. And we could refer him to many other instances of similar character, from Judas Iscariot to Mrs. Gardner.

***

A *Boston Traveler* correspondent departed Boston's Old Colony depot and rode the cars to Plymouth on a frigid Wednesday morning, January 13, 1858, to visit Abigail at the jail. He alighted from the train at Plymouth's terminal and ascended Depot Avenue's steep hill on foot to Court Street and the jail. A guard allowed him access through the main gate and escorted him to Sheriff Phillips's office. Phillips greeted the reporter and granted him permission to visit with Abigail. He was shown to her cell and was somewhat astonished to find her in a bright, cheerful mood. Abigail agreed to speak with him. The reporter noted "…a wildness in her expression, but no indication of insanity."

She spoke of her children, especially her daughter Abby, in loving terms. Her face softened when she said, "I miss them so. I haven't seen either of them since the trial."

She was reluctant to discuss the jury's indecision in her case except to say she was disappointed. She made no reference to her husband.

When the interview concluded and the reporter rose to leave, Abigail called after him.

"I am determined not to mourn," she said. "I hope to be released from confinement in the coming spring and as soon as I am freed, I intend to marry and start my life anew."

With a tip of his cap and a slight bow, the reporter stepped away and left the jail in the guard's charge.

***

According to *The Banner of Light*'s "The Messenger," Hosea Gardner's spirit revisited his earthly envoy soon after the mistrial with a message of compassion and forgiveness. Hosea pleaded with those in whose hands Abigail's fate was held to spare her life.

Vengeance is mine, and I will repay, sayeth the Lord.

Oh, how I wish that mortals would let God do His own work. How I wish they would not usurp the power that belongs to Him, for he distinctly says it is His to visit vengeance, not the work of mortals. Although I am free from the galling chains that for years bound me, although I suffer no pain, although I am a spirit, yet I cannot rest.

The secret agony felt by my children reaches me, and the terrible remorse of her who held the right of wife, reaches me also. Oh, she has hell enough without any further punishment. Can there not be something done to free her from the hell of earth? Place her in whatever position you may, surround her by all the wealth of earth, gratify every passion, still there will be hell enough left.

Four days ago I visited her in her desolate situation. And I found her actually cursing her Maker, because He had suffered her to be punished by a hell of Conscience. No prayer is offered to God for relief; although Remorse is like a viper in the soul, it brings no prayer. No, because the evil in her has overpowered all good, and she is lost to a sense of Truth.

Oh, Heaven forbid that she should longer suffer for trespassing upon the laws of my natural life. My blood does not cry for vengeance; no my soul cries for pity, and I thank God she has cut the cord which bound me to earth, and has made me free as I am.

But is there no way for me to benefit my children? Does not your channel reach them? Oh, can I not whisper peace to their souls? Can I not wipe away the stain upon their pure garments a parent has cast there?

It is for that I return; I must accomplish it. And my mother! She who was ever ready to throw off her own cares and take mine upon her soul. Can I not enter her soul, and inspire her spirit with Hope, with Joy Immortal? Can I not satisfy her that I am happy?

And her who, with a relentless hand, dealt me the potion of Death – can I not benefit her? Can I not avert the blow of that sword of Justice which seems hanging over her, ready to be dealt by mortals? Oh, you who now live in Right, take heed lest ye fall, for sin brings death – death of the soul – that of the body is nothing.

Oh, convey this message to her; say to her I freely forgive, and all I ask is that she obtains pardon from the God of Heaven. All He asks is repentance, but as long as she continues in this God-defying manner, she will not find Peace.

Oh, tell my children to love their mother, to be the lamp which shall guide her soul to Peace; let sweet words of love from their lips reach her spirit, and guide her to God. They may guide her steps; she can never be a guide to them.

And the public; oh, ask them to deal gently with the erring; they yet may turn her with words of holy love from misery's thorny track.

God of Wisdom, God of Power! If they on earth forget to pray, oh, do thou hear the prayer of the disembodied one? Do thou, oh Divine one, visit vengeance in thine own way? Oh, send angels to guide those who are left without an earthly guide, and, in thine own good time, give all to know, to see, and to praise Thee.

***

On March 26, 1858, the Massachusetts legislature repealed the murder statute. The new law established and defined two degrees of murder – one punishable with death and the other with imprisonment for life. The revised law placed the burden of deciding the degree of murder upon the jury.

On the same day, nearly six months after Abby had reached her twenty-first birthday, President James Buchanan's administration appointed her as Hingham Postmistress. Charles Siders resigned from the office as promised, and Abby assumed the business of the post and telegraph.

Although the post office appointment promised more income, it was still barely enough for her self-support, let alone for her thirteen-year-old brother. Marcus seemed happy in his place at Mr. Hunt's but his wages were meager. Abby was deeply concerned about Marcus's future and her ability to provide him with emotional and financial support. It seemed probable her mother would likely spend the remainder of her life in jail.

Abby sought Reverend Tilson's counsel when Sunday services concluded at the Baptist church, where she had continued to worship after her father's death.

"Reverend," Abby began, "I worry constantly about Marcus. He is at such a tender age. Mother's ordeal has been difficult for him. I speak with him often to soothe his fears and anxieties, but I'm not so sure my words have given him the comfort and relief he so desperately needs."

"I fully sympathize with your consternation, Abby," replied Tilson. "I do not doubt Marcus is under much duress trying to cope with overwhelming heartbreak and comprehend a tragedy even we as adults cannot understand."

"He misses Father terribly, as do I. He is without Father's love and guidance now, and I fear this hole in his heart will never be mended."

"God will provide, Abby," Tilson said, "and I will do everything in my power to guide and assure him of the Lord's bountiful love and mercy."

"Thank you, Reverend Tilson. Marcus is strong in his faith and prays daily. I'm sure he will welcome your intercession."

"How else can I help, Abby?"

"Mr. Hunt's generosity in providing Marcus with work and a place to stay has been wonderful, but Marcus can barely meet life's necessities with the wages he receives. I have done my best to support him with my income at the post office, but even with my recent appointment as postmistress, it is still difficult to make ends meet."

"Abby, it may be prudent to seek legal guardianship for Marcus. Have you ever considered this? There are many within the Baptist congregation who sympathize with your plight and who want to help in any way they can."

"What do you mean by guardianship?" Abby asked.

"A guardianship petition to the court is presented by a reputable person who meets the approval of you and Marcus. Since Marcus is under fourteen years old, the law considers him a minor and, because he is without parents, the court may appoint a guardian who is entrusted by law with his interests. The law recognizes that Marcus's youth and inexperience deter him from acting for himself in life's ordinary affairs," Tilson explained.

Abby's eyes misted.

"It is best, Abby. I have someone in mind. I will consult with him and let you know his answer."

"Thank you, Reverend Tilson. I will speak with Marcus at Mr. Hunt's after I leave here. I look forward to hearing from you."

Reverend Tilson met with Levi Hersey, a deacon and Sunday school teacher at the Baptist church. Thirty-five-year-old Hersey, a widower, lived with his father and sister on South Street near Marsh's Bridge in Hingham. Levi was a skilled cabinet maker, employed by the Hallet and Davis Piano Company on Harrison Avenue in Boston. He was also a staunch temperance advocate and co-founded Hingham's Sons of Temperance Corner Stone chapter, where he had befriended the Gardner children's father, Hosea. When Reverend Tilson approached Levi with the proposal to sponsor Marcus's guardianship, he readily accepted.

Attorney Henry E. Hersey, on behalf of Levi Hersey as principal and Reverend Jonathan Tilson and Joseph Ripley as sureties, petitioned the Plymouth County Probate Court to appoint Hersey as guardian to Marcus Gardner on May 17, 1858, two days before the start of Abigail's second trial. The court approved the petition after a brief hearing.

Chapter 10: Murder by Degrees

In 1855, an amendment to the state constitution had abolished the governor's power to appoint the state attorney general and established the position as an elective office. On Tuesday, November 3, 1857, Stephen H. Phillips, a thirty-four-year old Salem, Massachusetts, native and Harvard Law School graduate, defeated Attorney General John Clifford in the general election. Phillips's term commenced on January 1, 1858, and on the twenty-seventh of the same month, he appeared in his first-high profile case before the Supreme Judicial Court to prosecute William Joyce and William McNulty for the murder of Boston police officer Ezekiel W. Hodsdon.

The responsibility for the government's second prosecution of Abigail Gardner now rested with Phillips and the district attorney at the initial trial, James M. Keith. They were about to try the first person in the state under the newly defined murder statute.

Phillips had conferred with former attorney general Clifford for his perspective on the mistrial and had studied the transcripts at length. Phillips also reviewed the case with Keith.

"I see no reason to proceed any differently, Jim," said Phillips. "I have no question the evidence presented was more than sufficient to prove Mrs. Gardner's guilt."

"I agree, General. The facts as presented weighed heavily in the government's favor. Our most critical step in this new trial is ensuring we empanel a death-qualified jury."

"Yes, I concur. We will challenge judiciously. I fully intend to secure a first-degree conviction but would be satisfied with second-degree under the new statute. I believe we can expect a more favorable outcome."

***

Abigail's trial opened in Plymouth at eleven o'clock on a

mostly cloudy Wednesday morning, May 19, 1858. County officials had transferred all legal business to Davis Hall due to a renovation project underway at the courthouse. Justices Merrick, Metcalf, and Bigelow, as before, presided. Charles Davis and B. W. Harris continued in their roles as Abigail's defense counsel.

The second trial did not attract the feverish attention of the first. Fewer spectators and a handful of reporters was the norm each day. There was a marked absence of women in the gallery.

Abigail was dressed in the same mourning clothes. She appeared gaunt, her high cheekbones more pronounced, and her complexion sallow.

Attorney General Phillips moved for jury empanelment but before the court ruled, Attorney Davis made a motion to dismiss the indictment due to the 1858 repeal of the murder statute. The grand jury had indicted Abigail for murder under the previous statute; therefore, a trial under the new law was improper, he argued.

The court denied Davis's motion. Abigail would be tried under the new statute and the jury would, if they found evidence to convict her, determine if she was guilty of murder in the first or second degree.

The court proceeded with jury empanelment after Clerk of Court William Whitman read the indictment. Forty men appeared for jury duty and after examination by the court, the prosecution, and the defense, twenty-eight were dismissed. The court excused nineteen who were challenged peremptorily, four who had formed opinions about Abigail's guilt or innocence, and five who opposed capital punishment. Twelve men were empaneled and the court appointed Kingston resident James Foster, a sixty-four-year-old farmer, as jury foreman.

As he had at the first trial, Attorney Davis motioned for a sequestration of all but medico-legal witnesses and the court so ordered.

District Attorney Keith opened with the government's

statement when the last witness had exited the courtroom. His outline of the case varied little from the details he had offered during the first trial. At the conclusion of Keith's statement, the court adjourned for one hour.

When court resumed, the government called its first witness, Justice of the Peace and Coroner James Lewis. Lewis repeated his prior testimony, describing the inquest hearing and the autopsy performed on Hosea after his disinterment.

Dr. Calvin Ellis was sworn and established his expert qualifications as a physician. He testified about his post-mortem examination on Hosea's body and his removal of organs, including the stomach. The district attorney picked up the jar containing the stomach from the evidence table and presented it to the witness. Ellis identified it and stated the stomach was in the same state of preservation as it was during the first trial and expounded on arsenic's preservative effects. The jar and its contents were marked as evidence. Keith showed Ellis two vials containing fluid. Ellis identified both as evidence he had submitted to Dr. Jackson for analysis and they, too, were admitted as government exhibits without objection by the defense.

DA Keith presented the jar and vials to Dr. Charles Jackson. He identified the items as those he had received from Dr. Ellis. Then Jackson provided a detailed account of the chemical processes he had employed on the stomach and on the fluids to determine and confirm the presence of arsenic. The court here interrupted the district attorney and adjourned for the day.

***

On a cold, dreary Thursday, May 20, 1858, at 9:00 a.m., court reconvened. Deputies from Sheriff Phillips's office marched Abigail from the jail to Davis Hall, shielding her from the misty rain with an umbrella. Pedestrians going about their business in the town center stopped to stare at Abigail as the procession made its way down Main Street.

Court officers led Abigail to the prisoner's dock and Sheriff

206

Phillips called for order inside the sparsely occupied hall. The justices took their seats and the jury filed in.

"You may call your witness, Mr. Keith," Justice Metcalf directed.

"Thank you, Your Honor. The government calls Dr. Jackson to continue his testimony."

Jackson stepped to the witness chair and, after he was seated, Justice Metcalf reminded him he was still under oath. The district attorney presented Jackson with the copper vessel he had received from John Stephenson, which he identified. He also identified the vessel's contents and verified that his tests on the refuse had confirmed the presence of arsenic. The court admitted the vessel and contents as evidence with no objection from the defense.

"Dr. Jackson, if a person ingests a fatal dose of arsenic, how long can he expect to survive?" Keith asked.

"A fatal dose will cause death sometimes in twenty-four hours, sometimes after three or four weeks," Jackson replied.

"Is it possible something other than arsenic may have caused Mr. Gardner's death?" Keith asked.

"I heard Dr. Ellis's testimony of the autopsy. From his description, I saw no cause for death, except from the effects of arsenic. I have no doubt, assuming what Dr. Ellis testified to be true, and from what I saw myself, the death was produced in this case, by arsenic. I cannot account for the death in any other way. Arsenic is used as a preservative. The stomach here produced," Jackson said, holding the perfectly preserved evidence before him, "left in its natural state, without arsenic, or some preservative, would now be putrid liquid."

DA Keith indicated he had no further questions for the witness on direct examination and Attorney Davis rose for cross.

Davis questioned Jackson about the ulcers found on the stomach during the autopsy and if the ulcers had contributed in any way to Gardner's death.

"I should not place any great reliance upon the ulcers found upon the stomach alone," Jackson answered. "They might be produced by causes other than arsenic."

"Did you testify at the inquest held in February last?"

"Yes, I testified before the coroner."

"Have you seen the transcript of your inquest testimony?"

"Yes, and my testimony as written is mainly correct," said Jackson, "although there are some literary errors. But the facts are mainly correct."

"Have you ever treated a patient for arsenical poisoning, Doctor?" asked Davis.

"I have never had any case of poison by arsenic under my care," replied Jackson.

Davis hoped with his next question he would raise a doubt in the jurors' minds by introducing the possibility that someone had applied the arsenic externally and not internally as specified in the indictment.

"Doctor, if someone applied arsenic to an open wound or sore, would it have the same effect as an application by ingestion?"

"Arsenic by outward application, upon sores, would produce similar effects as if taken inwardly. It would affect the nervous system primarily; afterwards, the stomach."

"Thank you, Doctor. I have no further questions."

Davis returned to the defense table and DA Keith rose for rebuttal. He knew where Davis was going with this and he intended to make it clear to the jury that the only way arsenic could be found in the intestines and organs of the deceased was by ingestion and no other manner.

"Doctor, if arsenic was applied outwardly, would it be found in the intestines?"

"No," Jackson answered. "Arsenic taken in by absorption would not be found in the intestines," answered Jackson.

"Thank you, Dr. Jackson. I have no other questions for this

witness, Your Honors."

"Very well," said Justice Metcalf. "Doctor, you may step down."

The district attorney called druggist James Hunt to the witness chair and after he was sworn, Hunt recounted the circumstances under which he had sold poison to Charles Dodge and the boy's return to his drug store later to explain the poison was not for Mrs. Gardner but for a Paddy woman. He also confirmed his presence at the inquest the previous February and had heard the statement uttered by Abigail in which she denied ever having purchased arsenic at any time in her life. The defense challenged Hunt's recollection as to the exact date of Dodge's visit to his shop but Hunt remained firm about it being January twenty-second.

Davis indicated he had completed his cross-examination and the district attorney called eleven-year-old Charles Dodge. He was as terrified as he had been during the first trial.

The boy told the court about his meeting with Mrs. Gardner, the errand to Mr. Hunt's, and the procurement of the arsenic. In a third version of his story, Dodge this time said the arsenic was for Marcus Gardner. He returned to Mrs. Gardner with the poison and gave it to her. She asked him if he had told Mr. Hunt who the arsenic was for and he told her he said it was for her son, Marcus. She told him to return to Mr. Hunt and tell him the arsenic was for a Paddy woman. He went back and did as he was instructed. Frustrated, the district attorney turned over his witness to the defense for cross-examination. As far as the DA was concerned, it made no difference who Dodge said the arsenic was for. His testimony still showed he had received the poison from Hunt and given it to the defendant.

Attorney Davis asked the boy if he knew Marcus Gardner and Dodge confirmed he did; he said he used to live near him. The government had no questions for Dodge on redirect, and the court excused him.

Dr. Ezra Stephenson took the witness chair for the government and, after he was sworn, testified about his January 1857 meeting with Hosea at the post office, his examination of Abigail, her insistence about being pregnant, her admission of adultery, her disposal of Hosea's strange vomit, her indifference when asked about severing and straightening her husband's leg to fit the coffin, and her refusal to allow a post-mortem examination. Stephenson also testified about his involvement in Hosea's autopsy and his opinion of death by arsenic.

"Dr. Stephenson," Davis began on cross, "what was the true reason for your visit to Mrs. Gardner on the first occasion?"

"I went when I was first called to see if Mrs. Gardner was insane."

"Did you examine her for indications of insanity?"

"Yes."

"Doctor, you have testified about conversations you have had with the defendant. Are Mrs. Gardner's statements your words or hers?"

"I have usually given her statements in her own words."

"Did you treat Mr. Gardner for poisoning?"

"I did not."

"Did you ask anyone in the Gardner household to preserve Mr. Gardner's vomit?"

"I did not."

"Have you ever treated a patient who has been poisoned with arsenic?"

"I have never witnessed such a case; I have read of the symptoms in medical books."

"Who was taking care of Mr. Gardner when you were not there?"

"His mother acted as nurse."

"Who administered the medicine you prescribed?"

"I administered some of the medicine myself. I did not see anyone else give Mr. Gardner the medicine."

"You examined Mr. Gardner's leg after his fall. Did you observe anything unusual in the leg's appearance in relation to this fall?"

"I did not."

"How would you describe Mr. Gardner's overall physical health?"

"Mr. Gardner was not a strong man."

"What happens when arsenic is applied to a wound or sore, Doctor?"

"Arsenic, applied externally, where there is an abrasion, would be absorbed into the system."

"I'll ask you again, Doctor. Have you ever treated a patient poisoned with arsenic?"

"I have had no case of the kind and no experience."

"Thank you, Dr. Stephenson. I have no other questions."

"Mr. Keith, any redirect for this witness?" Judge Metcalf inquired.

"No, Your Honor."

"Call your next witness."

"Your Honors, the government calls John Stephenson."

Stephenson was sworn and settled himself into the witness chair. He repeated the testimony he had given at the first trial about statements he had heard Abigail utter at the inquest, his recovery of the slops behind the Gardner home with the copper container provided by Reed, and his delivery of the container and slops to Dr. Jackson.

"Mr. Stephenson, very briefly," Davis began on cross-examination. "What did the contents of the container look like after sitting for nearly nine months?"

"It was in liquid form and was of a dark color."

"Did it have a yellow color?"

"I don't know if the liquid had a yellow color."

"Thank you. Nothing else, Your Honors," Davis said.

"Redirect?" Metcalf asked.

"No, Your Honor," Keith replied.

The district attorney called Edwin Wilder, Otis Hersey, and Constable Gridley Hersey as witnesses in succession and all testified as they had at the first trial. Questions posed by the defense to each man elicited no new or conflicting testimony.

"The Commonwealth calls the daughter of the deceased, Miss Abigail Williams Gardner," said DA Keith at the excusal of Gridley Hersey.

An excited murmur rose in the gallery and the sheriff called for order. A court officer stepped out and after a few moments returned to the courtroom with Abby and guided her to the witness chair. She ignored her mother's stare as she passed the dock.

Abby repeated the testimony she had given at the first trial about her father's fall, Dr. Stephenson's medical treatment, and her grandmother's attendance and care for her father. Abby confirmed it was her father, and not her mother, who had requested her grandmother's presence.

"Did you administer any medicine to your father during his illness?" the district attorney asked.

"No, I did not. I took charge of the post office and store and was occupied all day and till late at night."

"You spent some time with your father on the Thursday before his death, did you not?"

"Yes."

"What was his condition then?"

"He was not well on Thursday morning. He vomited frequently and complained of a burning sensation of the stomach."

"Did your father say anything about the vomit he had purged?" the district attorney asked.

"Yes, he asked to have the vomit preserved."

"Was it preserved?"

"No," Abby replied. "Mother emptied it into a pail. She said she did not wish such smelling stuff in the house."

Abby nervously stole a glance in her mother's direction.

"Was your mother frequently with your father during his illness?"

"Yes. She was with him almost all the time."

"Did something happen between you and your mother at your father's bedside on the night he died?"

"Yes. I was standing by the bed when my father was dying. I was weeping. My mother asked me to stop and pulled me from the bedside."

"Thank you, Miss Gardner. I have no other questions at this time."

"Mr. Davis?" Justice Metcalf gestured.

"Yes. Thank you, Your Honor," Davis replied, shuffling the notes on his table before approaching the witness seat.

On cross-examination, Abby said she had last seen her father at noon the day before he died and she thought him sensible but weak.

"You said your mother was with your father almost all the time during his illness. Who took care of the household?"

"My mother attended to the household affairs and grandmother acted as nurse to my father."

"Is your mother meticulous in her household affairs?"

"She is, but not particularly so."

"Have you ever known your father to take medicine on his own?" Davis asked.

"Yes, he had been in the habit of taking pills, as he told me shortly before his last sickness," said Abby.

"Did you see anyone give your father medicine during his illness?"

"I did not."

There being no other questions from the defense or prosecution, the court excused Abby and the government called her brother Marcus to the witness chair. Marcus testified on direct examination about attending school during the week of his father's illness. He said he had picked up salts and liniments for his grandmother from Hunt's apothecary but had never applied any solution or given any medicine to his father. He also corroborated Abby's testimony about Abigail's refusal to save the vomit and its disposal in the slop pail.

"When was the last time you saw your father alive, Marcus?"

"I saw him Saturday night before he died."

"Thank you. No more questions," DA Keith said and returned to his seat at the prosecution table.

Attorney Davis began his cross-examination. "Master Gardner, did you run an errand to Mr. Hunt's store for your mother before your father died?"

"My mother asked me but it was school time and I could not go."

"Do you know if anyone did the errand for her?"

"Yes, I got one of the Miller boys to go for her."

"What time was that?"

"It was at noon."

"How can you be sure about the day?"

"I remember there had been heavy snow."

Attorney Davis stepped away and nodded to Justice Metcalf. Metcalf excused Marcus and the district attorney called Hosea's brother-in-law Reuben Reed.

Before he began direct examination of the witness, DA Keith once again presented the plan drawn by civil engineer Charles Seymour which the government had used at the first trial.

"Your Honors, for clarification purposes, the government proposes to introduce this plan if the defense has no objection."

"Mr. Davis?" Justice Metcalf inquired.

"We have no objection, Your Honor."

"Thank you," Metcalf replied. "Mr. Clerk, please mark the plan as an exhibit."

Reuben testified he was present when John Stephenson placed the materials found in Hosea's back yard into a container he had brought along for the purpose. Keith approached Reuben with Seymour's plan and asked him to point to the location where he had retrieved the materials and Reuben indicated.

Keith questioned him about the prisoner's conduct after Hosea's funeral and he said she did not seem affected by the solemnity of the affair and instead remained after the prayer to shake hands and converse with the people who had attended.

Attorney Davis had no questions for Reed on cross-examination.

Dentist Don Pedro Wilson was the government's final witness of the day and he testified how he had seen Mrs. Gardner burying the slops in the snow and explained how he had recovered the refuse with Reuben Reed and John Stephenson. Wilson indicated where he had seen the slops by referring to Seymour's plan.

On cross-examination the dentist testified he hadn't seen a pail in Mrs. Gardner's possession. Asked exactly where he had seen her, he said she stood on the path leading from the house to a shed in the backyard and, at Davis's request, pointed once again to the spot on the plan. Attorney General Phillips and DA Keith rose from their chairs at the prosecution table after the court dismissed Wilson.

"Your Honors, the government will present no further witnesses. We here rest our case," Phillips declared.

"Thank you, Mr. Attorney General," Judge Metcalf said. "Court will open tomorrow morning at nine o'clock and the defense will be prepared to present its opening statement. Court is adjourned."

**

The *Plymouth Rock* was compelled by the third day of proceedings to comment on the trial's tedium.

"The Gardner trial commenced on Wednesday and seems to create no excitement at all in our village – there being scarcely any attendance of out-of-town people except such as is obliged to attend. No new evidence has yet been put in, and the trial, which is being held in Davis Hall, proceeds as quietly and monotonously as the most stupid civil case ever put before a jury."

**

The third day of trial resumed promptly at nine o'clock on Friday, May 21. Justices Metcalf, Merrick, and Bigelow briskly ascended to the bench and called for the jury.

Abigail, seated in the prisoner's dock, her face still obscured by her mourning veil, watched intently as each juror entered the box.

Justice Metcalf called upon defense attorney Harris to present his opening statement.

"May it please Your Honors, Mr. Foreman, and gentlemen of the jury, I shall but give expression, to that which you all deeply feel," Harris began as he approached the jury box.

"I doubt not, when I say, that you were never before called, to the discharge of a more solemn or more fearful duty, than that which now engages your attention. You are charged with the issue of life and death, and upon you will at last be thrown, the responsibility for the verdict which you shall render. As no higher, more arduous or more important trust was ever before committed to your charge, so no greater care, calmer deliberation, or more fearless integrity and virtue were ever before demanded at your hands. And I doubt not gentlemen, that you have entered upon this grave and responsible appointment with minds subdued, judgments balanced, consciences quickened and enlightened, and hearts made prayerful, by anxious solicitude for the just issue of this trial.

"Thus far, your attention has been engrossed by the detail of the various proofs upon which the government rely, and upon which they propose by and by, to demand at your hands, the forfeiture of the defendant's life," Harris continued, now pacing to and fro before the panel with his hands tightly clasped behind his back.

"You have seen the web of their suspicion, woven from the fine fibers of trivial circumstance, with how much diligence and with what skill it has been forced upon your attention. And now it is announced that they have nothing more to charge – and at present nothing more to say – and I doubt not the learned and able gentlemen who conduct this cause on behalf of the government, wait patiently and willingly, yea, *hopefully* wait, that the unhappy prisoner may be heard in her defense. And I trust that I am justified in the belief, that no dreams of ambition, no allurements of fame will lead them to go beyond the clearly marked limits of high public duty that they may secure to themselves a personal triumph, at the fearful price of blood.

"It becomes my duty, first, to speak a humbler word in behalf of the helpless, lone woman, who has placed her life in your keeping. And it is not improper that I should say to you, that myself and my associate have been appointed by the Honorable Court, to speak and act here in behalf of this poor helpless female who has no money, and few friends, and who has thrown herself for protection upon the same government which also seeks her condemnation. We come before you gentlemen, actuated by no hope of pecuniary reward or expectation of personal honor, but only in obedience to that principle in the human heart, which always responds to the call of the helpless, in their hour of agony and peril.

"We know and feel how unequal is the contest and I pray in behalf of the prisoner at the bar, that the ultimate question of life or death to her may not be determined by a comparison of the merits of the efforts of the humble counsel for the defendant, with those of the learned, experience, and distinguished gentlemen who appear here for the government."

Here Harris went over the evidence in very much the same way he had done at the first trial. He challenged the competence and veracity of the Commonwealth's most important witness, Dr. Ezra Stephenson. He offered a lengthy explanation of the law and its application to the case at hand. He highlighted the defendant's presumption of innocence and the government's burden of proof and went into great detail explaining the difference between circumstantial, direct, and positive evidence.

"Every one of the circumstances from which the main inference is sought to be drawn, must be proved beyond a reasonable doubt, and independently of all others. Do not yield too much to circumstantial evidence. If any or all of the facts sustain naturally two distinct inferences, one of which is inconsistent with innocence, and the other consistent with innocence, I hardly need say which you must take. And here, at this point, gentlemen, lies a great and important part of your duty. Review the important part of the government's case, and see how it will bear the tests of this rule."

Harris closed his argument with a final appeal on his client's behalf and returned to the defense table where he was met with an approving nod from co-counsel. The court recessed.

***

The defense examined Drs. Stephenson and Jackson and James Hunt, when proceedings continued. All three men remained steadfast in their prior testimony. The prosecution had no questions on cross-examination.

Attorney Harris called fifty-two-year old Dr. Augustus Hayes, an eminent Boston consulting chemist and former state assayer. After he was sworn, Hayes testified to his qualifications as a chemist and his extensive knowledge of arsenic and its properties.

"Dr. Hayes, did you have an occasion to examine the stomach of the deceased?" Harris asked.

"Yes, I examined the deceased's stomach in Dr. Ellis's presence," Hayes replied.

"I show you this specimen previously admitted as evidence and ask you to identify it."

"This is the jar containing the stomach I examined."

"Please tell the court what you observed during your examination."

"First of all, I did not see any traces of sulphate of arsenic. I found a number of brownish-gray spots often observed in stomachs in which calomel has been found."

"Did you observe any other spots?"

"There were no other spots which could be referred to the action of any mineral poison."

"What else did you observe?"

"The stomach's lower part was covered with a yellowish, slimy substance having the same appearance found in other partially decayed stomachs, and especially where oil and fatty substances were present."

"Can you comment on the stomach's condition as it pertains to preservation?"

"I noticed nothing extraordinary in the stomach's preservation to the present and under the circumstances."

"Well, if the stomach did not contain arsenic as you have stated, to what do you attribute the stomach's preserved condition?" Harris inquired.

"Several stomachs left in my laboratory for twelve to sixteen months have kept as well preserved as this. The first stages of decay give rise to gases which are preservatives of subsequent decay to a certain extent when the stomachs are enclosed in a tight vessel. In these cases the decay proceeds very slowly. These, however, are remarkable cases, as in a majority of them decomposition is very rapid. Any metallic salt will retard and, in some cases, where death is caused by calomel, the parts in which the poison came in contact and could be detected were preserved from decay, while the rest of the stomach would rapidly decompose."

"What is your opinion as to the effects of substances such as castor oil, brandy and water, and anything else mixed with calomel?"

"Castor oil will retard decomposition, and so will brandy and water, but in a diminished degree as compared with pure alcohol. A mixture of calomel, castor oil, and lemon juice taken into the stomach would produce a bi-salt of mercury similar to corrosive sublimate and would act as an antiseptic or preservative of the stomach from decomposition. The bi-salt of mercury when taken tends to produce inflammation of the stomach, accompanied by a soreness of the throat," Hayes said.

"What about morphine? Would it have an effect?"

"I don't know the effect of morphine on a stomach."

"Let me understand then, Doctor. It is your opinion the stomach of the deceased did not contain arsenic?" Harris prompted.

"I found no traces of arsenic. In all cases of chemical examination of the stomachs of persons whose deaths were caused by arsenic, I have found a compound of arsenous acid and protein in the substance of the tissues. Arsenous acid has a strong tendency to combine with albuminous bodies and the fluids of the tissues in the stomach. Arsenous acid always combines with protein, either in life or in death, and forms a chemical compound, having certain chemical properties. This compound is recognized in cases of partial as well as complete poisoning. Where the proportion of arsenous acid is small in proportion to that of the protein or albuminous bodies, the compound ceases to be poisonous; on this fact is founded the administration of antidotes to the action of arsenous acid on the stomach in cases of poison. This compound would not affect the tissues of the stomach but would be ejected as fecal matter."

"What is the best test to determine the presence of arsenic, Doctor?"

"A careful chemical analysis of the stomach is the best test of the presence of poison; a physical examination would not be a satisfactory test, and the presence of sulphuret of arsenic in the stomach can only be proved by a chemical analysis. Where arsenic is found in fecal matter contained in the intestines, attended with little or no inflammation of the stomach, I should not be able to determine the cause of death unless a chemical analysis was made. By the facts disclosed by the autopsy and the subsequent discovery of arsenic in the intestines, I am not able to give an opinion as to the cause of Mr. Gardner's death."

"Thank you, Doctor. I have no further questions."

"Mr. Keith, do you wish to cross-examine the witness?" Justice Metcalf asked.

"Your Honor, I will examine the witness," said Attorney General Phillips, pushing back his chair. He then began, "Dr. Hayes, how did you perform a chemical analysis on the stomach of the deceased?"

"My examination was a physical one and not a chemical one."

"Well, then, Doctor, is a physical examination of the organ sufficient to prove or disprove the presence of arsenic?" asked Phillips.

"A chemical analysis is the only sure way to detect arsenic if taken internally."

"Thank you, Doctor. I have no other questions," Phillips said.

"Re-direct, Mr. Harris?" Metcalf inquired.

"No, Your Honor. At this point, the defense rests."

"Mr. Phillips?"

Phillips called Drs. Jackson and Ellis in rebuttal.

"Dr. Jackson, you have heard Dr. Hayes's testimony. Do you agree with his opinion?"

"First of all, I would say the so-called 'protein' referenced by Dr. Hayes is an artificial substance and is never found in a living body, but is produced by a chemical process. Secondly, there is no chemical known as 'bi-salt of mercury' alluded to by the doctor as produced by the mixture of calomel, castor oil, and lemon juice."

The defense had no questions for Jackson and he was dismissed.

The government called Dr. Ellis, asking, "…please tell the court whether you kept Mr. Gardner's stomach in an air-tight vessel or not."

"The stomach vessel was not air-tight."

Justice Metcalf interjected and corroborated Ellis's statement by saying, with a roll of his eyes, "The vessel certainly was not tight this morning when brought into court."

The judge's inference to the odor emitting from the specimen drew a smile from the audience in the gallery.

"Your Honors, the government has no further questions."

Metcalf gestured to the defense table and Attorneys Davis and Harris indicated they had no questions.

"We will adjourn for fifteen minutes," said Metcalf, "and at our return the defense will present its closing argument."

Attorney Davis's close was in many respects a repetition of his argument at the first trial. He ended his four hour oration with a final plea:

"I contend that the prisoner is presumed to be innocent; that the law in its tenderness to human life has placed the white robed angel of innocence at the side of every human being to guard and protect in the hour of peril. The government must prove beyond a reasonable doubt that Hosea J. Gardner was murdered and that he was killed with arsenic; and that the prisoner, with malice, and with intent to murder, administered, or caused to be administered arsenic to the deceased, before this angel leaves its charge and gives it up a victim for punishment and death."

Attorney General Phillips rose to present the prosecution's final argument when Davis concluded.

"Gentlemen of the jury, the crime with which the prisoner is charged is one at which humanity shudders, and from the contemplation of which the mind of man shrinks. You must put away all unmanly fear and resolutely resolve to do your duty. You must dismiss from your minds all prejudice and try this case calmly and conscientiously upon the law and the evidence."

Phillips next appealed to the jurors' sense of logic and reasoning asking, "Who had the motive to murder Hosea J. Gardner? The prisoner revealed to Dr. Stephenson the motive for murder, when she said she loved another man better than she loved her husband – that she had been intimate with him – that her husband was jealous of her, and had reason to be; and that this individual whom she loved had a wife and she a husband, and she must live on in her misery.

"Did she have the nerve to commit the crime? Think back to the witnesses who described her lack of love and tenderness of feeling when her husband fell and injured his limb.

"When the watchers, Wilder and Hersey, declined to give Mr. Gardner the brandy and water because it distressed him, the prisoner wished that the doctor's prescription should be followed, never faltering till the last moment of his life when she said, 'Let him die in peace.'

"After his death, her conduct was not subdued, but cold and unfeeling. At the funeral it was noticeable as cold and void of grief.

"Had she the means to commit the murder? The government has proved she had 180 grains of arsenic in her possession, and four grains were sufficient to destroy human life. Dr. Hunt says the boy Dodge bought the arsenic. Dodge says he bought it for Mrs. Gardner and put it into her hands.

"What did the prisoner do with the arsenic?" Phillips railed. "Where is it? For what did she obtain it? No explanation, except she said she bought it for a Paddy woman.

"Where is the Paddy woman? What was her name? How was she dressed? From where did she come, and to where has she gone?

"It is incumbent for the defense to answer these questions if they would have you, gentlemen of the jury, believe the statement was true – but no explanation is given.

"The government has therefore shown that the prisoner had the motive to commit the crime – that she had the means and the opportunity – and how was Hosea J. Gardner murdered? Poisoned by arsenic," the prosecutor submitted.

"The fact that Mr. Gardner had fallen and was confined to the house presented a favorable opportunity for the administration of the arsenic. There was nothing in the nature of the injury of the limb that was serious."

Phillips recited the symptoms manifested during Hosea's illness and commented on Abigail's conduct during that time – how she was unwilling to preserve the vomit and her constant presence in the sick room so as not to allow conversation out of her hearing; her conduct and protestation of innocence to Constable Hersey before she was accused; and her declarations at the examination before the coroner and to the constable that no one saw her give the poison and that it could not be proved.

"The conduct of the prisoner during the illness of the deceased, after his decease, at the funeral, and her declarations from time to time, unmistakably indicate her guilt. If Hosea J. Gardner died by poison, who was there who had a motive for the crime? Not the aged mother; there is no pretense whatever that she had a motive to murder her son. The daughter is above suspicion: dutiful, affectionate, and a model of filial tenderness and devotion.

"Gentlemen, you should believe the testimony of Drs. Jackson and Ellis, and if they are to be believed, if they are skillful and scientific men, and knew what they professed to know, then it must be taken to be proved that Hosea J. Gardner died of poison by arsenic.

"Was it suicide? All the circumstances negate the idea. There is no evidence that the deceased had arsenic in his possession, or ever contemplated self-destruction.

"Gentlemen, all the circumstances point to one person, and to one alone, who had a motive to commit the deed; to one person who had the opportunity; to one person who had the means to commit the crime; to one person whose conduct and conversation disclose guilt."

Phillips concluded, "The grand jury of Plymouth County has

presented the prisoner as the murderer of her husband, Hosea J. Gardner. We have placed before you the evidence of it, overwhelming and conclusive. It is for you to declare the effect of that evidence upon your minds. Can you escape the conclusion to which it inevitably leads? The awful responsibility is with you, and with you I leave it."

Chapter 11: A Lonely Life

Attorney General Phillips returned to the prosecution table. Justice Metcalf huddled with his colleagues then the three jurists nodded their heads simultaneously and drew back in their seats after a brief conversation. Metcalf turned to and addressed Abigail.

"Mrs. Gardner, the court will now allow you an opportunity to say what you please in relation to this case. The law gives you the right to be heard, but whatever you say is not to be considered legal evidence."

Abigail rose, nodded to Metcalf, lifted the veil she had kept drawn throughout the trial, and faced the jury to voice her last emotional plea.

"I am somewhat fatigued and excited from sitting here during the long days of this trial, and am unable to express my feelings as I should be glad to. I should be glad to convey to your minds, aside from falsehood and prejudice, the truth. I feel as though I could not rest until I let the world know what is true and what is false. I am not guilty."

Abigail faltered momentarily and dabbed at tears streaming down her face.

"I know the prejudice of many that are working against me. God knows my innocence – I am as innocent as any of you here of the charge. I feel like an outcast – unfortunate and friendless – without pity, and no one to pity me. I have no friends within two hundred miles of me. If I had, I think I could give you a very different opinion from that which I now have. I hope you will consider my case carefully. My husband was poisoned. God knows who did it. I know nothing about it, more than any of you here."

All eyes in the courtroom remained riveted on Abigail as she collapsed into her chair, overcome with her emotions. Justice

Merrick allowed a few moments for her to compose herself before delivering his charge to the jury. He reviewed the facts of the case as presented by the prosecution and defense and carefully explained the difference between first- and second-degree murder and how it pertained to the charge at hand.

"For instance, supposing the prisoner did poison her husband. If, at the time of the purchase of the arsenic, she contemplated that crime, then her act was murder in the first degree. If, on the other hand, she had, at that time, no such intention, but purchased it for some other object, and while preparing his drink, was seized by a sudden impulse, and dashed in a portion of the poison, that would be murder in the second degree. The degree of murder is to be found by the jury.

"With these instructions, gentlemen, I commit the case to you."

It was five o'clock when Merrick concluded and court officers escorted the jurors out of the courtroom for deliberation. The clerk of court transferred the exhibits marked during trial to the jury room and closed the door. A court officer remained outside to await the jury's decision.

Abigail remained in an anteroom with her attorneys to await the verdict. Phillips and Keith retired to the district attorney's temporary office off the main hall.

At ten o'clock, the jury foreman notified the officer posted at the door that he and his fellow jurors had reached a verdict. Twenty-five minutes later, the prosecution, defense, and Abigail were present in the courtroom. The jurors filed in after the justices were seated. All twelve men averted Abigail's gaze.

Clerk of Court Whitman rose and called each juror's name. Satisfied all were present, he addressed them.

"Gentlemen of the jury, have you agreed upon your verdict?"

"We have," foreman James Foster answered.

"Who shall speak for you?"

"Our foreman," replied the jury in unison.

Turning to the prisoner's dock, Whitman said, "Abigail Gardner, rise and hold up your right hand."

Abigail rose solemnly, leaned forward, and with her left hand supporting her on the dock's rail, raised her right. Attorneys Davis and Harris stood outside the dock and flanked her on both sides.

"Mr. Foreman, look upon the prisoner; prisoner, look upon the foreman. What say you Mr. Foreman? Is Abigail Gardner, the prisoner, guilty or not guilty?"

"Guilty," Foster pronounced.

The spectators gasped and turned their gaze to Abigail.

"In what degree?" Whitman asked.

"In the second degree," said Foster.

"So say you all?"

"So say us all," the jurors replied in unison.

The conviction was the first in Massachusetts under the new law.

Abigail was crestfallen. She breathed a heavy sigh and slumped into her seat. Attorney Davis spoke with her quietly and comforted her as the jury withdrew and assured her he would file an immediate appeal.

"Thank you, Mr. Davis, but I have little hope left. I am doomed to a life of misery behind prison walls; I'm sure the government will make sure of that," Abigail said.

Sheriff's deputies approached the dock, placed irons on Abigail's hands, and led her out of the courtroom.

A *Hingham Journal* reporter present at the verdict commented the next day on the final chapter of Abigail's long ordeal:

"Thus ends the public history of this terrible tragedy. In common with those of our citizens well acquainted with the circumstances of the case we have had the impression that Mrs. Gardner was guilty of the awful crime charged against her. We have no personal prejudice or ill will against her. We rejoice that the verdict was rendered "in the second degree." We hope that the discipline of the prison, that instruction and influences brought to bear upon her there, will awaken reflections of a moral character, and prove conducive to her spiritual good. Let us forgive her, and draw the palliative veil of charity over her sins, for she is human and a woman. And may we learn from her case the great lesson of human frailty – the importance of regulating our tempers, passions, and conduct by the high standard of Christianity, and resisting even the appearance and beginnings of evil."

The *Plymouth Rock* also commented on the trial's outcome and the revised murder statute's significance.

"It is difficult to believe that, if Mrs. Gardner was guilty of any offence at all, if she did actually administer arsenic to her husband, it was not done with premeditation and malice, so that under the old law, the jury would have brought in a verdict of murder or have acquitted her altogether. The latter would probably have been the result, under a plea of insanity, or some doubt in the minds of the jury in regard to the evidence. So that we think ourselves justified in saying that hanging is practically abolished in Massachusetts and that after those now under sentence of death shall have suffered the penalty of the law it will be a long time before a human being will be again deprived of life under its sanctions. We rejoice at this step in advance, believing that human life will be quite as safe as hitherto, and the punishment of crime will be much more certain."

***

Attorney General Phillips moved for sentencing as soon as the last juror departed. Attorney Davis immediately stood and objected. He and junior counsel Harris had prepared a motion to submit to the court in the event of a conviction.

Davis revisited his argument submitted at the outset of the trial, challenging the court's jurisdiction and the validity of the murder statute enacted the previous March.

"Your Honors, may it please the court; the defense moves for an arrest of judgment on the ground that the act of 1858 repealed the law of murder, under which the prisoner was indicted."

Davis next filed a motion for a new trial. First, Davis noted, the stomach of the deceased, which was introduced as evidence, was not sent out with the jury when the case was closed, it having been taken previously by Dr. Ellis to Boston; second, the vials containing arsenic which were exhibited to the jury by Dr. Jackson, were taken by him to Boston and were not with the jury in the jury room.

"May I approach the bench, Your Honors?" asked Davis.

The court consented and Davis presented his handwritten motion at sidebar.

Plymouth: Supreme Judicial Court
May Term, 1858
Commonwealth v. Abigail Gardner

And now the defendant comes after verdict and before judgment and moves for a new trial, because the court instructed the jury that the crime to be tried by them was whether the defendant was guilty of murder in the first or in the second degree, or not guilty of murder, as provided and declared in Chapter 154 of the laws of 1858.

Because a certain bottle alleged to contain a stomach, or the remains of a stomach, was exhibited to the jury as the stomach of Hosea J. Gardner, deceased, and one of the questions involved in the crime was whether said stomach was in a certain state of preservation, and whether it exhibited manifestations of the presence of arsenic; and certain vials alleged to contain sulphuret of arsenic and to exhibit arsenous acid were in evidence before the jury; and it was in crime whether the viscera contained sulphuret of arsenic, or exhibited arsenous acid, and whether the weight of said arsenous acid and said sulphuret of arsenic was more or less; and whether said bottle was air tight or not, and said bottle and said vials were not presented to the jury

230

when they retired to deliberate upon their verdict, but were removed and not presented by the government though requested and demanded by the defendant, and the same was called to the attention of the court before the jury retired.

By her attorney,
Charles G. Davis

Merrick, Metcalf, and Bigelow conferred and immediately overruled Davis's motion regarding the absence of the bottle and vials in the jury room during deliberation.

"Mr. Davis," Justice Metcalf replied. "The full court will hear your motion for arrest of judgment and a new trial at the October session. In the meantime, the prisoner is remanded to Plymouth Jail to await the decision of the court. Court is now adjourned."

Deputies removed Abigail from the dock and whisked her from the courtroom to the jail and her cell. She frantically looked over her shoulder at her lawyers, but the two men could only nod in a gesture of reassurance. A sullen, forlorn, five-month stretch in stark confinement at Plymouth Jail loomed. Her fate now rested on her lawyers' legal skill and the Supreme Judicial Court's ultimate opinion.

***

Abigail's conviction came across the wires, and Abby read the words with a touch of sadness but little sympathy for her mother.

She walked over to the bakery when the post office closed to share the news with Marcus.

"Mr. Hunt, may I have a word with my brother?"

Noting her unexpressive eyes, the gentleman was prompted to call for the young man as requested.

Marcus came out from behind Hunt's counter – his hair, face, and clothing covered with flour. He stepped outside with his sister.

She explained to him, "The jury found mother guilty. She will spend the rest of her life in prison. May God forgive her for what she has done to Father."

231

Near tears and with his shoulders slumped, he did not reply, just turned and went back inside.

Hunt sensed what had happened and asked the boy if he needed time alone.

Marcus shook his head and returned to his work.

***

Abigail bided time in her cell as the world passed her by.

Attorney Harris assisted senior counselor Davis in preparing arguments in support of an arrest of judgment and a new trial until July when Governor Nathaniel Banks appointed him District Attorney for the Southeastern District. He would, ironically, replace Abigail's prosecutor, James Keith, who had resigned to enter private practice.

Attorney General Phillips remained occupied with the business of the state, most prominently with the much-publicized prosecution of siblings Francis and Miriam Heath for the January murder of their father, Joshua Heath, in Dracut.

Defense Attorney Davis filed his motions on Abigail's behalf in early October and, on the twenty-seventh of the same month, presented his case before the Supreme Judicial Court in session at Taunton, Massachusetts.

Attorney General Phillips challenged Davis's argument by citing eight cases to support the government's position and to uphold the constitutionality of the 1858 statute.

The Supreme Judicial Court weighed the arguments of both sides and Chief Justice Lemuel Shaw, in writing the court's opinion, overruled Davis's motion for an arrest of judgment and new trial and ordered the defendant to appear before the court on November third for sentencing.

A few days after the court overruled his motion, Attorney Davis visited Abigail at her cell in Plymouth Jail.

"Abigail," Davis began, "I'm afraid we have failed in our attempt to prevent your sentencing and obtain a new trial. The court has directed your sentence be implemented immediately."

232

"Oh dear," Abigail moaned. "Is there not any other appeal we can make to overturn the court's decision?"

"I'm afraid not, Abigail. The court's decision is final."

"What about a pardon? Can't we appeal to the governor's sense of mercy?"

"Yes, we can try Abigail. But it is doubtful the governor would consider it."

Abigail was devastated. She had so looked forward to a new trial and exoneration. Her fate now rested with the governor and she realized, for the first time, she would likely spend the rest of her life in prison.

Few people had visited her as the trial wore on. Even her children had stayed away.

On Wednesday, November 3, 1858, Plymouth County deputy sheriffs transported Abigail from the House of Correction to the courthouse in Taunton where she was met by Attorney Davis. Abigail was terrified at the thought of having to spend her life in Charlestown State Prison.

"Mrs. Gardner, you needn't worry," said Davis. "The court, by law, can only commit men convicted of murder to the state prison. Women serve their time at a house of correction."

Abigail's case was called and the court sentenced her to hard labor for the term of her natural life and, as Davis had promised, committed her to the Plymouth House of Correction.

"It has now been demonstrated to the satisfaction of the skeptical," said the *Hingham Journal* several days after sentencing, "that a woman cannot escape through the meshes of law from the penalties of justice. We hope our town will never again be the theater of the commission of a crime so dark and dreadful as the one for which Mrs. Gardner is now suffering the merited penalty."

***

When fifty-year-old James Bates of East Bridgewater was elected to a three-year term as sheriff in November 1859, he also assumed the title of Plymouth County Jailer and Master of the

House of Correction. He lived with his wife and two children inside the prison walls in a house constructed for his use at county expense.

There were forty-five prisoners incarcerated at the jail and house of correction when Bates began his term in January. Most were serving time for minor offenses such as liquor law violations, drunkenness, and, in one instance, injuring a fruit tree. Some felons were committed for such diverse crimes as forgery, assault, burglary, attempted rape, larceny, bigamy, keeping a nuisance, and mutiny. The majority of offenders were men, but fifteen women were also confined to the facility. Seven children, ranging in age from two months to two years old, were confined with their unwed mothers or parents. Only Abigail Gardner was serving a life sentence for murder.

Attorney Davis's petitions for a governor's pardon failed.

An unforgiving Abby had refused to consent on each occasion.

"Surely you can find some mercy in your heart, Miss Gardner," said Davis.

"Mr. Davis, I would be in fear of my own life if Mother was freed."

***

Marcus remained under Levi Hersey's guardianship and continued to live with and work for Mr. Hunt until 1860, when he abandoned the baker's trade to pursue adventure on the high seas. He signed on as a seaman aboard a sailing ship bound for destinations far and wide. The year before Marcus set sail from Hingham Harbor, he had enrolled in the temperance division at Levi's urging.

On October 11, 1861, Abby Gardner received a shocking telegram from Marcus's ship captain. Marcus had accidentally fallen overboard and had drowned off the coast of Nova Scotia. Shipmates had recovered Marcus's body. Abby replied through tears with an acknowledgement, closed the post office and shop, and raced to Levi Hersey's South Street home.

Abby knocked on the door and Levi's seventy-six-year-old father, Noah, appeared.

"I'm so sorry, Abby," said Noah after Abby told him of Marcus's plight. "I will send Levi to you as soon as he arrives from work in Boston. Please, if there is anything I can do…"

"Thank you, Mr. Hersey. I appreciate your kindness, but I don't want to trouble you."

Levi alighted from the Cohasset bound train at West Hingham an hour later and walked the short distance to his home.

"Oh, Levi," Noah said as his son entered the door. "Something terrible has happened. Marcus has drowned. Abby was here in tears. She asked me to send you to her as soon as you returned."

Levi was stunned and asked, "Is there any end to the tragedies this poor, young woman must endure?" He made haste to the post office where he found Abby weeping and tried to comfort her. Levi read the grim, transcribed telegraph message Abby had received from the ship's captain.

"Abby, it pains me to hear such news. We have lost a wonderful young man."

"I have realized my worst fears, Levi. I pleaded with him to stay, but he would not be dissuaded from his dreams. I regret now I had not been more firm with him."

"Do not labor yourself with guilt, Abby. Marcus had a life of his own and lived it as he wished."

"Levi, I do not want him buried at sea. I want him here at home with Father."

"We must telegraph the ship's captain before he leaves port, Abby. I'm sure the captain will honor your wishes and as soon as the ship arrives here at Hingham, the Sons will see to a proper burial."

"Thank you, Levi."

"Do you want me to notify your mother, Abby?"

"No, Levi; as far as I'm concerned, she does not have a right to know. She severed her ties from us with her cruelty and is not our mother anymore."

***

The vessel bearing Marcus's body docked at Hingham, and shipmates ceremoniously carried Marcus's body, sewn in sailcloth, down the vessel's plank to a waiting wagon and a contingent of Sons led by Levi. Marcus was laid to rest after brief services in Hingham Centre Cemetery.

On October 25, 1861, the Corner Stone Division publicly offered its condolences with a proclamation in the *Hingham Journal*:

> *Whereas, through the mysterious dispensation of Divine Providence, a beloved brother has been suddenly removed from our midst by the hand of Death,*
> *Resolved – That in this afflictive event we recognize the hand of Him "who doth not willingly afflict or grieve the children of men," and "whose ways are not as our ways."*
> *Resolved – That we remember with pleasure his many virtues and steady adherence to the principles of our Order while peculiarly exposed to temptation.*
> *Resolved – That we tender to the deeply stricken sister, whose young life has been so clouded, and to the remaining relatives, our heartfelt sympathy with them in this their day of sorrow, and may Our Father visit them in mercy and heal the wounds of the broken-hearted.*
> *Resolved – That a copy of these resolutions be forwarded to the sister of the deceased, and published in the Hingham Journal and South Shore Advertiser.*
> *Signed, George H. Everett, Levi Hersey, Committee;*
> *C. B. Leavitt, R. S [Recording Scribe]*

Abby and Levi grew closer after Marcus's death. Levi, a widower, had been married twice before. His first wife, Caroline Gates Whitmarsh, gave birth to their only child, Levi Junior, who

236

died in 1848 at age two of cholera infantum. Mortification (gangrene) took thirty-one-year-old Caroline's life in 1855. Levi married Caroline's younger sister, Mary Whitmarsh, three years later, and to this union their first and only child, Ira Grover Hersey, was born in 1860. Mary died three months after Ira's birth of physical and mental exhaustion.

On October 12, 1863, Levi and Abby filed their intention to marry. Reverend Jonathan Tilson united them on the same day at the First Baptist Church.

Abby made her home with Levi, his sister, and Levi's young son, Ira, at the Hersey house on South Street after the wedding. She resigned from her position as postmistress two weeks later and old family friend Edwin Wilder was appointed postmaster. He moved the post office to the newly constructed Lincoln building on South Street.

The following August, Abby gave birth to a daughter, christened Mary Caroline, in memory of Levi's late wives. A son, Allen, was born on July 2, 1868, and died the next day. Two other daughters, Annie Ives, born in 1871, and Alice Bradford, born in 1874, followed.

***

Abigail had relinquished any hope for release from prison and had mended her intractable ways. By 1865, her strength had deteriorated with age. When the prison matron informed the sheriff about Abigail's declining productivity, Bates took Abigail into his prison quarters and assigned her to domestic duties.

Abigail remained incarcerated at Plymouth's House of Correction until September 6, 1871, when the state's prison commission ordered her transferred to the Bristol County House of Correction at New Bedford since statewide reforms established by the commission resulted in the segregation of women from men in separate buildings and cells. Women were placed under the supervision of matrons regardless of age or seriousness of offense. The commission also ordered county commissioners to improve the conditions of cells and to create spacious and airy workrooms to train the women in a useful trade or other employment. County authorities who held a female inmate in a facility and failed to meet the new standards were obliged to transfer the prisoner to an approved institution and to provide compensation for associated inmate expenses to the receiving institution.

The new women's building at New Bedford's house of correction contained forty cells, each measuring four by seven by seven feet high, slightly smaller than the cells at Plymouth. Inmates were allowed access to the prison library and could attend religious services every Sunday morning. The women were kept busy in a segregated workroom manufacturing baskets which were sold to the general public to offset the institution's expenses. Charles Burt, master of the New Bedford jail and house of correction, managed with efficiency.

A prison deputy admitted Abigail to the house of correction and assigned her prisoner number 3357. Matron Caroline Morse escorted her to a private area and ordered Abigail to remove her clothes and change into prison garb. There was a repeat of the scene in Plymouth years ago. Abigail was angered by her transfer. She had established a bearable existence there and had befriended several women.

"I will not wear that deplorable dress you call a uniform. It's not fit for a vagrant."

"Mrs. Gardner, if you do not obey me, I will place you in solitary confinement until you comply. Do you understand?" asked Morse.

"Oh, I understand full well, but I refuse. You can send me to your dungeon. I don't care."

"Then you've given me no choice."

Abigail railed, attracting the attention of other inmates on the ward. Morse called for assistance and Officer Isaac Tompkins quickly responded. The two struggled to restrain Abigail as she cursed and shouted. They were surprised by the frail woman's strength. When they finally had her somewhat under control, they ushered her to a cell in the prison's darkest corner.

"You have no right to treat me this way," Abigail said. "I'll speak to the warden about your cruel treatment."

Morse slammed the cell door and left Abigail alone in the dank cell, secluded from the rest of the prison's population. Morse returned to the women's ward and inventoried the items in Abigail's travel bag. There she found a hat, a dress, six chemise skirts, two pairs of drawers, three nightgowns, stockings, boots, skirt hoops, and a shawl. The bag also contained about twenty-two dollars in cash, which along with the clothing, Morse turned over to the warden for safekeeping. Burt later deposited the cash in an account under Abigail's name in a local bank.

The next day, Morse returned to Abigail.

"Are you ready to do as you are told, Mrs. Gardner?" the matron asked through the small, barred opening in the door.

"I am, but I still don't appreciate this treatment. I'm cold and I'm hungry and thirsty."

Morse opened the cell door.

"I'll take you up to your assigned cell in the women's ward now, Mrs. Gardner, and I'll have the kitchen prepare a breakfast."

A haggard Abigail followed the matron silently and in the cell she undressed and donned the prison uniform. An orderly arrived with breakfast, and Abigail ate voraciously. The matron gathered Abigail's clothing, closed the cell door, and secured them with her other property.

Abigail continued "to give prison authorities no end of trouble…her life went forward pretty evenly but was very regularly interspersed with rebellious fits and half-relentings," according to the *Boston Herald*. Despite Abigail's conduct, she was punished on only one other occasion, ten months after her admission to New Bedford, for talking in her cell. The matron confined her there for a day without privileges.

***

Levi received a letter from Sheriff Bates a week after Abigail's transfer to New Bedford. Bates suggested Levi contact the warden, Charles Burt, for further information.

"Abby, the state has transferred your mother to the house of correction in New Bedford. I received notification from the sheriff at work today," Levi said when he returned home in the evening.

"That's odd, Levi. Did he say why she was sent there?" Abby asked, puzzled by the change.

"He did not, but he gave me the name of the new warden, and I intend to send him a telegram in the morning."

"Levi, make sure you tell the new warden to send any correspondence from or about Mother to you at the factory. I want to resume the same arrangement we had with Sheriff Bates. I don't want to know anything about her."

"I will, Abby."

***

Abigail eventually settled into the routine of her prison life and found some peace in the workroom where she preferred to sit apart from the other workers while she sewed or darned prison clothing in a space by a southerly window in the top story of the women's building. She spent much of her time in silent reflection and faithfully attended Sunday services in the prison chapel where she befriended prison chaplain Isaac Henry Coe, the pastor of the Bonney Street Christian Church in New Bedford.

Chronic illness plagued her as she approached old age and for months in 1884 she was confined in the prison's infirmary. Her condition was incurable and there was little the infirmary's physician could do for her other than treat her pain. By early March 1885, death was imminent. Devastated by this prognosis, Abigail sent an orderly with an urgent request for Chaplain Coe.

"Reverend Coe, I am told my end is near. There are many things weighing on my conscience, and I feel a need to confide in you. I don't know of any other way to lift me from my burden and bring me solace," Abigail said with tears in her eyes.

"I am sorry to learn of your illness, Abigail, and I'm more than happy to listen and help in any way I can. The Lord looks upon us with favor when we cleanse our souls of our misgivings," Coe replied.

"Soon after I began my prison sentence at Plymouth," Abigail began in a tremulous whisper, "the jail keepers brought in an old woman sentenced for a liquor offense. The keepers asked me to assist this old woman with a bath and a change of clothes, but she was obstinate and refused to remove her clothing. A keeper intervened and a struggle ensued and in the course of this struggle the woman's dress came unloosed and out dropped a great wad of bank bills. They were scattered upon the floor and, in the confusion, I took a twenty-dollar bill and secreted it in my clothing. The keeper gathered up all the rest and secured it with the warden until such time as the woman had completed her sentence.

"When I was transferred to New Bedford, I still had the twenty-dollar bill and handed it over to Mr. Burt. He deposited the money for me in a bank account to my credit. I have since learned he intends to use it for my funeral expenses.

"Reverend Coe, if the money is spent in this way, it will sink me to hell. I cannot allow it. Please speak with Mr. Burt and see if he'll return it to the woman I stole it from."

"Of course, Abigail," said Coe.

"Thank you. And now I wish to confess to you my deepest shame. For many years I have denied poisoning my husband, but now I must tell you it is true. I cannot tell you why I committed this unspeakable act, other than to say I believe a demon stood by my side and continually urged me on until the deed was done. Hosea was a good, kind man and I never had reason to complain of his treatment toward me. I am filled with remorse for what I have done and can only hope the good Lord will forgive me."

"The Lord our God is merciful, Abigail. Let us recall John, Chapter 1, Verse 9, 'If we confess our sins, He is faithful and just and will forgive our sins and purify us from all unrighteousness.'"

Chaplain and penitent joined in prayer until Abigail's medication overtook her. Coe quietly left her bedside and visited with the warden in his office.

"Charles, I've just left Mrs. Gardner. She is dying. It pains me to violate the sanctity of her confidence, but I believe it's important for you to know she has confessed to the murder of her husband."

"After all these years," Burt replied, shaking his head. "I suppose I should not be surprised. It's not the first time I've heard or seen prisoners about to meet their Maker admit their transgressions."

"She was quite remorseful, Charles. May God forgive her," said the chaplain.

Coe informed Burt about Abigail's theft in Plymouth.

"She does not want the money used for her funeral and burial. She wants it returned to the rightful owner," the chaplain said. "She said it would sink her to hell if the money was expended in that way."

"Sink her to hell?" Burt asked incredulously. "That ship has already sailed, Reverend."

Coe bowed his head.

"I'll contact Plymouth authorities to see if they can locate the woman, but it's doubtful," said Burt. "So many years have passed. If we can't return the money, we will have no alternative but to use it for Mrs. Gardner's interment; unless, of course, her family claims the body."

Burt telegraphed the Plymouth County sheriff. The sheriff searched his records but efforts to identify the woman from whom the money was stolen proved fruitless.

***

At half-past four on Friday afternoon, June 19, 1885, Abigail Gardner died of uterine cancer. Warden Burt notified Abby's husband Levi and asked if he wished to claim the body for burial.

"Abby, I received word of your mother's death today," Levi

said when he returned home the same evening. "The warden wants to know if we wish to claim the body for burial."

"I'm afraid Mr. Burt will have to take responsibility for it, Levi. I want nothing to do with it."

Levi telegraphed Burt the next morning and informed him of Abby's decision. Burt contacted New Bedford undertaker Edward Wilson and made arrangements for Abigail's burial. The sheriff expended a portion of the proceeds from Abigail's account at the New Bedford Savings Bank to compensate Wilson. He depleted the eleven-dollar balance in the account to settle her prison debts and to ship Abigail's clothing by express to Abby's husband, Levi, at the piano factory in Boston.

Several inmates who had befriended Abigail attended a funeral service conducted by Reverend Coe in the prison chapel. No one from Abigail's family was present. Warden Burt purchased a small flower bouquet and placed it atop Abigail's plain pine coffin. When the modest service concluded, undertaker Wilson and his assistants prepared the coffin for transport from the jail on Court Street to Oak Grove Cemetery. People celebrating life's gaiety and enjoying the sun's warmth paid little heed to the somber hearse as it passed. The pitiful, penitent woman whose corpse lay within would soon be interred without fanfare in the ignominy of a solitary, unmarked grave.

Acknowledgements

This book would not have been possible without the invaluable assistance and encouragement of many people, institutions, and organizations. I especially thank Michael Achille, Hingham Historical Society, for sharing his vast knowledge of Hingham history and for reviewing my text for accuracy. I also thank Robert Malme, archivist, Hingham Historical Society, for locating and sharing documents and photographs of Hingham as it was in the mid-nineteenth century. Thank you to Caitlin Jones, Reference Archivist, Massachusetts State Archives, and Jodi Goodman, Head of Special Collections, New Bedford Public Library, for help with records related to the New Bedford House of Correction.

Thanks to M. J. Molinari of Granville, MA, for kindly sharing Hersey family photographs and newspaper clippings. They are now part of the Hingham Historical Society's Archives.

Colleen D'Alessandro edited photographs and maps; Suzanne Gallagher reviewed legal issues; my siblings, Jim and Dan Gallagher and Christine Flatley, friends Marianne Lord and Betty Joy, and my wife, Jeanne, reviewed my manuscript for content and grammatical errors and provided constructive feedback. I thank you all. I also extend my gratitude to Annie Hartnett, noted author of *Rabbit Cake*, who critiqued my manuscript and offered her perspective and indispensable guidance. Thank you again, Stephanie Blackman, Riverhaven Books, for publishing this, my fourth book.

Many thanks to the New England Historic and Genealogical Society, Boston, MA; Peabody Essex Museum, Salem, MA; Ancestry.com; Boston Public Library, Special Collections and Microtext Department; Boston City Archives; Massachusetts Bureau of Vital Records and Statistics, Boston, MA; Plymouth County Registry of Deeds, Plymouth, MA; New Bedford Historical Society; Edward T. Wilson Funeral Chapel, New Bedford, MA; Hingham Public Library; Plymouth Public Library; Massachusetts Historical

Commission; Massachusetts Historical Society; New Bedford Town Clerk's Office; MA Supreme Judicial Court Archives and Records, Boston, MA; Library of Congress, Washington, DC; and Francis A. Countway Medical Library, Harvard University, Boston, MA.

Notes

Chapter 1

1   the trains and coaches delivering mail: "The Weather; Further Trouble upon the Railroads; Condition of the Harbor." *Boston Post*, January 24, 1857. See also, Joshua Tower Diaries, 1857; Hingham Public Library, Hingham Histories, Reel 80-9.

1   gave her little consolation: "City Matters; Meteorological." *Boston Traveler*, January 28, 1857.

1   causing a permanent, crooked deformity: "The Hingham Tragedy; Our Boston Correspondent, Boston, February 12, 1857; Situation of Hingham; Popular Alarm and Excitement; Sketches of the Murderess and her Victim; How the Poison was Administered; Latest Reports." *New York Herald*, February 16, 1857.

1   Gentle rain had begun to fall": "City Matters; Meteorological." *Boston Traveler*, January 28, 1857.

1   and Sophia Cole Gardner: "Massachusetts, Town Clerk, Vital and Town Records, 1626-2001," database with images, *FamilySearch*(https://familysearch.org/ark:/61903/1:1:FHX 7-LVC : 5 November 2017), Hosea James Gardner, 30 Oct 1810; citing Birth, Hingham, Plymouth, Massachusetts, United States, town clerk offices, Massachusetts; FHL microfilm 423,520.

1   died in 1840 at the age of fifty-three: "Massachusetts, Town Clerk, Vital and Town Records, 1626-2001," database with images, FamilySearch (https://familysearch.org/ark:/61903/3:1:3QS Q-G97M-YHG7?cc=2061550&wc=Q4D7-PTG%3A353350201%2C353451301%2C353453801: 13 July 2016), Plymouth > Hingham > Births, marriages, deaths 1635-1844, 1840, page 60 > image 277 of 546; citing Massachusetts Secretary of the Commonwealth, Boston.

2   no real estate and few personal assets: Ancestry.com: Massachusetts Wills and Probate Records, 1635-1991; Plymouth County, Probate Estate File 8402, Hosea Gardner, 1840.

2   her husband, John Wade, after his father's death: Ancestry.com: 1850 United States Federal Census: Hingham, Plymouth,

Massachusetts; Roll: M432_332; Page: 33A; Image: 71; August 22, 1850.

2   Abigail was born in Islesboro: "Our Hingham Correspondence; The Late Murder Case; Conduct of Mrs. Gardner; Her Antecedents." *Boston Herald*, February 19, 1857. See also, Abigail's place of birth, Islesboro, is recorded on the 1852 birth record of her son, James Otis, in Hingham (Massachusetts Vital Records, Massachusetts State Archives, Births, Hingham, 1852, volume 64, page 263).

2   off the coast of Maine: Islesboro Historical Society: Warren Survey Map, Islesboro, Waldo County, Maine, from a circa 1799 map by Samuel Warren, Jr., created circa 1893; https://www.mainememory.net/artifact/28353. Abigail was raised on a small farm located on the island's norther point, near Meadow Pond.

2   raised by her parents as a Free Will Baptist: John Pendleton Farrow, Master Mariner, *History of Islesborough, Maine* (Bangor: Thomas W. Burr, Printer, 1893), 232. Abigail was one of ten children born to Zachariah and Rebecca (Williams) Marshall, devout Free Will Baptists. Abigail's maternal great-grandfather, Shubael Williams of Connecticut, first settled the island in 1764. John Pendleton Farrow, Master Mariner, *History of Islesborough, Maine* (Bangor: Thomas W. Burr, Printer, 1893), 9, 298, 312.

2   found work as a dressmaker in a tailor's shop: "Generalities." *Republican Journal* [Belfast, Maine], February 20, 1857.

2   domestic servant in his Hingham home: "The Hingham Tragedy; Our Boston Correspondence, Boston, February 12, 1857; Situation of Hingham ; Popular Alarm and Excitement; Sketches of the Murderess and her Victim; How the Poison was Administered; Latest Reports." *New York Herald*, February 16, 1857. Woodward's financial commitments and frequent absences from home motivated him to obtain the services of a live-in domestic servant.

2   master mariner and Islesboro native: John Pendleton Farrow, Master Mariner, *History of Islesborough, Maine* (Bangor: Thomas W. Burr, Printer, 1893), 12. His father, Joseph Woodward, was a Hingham native and settled in Islesboro in 1784. He later bought property near Gilkey's Harbor in Islesboro, and another lot which he sold to Derby Academy. He drowned in Belfast Bay off the Maine coast.

2   up and down the New England Coast: Captain Woodward's business flourished over the years and in 1826 he acquired a one-half share in one of the dozen wharves along Hingham harbor:

247

Plymouth County Registry of Deeds, Samuel Sprague to Joseph Woodward, document 856, book 156, page 250, July 28, 1826; Benjamin King to Joseph Woodward, document 796, book 166, page 137, January 19, 1829; purchase and sale of Commercial Wharf. Woodward co-owned Commercial Wharf in the cove with Hingham cooper Samuel Sprague.

2 in 1820 built a large, Federal-style house: Massachusetts Historical Commission; MACRIS Inventory #HIN.1231; Local #243.81-113; Captain Joseph Woodward House, 1820; http://mhcmacris.net/Details.aspx?MhcId=HIN.1231. The house is located at 44 Spring Street.

2 for his wife and growing family: Ancestry.com: 1830 United States Federal Census: Hingham, Plymouth, Massachusetts; Series: M19; Roll: 64; Page: 210; Family History Library Film: 0337922. Lower Plain is now Hingham Centre.

2 set sail for Hingham aboard Woodward's schooner, *George*: "The Hingham Murder." *Boston Daily Advertiser*, February 12, 1857. See also, *Plymouth Rock*, February19, 1857. See also, "Our Hingham Correspondence; The Late Murder Case; Conduct of Mrs. Gardner; Her Antecedents." *Boston Herald*, February 19, 1857. See also, "Marine List." *Bangor Weekly Register*, June 9, 1829, Vol. XIV, Issue 23, page 3; Woodward captain of schooner *George* bound from Hingham. https://www.genealogybank.com/doc/newspapers/image/v2%3A11 92176E56672B20%40GB3NEWS-1413E4E1C4DCC428%402389248-1413DCA20EB263E0%402-1417361F48D9A494%40Shipping%2BNews?h=2&fname=&lname =&fullname=&kwinc=george&kwexc=&rgfromDate=06/09/1829& rgtoDate=06/09/1829&formDate=&formDateFlex=exact&dateType =range&processingtime=&addedFrom=&addedTo=&sid=dtolifeqtk gcjffjdaoswcnhebpefvty_wma-gateway011_1590863018684.

2 married Hosea Gardner in 1833: Vital Records, 1637-1845, volume 3, page 123; (*Online database: AmericanAncestors.org*, New England Historic Genealogical Society, 2016; *Vital Records of Hingham, Massachusetts, ca. 1639-1844*). Hersey, Reuben. Mss. 901, R. Stanton Avery Special Collections Department, New England Historic Genealogical Society. They married on January 29, 1833.

2 six months pregnant: Hingham, MA: Vital Records, 1637-1845, volume 3, page 106. (*Online database: AmericanAncestors.org*, New England Historic Genealogical Society, 2016. *Vital Records of Hingham, Massachusetts, ca. 1639-1844.*; Hersey, Reuben. Mss.

901. R. Stanton Avery Special Collections Department, New England Historic Genealogical Society. She gave birth to Andrew Marshall Gardner in Hingham on May 7, 1833.

2   died four months later: "Massachusetts, Town Clerk, Vital and Town Records, 1626-2001," database with images, *FamilySearch*(https://familysearch.org/ark:/61903/1:1:FH1 Q-PBC : 5 November 2017), Andrew Marshall Gardner, 27 Sep 1833; citing Death, Hingham, Plymouth, Massachusetts, United States, , town clerk offices, Massachusetts; FHL microfilm 423,520.

2   four more children were born over the next two decades: Abigail Williams Gardner: "Massachusetts, Town Clerk, Vital and Town Records, 1626-2001," database with images, *FamilySearch*(https://familysearch.org/ark:/61903/1:1:FHX W-X99 : 5 November 2017), Abigail Williams Gardner, 10 Oct 1836; citing Birth, Hingham, Plymouth, Massachusetts, United States, , town clerk offices, Massachusetts; FHL microfilm 423,520; Marcus Morton Gardner in Weymouth in 1839: Massachusetts: Vital Records, 1621-1850 (Online Database: AmericanAncestors.org, New England Historic Genealogical Society, 2001-2016). Weymouth, volume 1, page 116; Marcus Morton died of "inflammation of the bowels" on April 9, 1843: Massachusetts: Vital Records, 1621-1850 (Online Database: AmericanAncestors.org, New England Historic Genealogical Society, 2001-2016). Weymouth, volume 2, page 273; Marcus Henry Gardner: Massachusetts Vital Records, Massachusetts State Archives, Births, Weymouth, 1844, volume 1, page 116; Marcus Henry Gardner was born on June 28, 1844; James Otis Gardner, born in Hingham, January 26, 1852: Massachusetts Vital Records, Massachusetts State Archives, Births, Hingham, 1852, volume 64, page 263, #2, died twenty months later of dysentery: Ibid. volume 76, page 204, #55. He died on September 21, 1853.

2   had been a shoemaker and a public school teacher: Ancestry.com.: 1850 United States Federal Census: Hingham, Plymouth County, Massachusetts- Roll: M432-332 Page: 7A; Image: 19; "Our Boston Correspondent, Boston, February 12, 1857; Situation of Hingham; Popular Alarm and Excitement; Sketches of the Murderess and her Victim; How the Poison was Administered; Latest Reports." *New York Herald*, February 16, 1857.

2   when he declined a nomination for another term: *Hingham Town Reports*. See also, "Town Meeting." Hingham *Patriot*, March 10, 1848; and *Hingham Journal and South Shore Advertiser*, February 24, 1854.

2   Pierce as Hingham's postmaster: *Record of Appointment of Postmasters, 1832-1971*. NARA Microfilm Publication, M841, 145 rolls; Records of the Post Office Department, Record Group Number 28; volume 27, page 91, Plymouth County, Massachusetts; Washington, D.C., National Archives. Hosea was appointed on January 7, 1854.

2   was established in Hingham in 1846: *Hingham Patriot*, May 1, 1846. The order was established on April 24, 1846. See also, "Sons of Temperance." *Hingham Patriot*, October 8, 1847. Note: According to Francis H. Lincoln in a chapter on "Lodges and Societies" in *History of the Town of Hingham, Massachusetts*, volume 1, part 2, page 298, this society was formed in April 1852.

2   elected him an officer the following year: "Sons of Temperance." *Hingham Patriot*, October 8, 1847.

3   the village center and the train depot: Bouvé, et al. *History of the Town of Hingham, Massachusetts, in Three Volumes; Volume 1, Part 2, Historical* (Hingham, MA: Published by the town; printed by University Press, John Wilson and Sons, 1893), 384.

3   "...after religious services had ended:" Claire Prechtel-Kluskens, "The Nineteenth-Century Postmaster and His Duties." *NGS NewsMagazine*, January/February/March 2007, 35-39. https://twelvekey.files.wordpress.com/2014/10/ngsmagazine2007-01.pdf

3   moneys received, and expenses paid: *The United States Postal Service-An American History, 1775-2006*; United States Postal Service, Publication 100; https://about.usps.com/publications/pub100.pdf.

3   his $400 annual government salary: D. D. T. Leech. *Post Office Directory or Business Man's Guide to the Post Offices in the United States* (New York: J. H. Colton & Co., 1856), 85. See also, "The Hingham Tragedy; Our Boston Correspondence, Boston, February 12, 1857; Situation of Hingham; Popular Alarm and Excitement; Sketches of the Murderess and her Victim; How the Poison was Administered; Latest Reports." *The New York Herald*, February 16, 1857.

3   responsibility for its operation: "The Telegraph." *Hingham Journal and South Shore Advertiser*, May 2, 1856.

3   4,300 inhabitants living there in 1857: Ancestry.com: 1860 United States Federal Census; Hingham, Plymouth, Massachusetts; Roll: M653-519.

3   built the Lincoln home in 1638: Bouvé et al. *History of the Town of Hingham, Massachusetts, in Three Volumes; Volume 1, Part 1 –*

Military History (Hingham, MA: Published by the town; printed by University Press, John Wilson and Sons, 1893), 215, 223.

3 during the Pequod and King Philip's Wars: Ibid. 187, 214-215.

3 hanged himself in the shed: *Boston Daily Atlas*, April 16, 1856, 2.

4 Henry Hersey's law office: Hingham Historical Society, Hingham, MA, Map of Hingham Village, 1857.

4 Loring Hall, the "Old Ship Church," and Derby Academy: Ibid.

4 "...while the bells ring": Hingham Historical Society, Judy Kimball Lantern Slide Collection, Acc#54, "Broad Bridge, Early 1860s;" PH Box 10 – 004\ph389.jpg.

4 considered the finest in town: "Advertisements - Hingham Market.*" Hingham Journal and South Shore Advertiser*, March 27, 1857.

4 for its scheduled 4:10 p.m. arrival: "Train Schedule." *Hingham Journal and South Shore Advertiser*, January 16, 1857.

4 newly inaugurated South Shore Railroad: Plymouth County Registry of Deeds, book 235, pages 55-56, December 14, 1849. See also comments on the financial panic of 1857-58 in Lorena Laing Hart and Francis Russell Hart. *Not All Is Changed: A Life History of Hingham* (Hingham, MA: The Hingham Historical Commission, 1993), 147.

4 closing of his hat and cap business: "To Let." *Hingham Journal and South Shore Advertiser*, January 30, 1857.

5 culvert constructed by the railroad: Lorena Laing Hart and Francis Russell Hart. *Not All Is Changed: A Life History of Hingham* (Hingham, MA: The Hingham Historical Commission, 1993), 109; see also, "The Town Brook." *Hingham Patriot*, June 16, 1848.

5 Burr & Brown's cord and tassel dye house: Bouvé, et al. *History of the Town of Hingham, Massachusetts, in Three Volumes; Volume 1, Part 2* (Hingham, MA: Published by the town; printed by University Press, John Wilson and Sons, 1893), 162. See also, Lorena Laing Hart and Francis Russell Hart. *Not All Is Changed: A Life History of Hingham* (Hingham, MA: The Hingham Historical Commission, 1993), 136.

8 "...not trouble Mr. Todd:" "Trial of Mrs. Gardner, at Plymouth, for the Murder of her Husband, Hosea J. Gardner, on the 28th of January, 1857; Supreme Judicial Court; Special Session; Holden at Plymouth; Metcalf, Bigelow and Merrick, Justices; For Government – Attorney General Clifford and District Attorney Keith; For Defense – Charles J. Davis of Plymouth and Hon. B. W. Harris of Plymouth; (Reported for the *Boston Post*) – Plymouth, September 1; Conclusion of Tuesday's Proceedings." *Boston Post*, September 3, 1857.

9   "...twenty feet and not get hurt:" "Trial of Mrs. Gardner, at
        Plymouth, for the Murder of her Husband, Hosea J. Gardner, on the
        28th of January, 1857; Supreme Judicial Court; Special Session;
        Holden at Plymouth; Metcalf, Bigelow and Merrick, Justices; For
        Government – Attorney General Clifford and District Attorney
        Keith; For Defense – Charles J. Davis of Plymouth and Hon. B. W.
        Harris of Bridgewater." *Plymouth Rock*, September 10, 1857.

9   Gordon after his retirement: Bouvé et al. *History of the Town of
        Hingham, Massachusetts, in Three Volumes; Volume 1, Part 2 –
        Historical* (Hingham, MA: Published by the town; printed by
        University Press, John Wilson and Sons, 1893), 322.

9   "...showed little sympathy for him:" "The Hingham Murder."
        Boston Daily Advertiser, Thursday, February 12, 1857.

10   "...get plenty of rest:" Ibid.

13   "...should be back on his feet soon:" Sir Anthony Carlisle, F. R. S.,
        *Practical Observations on the Preservation of Health and the
        Prevention of Diseases; Comprising the Author's Experience on the
        Disorders of Childhood and Old Age, on Scrofula, and on the
        Efficacy of Cathartic Medicines* (London: John Church, 1838)
        pages 146-147.

13   "...spirits as a medicinal remedy:" Forbes, John, M.D., F.R.S.,
        F.G.S. *Temperance and Teetotalism: An Inquiry into the Effects of
        Alcoholic Drinks on the Human System in Health and Disease*
        (London: John Church, Prince Street, SoHo, 1847), 30.

14   next to his bed and heaved: "The Hingham Murder Case; Arrest of
        Abigail Gardner on Charge of the Murder of her Husband;
        Coroner's Inquest; Testimony before the Magistrate; The Accused
        Committed" (From the *Boston Traveler*, Feb. 11). *New York
        Herald*, February 13, 1857.

15   completed most of the postal quarterly: Ibid.

16   "...little firewood to spare:" "The Murder Case in Town." *Hingham
        Journal and South Shore Advertiser*, February 12, 1857.

18   "...evil enough to do such a thing:" Ibid.

18   "...as though I was spewing spiders:" Ibid.

Chapter 2

20   Swirling snow and a brisk wind: "City Matters; Meteorological."
        Boston Traveler, January 31, 1857, and February 2, 1857.

21   opposite the Second Parish Church in South Hingham: Hingham
        Historical Society online; 688 Main Street, Edward Wilder House,
        built 1805, acquired by son, Edwin, in 1853.

https://hinghamhistorical.org/project/688-main-street/ ; See also,
1860 United States Federal Census, Hingham, Plymouth,
Massachusetts, Family #478, Dwelling # 504, Page: 488; Family
History Library Film: 803519; See also, Hingham Historical
Society, 1857 map, Hingham Village.

21 Wind and hail pattered: "City Matters; Meteorological." *Boston
Traveler*, February 2, 1857.

22 forty-year-old silk and tassel maker: Massachusetts State Census,
1855, Hingham, August 15, 1855, page 70, house #86. Otis is living
with his brother, Franklin, and his family. Franklin Hersey is
enumerated two households from Isaac Little, owner of the Union
Hotel.

23 steady rain had melted much of the earlier snow: "City Matters;
Meteorological." *Boston Traveler*, February 2, 1857.

24 "Let him die in peace:" "Trial of Mrs. Gardner, at Plymouth, for the
Murder of her Husband, Hosea J. Gardner, on the 28th of January
1857; Conclusion of Tuesday's Proceedings." *Boston Post*,
September 3, 1857.

24 "…you must try to be resigned:" Ibid. See also, "Trial of Abigail
Gardner for the Murder of her Husband, Hosea J. Gardner, before
the Supreme Court at Plymouth." *Boston Daily Bee*, September 3,
1857.

25 die within the year: James K. Crissman. *Death and Dying in
Central Appalachia: Changing Attitudes and Practices* (Urbana and
Chicago: University of Illinois Press, 1994), 25.

25 lowered it onto the sofa: "Trial of Mrs. Gardner, at Plymouth, for
the Murder of her Husband, Hosea J. Gardner, on the 28th of
January 1857; Conclusion of Tuesday's Proceedings." *Boston Post*,
September 3, 1857.

26 "…certainly seemed suspicious," Wilder speculated: Ibid.

26 entitled to it as a chapter member: Sons of Temperance of North
America. *Constitutions of the Order of the Sons of Temperance of
North America* (Philadelphia: Craig and Young, Printers, 1849), 14.

28 with his partner, Joseph Ripley, since 1845: "Co-partnership Notice;
Ripley and Newhall; Undertaking Business Continued as
Heretofore." *Hingham Patriot*, February 6, 1846.

28 in their shop on South Street: "Ripley and Newhall, South St.,
Hingham." *Hingham Journal and South Shore Advertiser*, January
16, 1857.

28 in partnership with his brother, Nehemiah: "Co-partnership Notice."
Hingham Patriot, May 14, 1842. Nehemiah Ripley, Jr., announced
a partnership with his brother, Joseph Ripley, in his cabinet and

furniture manufacturing business. The brothers owned a shop at Ford's Building on South Street. See also, Plymouth County Registry of Deeds, document #1894, book 267, page 116, dated May 15, 1855; The cabinet business of Ripley and Newhall is now located at a new location on South Street. Joseph Ripley sold one-half of the new building to his partner, Joseph Newhall.

29   "...laid out before I leave:" "The Hingham Murder Case; Arrest of Abigail Gardner on Charge of the Murder of her Husband; Coroner's Inquest; Testimony before the Magistrate; The Accused Committed" (From the *Boston Traveler*, Feb. 11). *New York Herald*, February 13, 1857.

30   "...if it sees its reflection:" Gary Laderman. *The Sacred Remains: American Attitudes toward Death, 1799-1883* (New Haven: Yale University Press, 1996), 31.

30   some sign of grief, but it was not to be: "Second Trial of Mrs. Gardner, of Hingham, for the Murder of her Husband; Second Day." *Boston Daily Evening Traveler*, May 20, 1858.

31   "...I refused to abide by his wishes: "Legislative Visit to Plymouth." *Boston Traveler*, April 18, 1857.

32   boarded with her daughter, Catherine: Massachusetts, State Census, 1855, Hingham, August 15, 1855, page 4; Hingham Historical Society, Hingham, MA, Map of Hingham Lower Plain, 1857.

33   "...coursing through my mind: "The Hingham Murder." *Boston Daily Advertiser*, February 12, 1857.

34   "...abusive toward both children:" *Hingham Journal and South Shore Advertiser*, February 11, 1857.

35   "...allowing such a thing to happen:" "The Hingham Murder Case; Arrest of Abigail Gardner on Charge of the Murder of her Husband; Coroner's Inquest; Testimony before the Magistrate; The Accused Committed." (From the *Boston Traveler*, Feb. 11) *New York Herald*, February 13, 1857.

36   "...this child killed for the world:" "Trial of Mrs. Gardner, at Plymouth, for the Murder of her Husband, Hosea J. Gardner, on the 28th of January 1857; Conclusion of Wednesday's Proceedings." *Boston Post*, September 4, 1857.

36   horse-drawn, black-draped hearse: Loring and Wilder Collection, Hingham Public Library, Hingham, MA; "Cemeteries, 76-13-1, The Hearse Account Book, 1830-1862; entry on February 3, 1857 bill due and paid $1.00 from Estate of Hosea J. Gardner for use of hearse.

36   black mourning badges and cockades: D. Tulla Lightfoot. *The Culture and Art of Death in 19th Century America* (Jefferson, NC: McFarland & Company, 2019), 81-82.

37   dark tomb's narrow opening and sealed it: Massachusetts Vital Records, Massachusetts State Archives, Deaths, Hingham, 1857, volume 112, page 291, #10.

37   until she reached age twenty-one in October: "All Sorts of Paragraphs." *Boston Post*, March 5, 1857.

37   fancy goods, cigars, and tobacco: "Books, Stationery, and Fancy Goods Store." *Hingham Journal and South Shore Advertiser*, March 27, 1857.

39   "…will not permit it," Abigail declared: "The Hingham Murder." *Boston Daily Advertiser*, February 12, 1857.

42   "…prepared to remove the body in the morning:" Ibid.

43   on Pleasant Street after Reed's departure: Plymouth County Registry of Deeds, Document #1600, book 189, page 104, October 24, 1836, Deed, Francis Cushing to James S. Lewis; the house is located at 63 Pleasant Street and was built by Captain Adna Cushing in 1811.

43   "…he had ingested enough to cause death:" Alfred S. Taylor, F.R.S. *On Poisons, in Relation to Medical Jurisprudence and Medicine* (Philadelphia: Lea and Blanchard, 1848), 336-337. https://books.google.com/books?id=WLQ0AAAAIAAJ&pg=PA33 7&dq=calomel+poisonous&hl=en&newbks=1&newbks_redir=0&s a=X&ved=2ahUKEwi7namuh9TnAhUDw1kKHSIIB6oQ6AEwAX oECAMQAg#v=onepage&q=calomel&f=false

43   "…all manner of compounds, most notably arsenic:" Mark Harris. *Grave Matters: A Journey through the Modern Funeral Industry to a Natural Way of Burial* (New York: Scribner, 2007), 38.

Chapter 3

45   a hat rack attached to each: *Reports of the Town of Hingham, 1833-1860, Contract and Specifications for Building a Town Hall for the Inhabitants of the Town of Hingham* (Hingham, MA: Jedediah Farmer, Printer, 1844).

45   "…nothing but the truth; so help you God:" *The Revised Statutes of the Commonwealth of Massachusetts, passed November 4, 1835: to which are subjoined, an act in amendment thereof, and an act expressly to repeal the acts which are consolidated therein, both passed in February 1836, and to which are prefixed the Constitutions of the United States and of the Commonwealth of*

Massachusetts; Part IV, Title II, Chapter 140, of coroners inquests, Section 4, page 769.
https://books.google.com/books?id=UA5HAQAAIAAJ&pg=PA768
&dq=massachusetts+revised+statutes+chapter+140+coroner+inques
t+1836&hl=en&sa=X&ved=2ahUKEwip6ZG_0pHlAhXtmOAKH
YP3CVsQ6AEwAHoECAEQAg#v=onepage&q=massachusetts%2
0revised%20statutes%20chapter%20140%20coroner%20inquest%2
01836&f=false.

46   "…to an examination of his body:" "The Murder Case in Town."
       Hingham Journal and South Shore Advertiser, February 12, 1857.

47   "…nothing to hurt anybody:" Ibid.

47   Dr. Calvin Ellis, a pathologist at Massachusetts General Hospital:
       George B. Shattuck, Ed. Obituary. Calvin M. Ellis, M. D.; The
       Boston Medical and Surgical Journal, volume 109 (Boston:
       Houghton Mifflin Co., 1883), 598.
       https://books.google.com/books?id=aK41AQAAMAAJ&pg=PA59
       8&lpg=PA598&dq=dr.+calvin+ellis+ma+general+hospital&source
       =bl&ots=W70ugIl0FD&sig=ACfU3U27PHVJDTAXoz-
       0a2HHMuolGesgsA&hl=en&sa=X&ved=2ahUKEwiCo6Pv8LPlAh
       XGY98KHXEJATAQ6AEwB3oECAYQAQ#v=onepage&q=ellis&
       f=false. The thirty-year-old physician was a Boston native. He
       graduated from Harvard College in 1846 and Harvard Medical
       School in 1849.

47   Dr. Charles Jackson, the state assayer: Thomas Francis Harrington.
       *The Harvard Medical School; A History, Narrative and
       Documentary, Volume 2* (New York: Lewis Publishing Company,
       1905), 604. See also, Richard J. Wolfe and Richard Patterson.
       Charles Thomas Jackson, the Head behind the Hands (Novato, CA,
       HistoryofScience.com, 2007), 40-41, 123-125, 225. See also,
       George Bemis, Esq. *Report of the Case of John W. Webster,
       Indicted for the Murder of George Parkman, before the Supreme
       Judicial Court of Massachusetts* (Boston: Charles C. Little and
       James Brown, 1850), 72-79. Fifty-two-year-old Jackson, a
       Plymouth native, graduated from Harvard Medical School in 1829.
       In 1836, he shifted his focus from the practice of medicine to the
       science of geology and chemistry. His claims of credit for the
       discovery of ether as a surgical anesthetic and the invention, along
       with Samuel F. B. Morse, of the electromagnetic telegraph were the
       subject of much controversy. Jackson had testified as an expert
       witness for the prosecution in numerous capital cases, including the
       much-publicized 1850 trial of his former Harvard professor, John
       Webster, for the murder of Dr. George Parkman.

48   the air was thick and foggy: "City Matters; Meteorological." *Boston Traveler*, February 7, 1857.

48   "...whose mortal remains lie within?:" *The Revised Statutes of the Commonwealth of Massachusetts, passed November 4, 1835: to which are subjoined, an act in amendment thereof, and an act expressly to repeal the acts which are consolidated therein, both passed in February 1836, and to which are prefixed the Constitutions of the United States and of the Commonwealth of Massachusetts*; Part IV, Title II, Chapter 140, of coroners inquests, Section 4, page 769.

49   helped retard further decomposition: Kate Sweeney. *American Afterlife: Encounters in the Customs of Mourning* (Athens, GA: University of Georgia Press, 2014), 4-5.

50   to state assayer Jackson for chemical analysis without delay: "Trial of Mrs. Abigail Gardner for the Murder of her Husband." *Plymouth Rock*, September 10, 1857.

51   local express man Eli Kenerson: "The Hingham Tragedy; Our Boston Correspondent; Boston, February 12, 1857; Situation of Hingham; Popular Alarm and Excitement; Sketches of the Murderess and her Victim; How the Poison was Administered; Latest Reports." *New York Herald*, February 16, 1857. See also, 1860 United States Federal Census: Census Place: Hingham, Plymouth, Massachusetts; Roll: M653_519; Page: 451; Family History Library Film: 803519; Plymouth County Probate Court, Probate Estate File #12028, 1879, Eli H. Kenerson, express man – Schedule of property describes his ownership of house and part of a barn on North Street.

51   "...seen her sneaking into the man's stable:" "Suburban News; The Hingham Murder Case; Highly Important Evidence; New and Astounding Developments; Medical Testimony; Mrs. Gardner Fully Committed for Trial; Verdict of the Coroner's Jury; Second Day." *Boston Traveler*, February 12, 1857.

51   "...fancy dishes and confections:" Ibid.

51   "...Mrs. Kenerson sees to him:" Plymouth County Probate Court, Probate File #9049, 1865, Last Will and Testament of Loring Hammond of Hingham, dated May 19, 1860 – In the will, Hammond bequeaths his personal possessions to Aseneth H. Kenerson, wife of Eli H. Kenerson, "as some return for her care for me in my affliction."

52   "...diverse opinions about the Sabbath: "Letter from Plymouth; Trial of Mrs. Gardner." *Boston Traveler*, September 1, 1857.

52 "...where the poor woman soon died:" "Our Hingham Correspondence; The Late Murder Case; Conduct of Mrs. Gardner; Her Antecedents." *Boston Herald*, February 19, 1857.

53 *by all the approved methods*: "The Murder Case in Town." *Hingham Journal and South Shore Advertiser*, February 12, 1857.

54 "Are you ready to start?": "Trial of Mrs. Gardner at Plymouth for the Murder of her Husband, Hosea J. Gardner, on the 28th of January, 1857." *Boston Post*, September 4, 1857.

55 a voice trembling with emotion: "The Hingham Murder." *Boston Daily Advertiser*, Thursday, February 12, 1857.

55 "...a mite of arsenic in my life:" "Suburban News; The Hingham Murder Case; Further Important Developments; Arrest of Abigail Gardner on Charge of the Murder of her Husband; Great Excitement; Coroner's Inquest; Testimony before the Magistrate; The Accused Committed." *Boston Traveler*, February 11, 1857.

57 "...turn this house inside out:" "The Hingham Murder." *Boston Daily Advertiser*, Thursday, February 12, 1857.

57 "...since the snow was so deep:" Ibid.

58 "...so wanted me to go:" Ibid.

58 he lived with them and his cousins: "Trial of Mrs. Gardner, at Plymouth, for the Murder of her Husband, Hosea J. Gardner, on the 28th of January, 1857." *Boston Post*, September 3, 1857.

59 "...only about twelve feet away:" "The Hingham Murder." *Boston Daily Advertiser*, Thursday, February 12, 1857.

62 "...some depredation or other:" Ibid.

63 ...Sir Walter Scott's "Guy Mannering": "The Hingham Tragedy; Our Boston Correspondence; Boston, February 12, 1857; Situation of Hingham; Popular Alarm and Excitement; Sketches of the Murderess and her Victim; How the Poison was Administered; Latest Reports." *New York Herald*, February 16, 1857.

63 "...for you to advocate in a different arena:" The son of local militia captain Stephen Hersey, Henry attended Hingham public schools and Hingham's Derby Academy. He graduated from Harvard College in 1850. He was a private tutor in Charlestown, New Hampshire, and studied law in the office of Honorable Peleg W. Chandler and Judge John P. Putnam. He was admitted to the Suffolk Bar in September, 1854, and immediately set up practices in Boston and Hingham. Contemporaries described him as "...gentle, quiet, modest, and unobtrusive, yet very social and genial in his nature. He was refined in his tastes, diligent and methodical in his habits, and upright in all his dealings." Bouvé et al. *History of the Town of Hingham, Massachusetts, in Three Volumes; Volume 1,*

Part 2 – *Historical* (Hingham, MA: Published by the town; printed by University Press, John Wilson and Sons, 1893), 331.

65 "...confer with me quietly and I will advise you:" "The Hingham Murder Case: Commitment of Mrs. Gardner for Trial; Strong Proofs." *Boston Evening Transcript*, February 12, 1857.

Chapter 4

66 see the accused and hear the testimony: "The Hingham Tragedy; Our Boston Correspondence; Boston, February 12, 1857; Situation of Hingham; Popular Alarm and Excitement; Sketches of the Murderess and her Victim; How the Poison was Administered; Latest Reports." *New York Herald*, February 16, 1857.

67 *as to be avoided if possible*: "The Hingham Murder Case; Highly Important Evidence; New and Astounding Developments; Medical testimony; Mrs. Gardner Fully Committed for Trial; Verdict of the Coroner's Jury." *Boston Traveler*, February 12, 1857.

69 "...he was so senseless:" "Traveler Extra; The Hingham Murder Case; Continuation of the Examination of Mrs. Gardner." *Boston Traveler*, February 11, 1857.

69 "...he requested me to stay:" Ibid.

71 "...the idea of going further:" Ibid.

73 "as social and cheerful as usual:" "The Husband Poisoner at Hingham." *Connecticut Courant*, (Hartford) February 21, 1857.

74 Dr. Fiske's statements under oath: "The Hingham Murder Case; Highly Important Evidence; New and Astounding Developments; Medical testimony; Mrs. Gardner Fully Committed for Trial; Verdict of the Coroner's Jury." *Boston Traveler*, February 12, 1857.

76 "...have it pass through the stomach," Jackson concluded:" "The Hingham Murder; Interesting Testimony; Dr. Jackson Testifies to Finding a Large Quantity of Arsenic in the Intestines of the Deceased; Mrs. Gardner, the Accused, Fully Committed to Trial; Her Appearance, etc. etc." *Boston Herald*, February 12, 1857.

76 "...looked upon a granite statue:" Ibid.

76 "...between the twenty-seventh and thirty-first days of January last past:" Ibid.

77 "...remand her to Plymouth Jail in the morning:" Ibid.

78 "...place you in irons:" "Our Hingham Correspondence; The Late Murder Case; Conduct of Mrs. Gardner; Her Antecedents." *Boston Herald*, February 19, 1857.

80   "…just penalty for her high crime:" "The Hingham Murder Case; Commitment of Mrs. Gardner for Trial; Strong Proofs of Guilt." *Boston Evening Transcript*, February 12, 1857.

80   "…that iron leg fell to:" "The Hingham Murder." *Lowell Daily Citizen and News*, February 12, 1857.

81   "…on occasions when he was there:" "The Hingham Murder Case; Highly Important Evidence; New and Astounding Developments; Medical Testimony; Mrs. Gardner Fully Committed for Trial; Verdict of the Coroner's Jury." *Boston Traveler*, Evening Edition, February 12, 1857.

81   Abigail in the February 1857 edition: "The Hingham Tragedy! Murder by Poison! A Wife Charged and Arrested; Evidence Against Mrs. Gardner; The Result." *National Police Gazette* [New York, NY], February 21, 1857.

83   his mouth agape, as the carriage pulled away: "Mrs. Gardner." *Hingham Journal and South Shore Advertiser*, February 20, 1857.

83   recently constructed house of correction: D. Hamilton Hurd. *History of Plymouth County, Massachusetts, with Biographical Sketches of Many of its Pioneers and Prominent Men* (Philadelphia: J. W. Lewis & Co., 1884), 5. The jail, a granite structure, was built in 1819; the house of correction was added as a separate building in 1852.

83   approached the jail's entrance at noontime: "Our Hingham Correspondence; The Late Murder Case; Conduct of Mrs. Gardner; Her Antecedents." *Boston Herald*, February 19, 1857.

84   "…when my friends call to see me:" "Mrs. Gardner." *Hingham Journal and South Shore Advertiser*, February 20, 1857.

85   "…husband did away with himself:" "Mrs. Gardner." *Hingham Journal and South Shore Advertiser*, February 20, 1857.

Chapter 5

86   to discuss the Gardner case: *Memorial Biographies of the New England Historic Genealogical Society, Vol. IX, 1890-1897* (Boston: New England Historic Genealogical Society, 1908), 188. Thirty-seven-year-old James Monroe Keith graduated from Brown University in 1845 and three years later was admitted to the Suffolk County Bar. In 1855, Massachusetts Governor Henry Gardner appointed him District Attorney of the Southeastern District, which at that time comprised Norfolk and Plymouth Counties. When the position became elective the following year, Keith won a three-year term.

87   at the Hingham wharves with John Mayhew: Ancestry.com; Massachusetts Wills and Probate Records, 1635-1991; Plymouth County, Probate Estate File 8403, Hosea J. Gardner, 1857.

88   for the support of Abby and Marcus: Ibid.

88   "...Mrs. Davis's home on Main Street:" 1860 United States Federal Census: Hingham, Plymouth, Massachusetts- Roll: M653-519; Page 497. See also, Hingham Historical Society, Hingham, MA, Map of Hingham Village, 1857.

88   "...as an apprentice in his bakery:" 1860 United States Federal Census: Hingham, Plymouth, Massachusetts- Roll: M653-519; Page 468. See also, Hingham Historical Society, Hingham, MA, Map of Hingham Village, 1857.

89   completely equipped American station of its day: Carroll L. V. Meeks. *The Railroad Station: An Architectural History* (New York: Dover Publications, 1995), 51.

90   purchased the fifteen-cent fare: Charles Eben Fisher. *The Story of the Old Colony Railroad* (Taunton, MA: C. A. Hack & Son, 1919), 25.

91   "...Hanover Street, opposite Portland:" "Amusements." *Boston Herald*, March 13, 1857, page 3.

92   "...the mediumship of Mrs. J. H. Conant:" "New Advertisements." *Boston Herald*, morning edition, March 30, 1857.

92   settled in Boston's North End: J. W. Day, T. Parker, Harry Houdini Collection (Library of Congress). *Biography of Mrs. J.H. Conant, the world's medium of the nineteenth century: being a history of her mediumship from childhood to the present time, together with extracts from the diary of her physician, selections from letters received verifying spirit communications given through her organism at the Banner of light free circles: specimen messages, essays, and invocations from various intelligences in the other life, etc., etc., etc..* (Boston: William White and Co., 1873), 17-35.

94   *...and together as forgiveness*: "The Messenger." *Banner of Light* [Boston, MA], April 11, 1857, page 6. http://www.iapsop.com/archive/materials/banner_of_light/banner_o f_light_v1_n1_11_april_1857.pdf, accessed August 1, 2019.

94   "...the 'Message Department' of the '*Banner of Light:*' P. T. Barnum. *The Humbugs of the World: An Account of Humbugs, Delusions, Impositions, Quackeries, Deceits and Deceivers Generally, in all Ages* (New York: Carlton Publisher, 1866), 119-124.

95   handed up a true bill: Indictment of Abigail Gardner, April 13, 1857; Massachusetts Supreme Judicial Archives, Pemberton

Square, Boston, MA; See also "Trial of Mrs. Gardner, at Plymouth, for the Murder of her Husband, Hosea J. Gardner, on the 28th of January, 1857; Supreme Judicial Court; Special Session; Holden at Plymouth; Metcalf, Bigelow and Merrick, Justices; For Government – Attorney General Clifford and District Attorney Keith; For Defense – Charles J. Davis of Plymouth and Hon. B. W. Harris of Bridgewater." *Plymouth Rock*, September 10, 1857.

95   ordered her held without bail: "Arraignment of Mrs. Abigail Gardner." *New Bedford Mercury*, April 24, 1857.

95   among his peers in the legal profession: D. Hamilton Hurd, *History of Plymouth County, Massachusetts, with Biographical Sketches of many of its Pioneers and Prominent Men* (Philadelphia: 1884, J. W. Lewis & Co.), 48-49. Davis was born in Plymouth and attended Derby Academy in Hingham and Plymouth High School. In 1840, he received a Bachelor's degree at Harvard. He studied law in the office of Hon. Jacob H. Loud of Plymouth and at the Dane Law School of Harvard, and was admitted to the Plymouth County bar in 1843.

95   parts of Plymouth County as a state senator: Ibid. 44-45. Attorney Harris was born in East Bridgewater in 1823 and received his early education in the town's public schools, the East Bridgewater Academy, and Phillips Academy in Andover, Massachusetts. After graduation he taught school in various South Shore towns until 1847, when he entered Harvard Law School. He was admitted to the Massachusetts bar in 1850.

95   with walls eight feet high: Documents printed by order of the House of Representatives of the Commonwealth of Massachusetts during the session of the General Court, 1872; House Number 30: First Annual Report of the Commissioners of Prisons, January 1872 (Boston: Wright and Potter, Printers, 1872), 17. https://books.google.com/books?id=GsQXAAAAYAAJ&pg=PA1 &dq=first+annual+report+of+the+prison+commissioners+1872&hl =en&newbks=1&newbks_redir=0&sa=X&ved=2ahUKEwjSieyvo- jnAhWTj3IEHTsHCKsQ6AEwAXoECAMQAg#v=onepage&q=fir st%20annual%20report%20of%20the%20prison%20commissioners %201872&f=false.

95   were lighted by gas: "Legislative Visit to Plymouth." *Boston Traveler*, April 18, 1857.

95   services were conducted once a week: Ibid.

96   the "Lucrezia Borgia of Hingham:" "The Legislative Excursion." *Boston Herald*, April 17, 1857.

96 "...took his own life," said Abigail: "Legislative Visit to Plymouth." *Boston Traveler*, April 18, 1857.

99 a one-term Massachusetts governor: Conrad Reno, LL.B., *Memoirs of the Judiciary and Bar of New England for the Nineteenth Century with a History of the Judicial System of New England*, Volume III (Boston: The Century Memorial Publishing Company, 1901), 164. Clifford was born in Providence, Rhode Island, in 1809, graduated from Brown University in 1827, and studied law with future Supreme Judicial Court justice Theron Metcalf in Dedham, Massachusetts. He also studied with noted defense attorney Timothy Coffin and became a partner in Coffin's office after he was admitted to the Massachusetts bar in 1830. In 1849, Governor Nixon Briggs appointed Clifford attorney general of Massachusetts. In that role, Clifford and District Attorney George Bemis prosecuted Harvard Medical School professor John Webster in the 1850 Parkman murder trial. Clifford was swept into the office of governor in 1852 following his high-profile prosecution of Webster and served one year. He declined his party's nomination for a second term, and newly elected Governor Emory Washburn reappointed him as the Commonwealth's attorney general in 1854.

99 sensational 1850 Parkman murder trial: See Paul Collins. *Blood & Ivy: The 1849 Murder that Scandalized Harvard* (New York: W. W. Norton, Inc., 2019).

99 where the crime occurred assisted him: Joel Parker; William A Richardson; Andrew Augustus Richmond; George Partridge Sanger; Massachusetts. *The General Statutes of the Commonwealth of Massachusetts* (Boston: Wright & Potter, 1860), 129-130; Chapter 14, "of Certain State Officers," Attorney-General and District-Attorneys; Section 17-[Attorney General] "shall appear for the commonwealth, in the supreme judicial court, when held by three or more justices in all, prosecutions for crimes punishable by death; Section 31-"The district attorneys within their respective districts shall appear for the commonwealth in the supreme judicial court and superior court in all cases, criminal or civil, in which the commonwealth is a party or interested; shall aid the attorney general in the duties required of him, and perform all the duties which he is authorized to perform, when he is not required to do the same personally...

101 "...the Commonwealth has hanged one:" Massachusetts Historical Society, *Proceedings of the Massachusetts Historical Society*, Second Series, Volume XIX (Boston: by the Society, 1906), 178-185. The last woman executed in Massachusetts for any crime was

Rachel Wall in 1789. A Suffolk County jury convicted Wall of
highway. See also, Daniel Allen Hearn. *Legal Executions in New
England, 1623-1960* (Jefferson, NC and London: McFarland & Co.,
1999), pages 16, 104, and 122. Alice Bishop was convicted of
murder and hanged in Plymouth in 1648; Esther and Susannah
Andrews were convicted of murder and hanged in Plymouth in
1696; Elizabeth Colson was hanged in Plymouth in 1727 after her
conviction for murder.

102   treat Sophia with zinc oxide ointment, glycerin, and laudanum and
water: John Irvine McKelway, M.D., "Erysipelas," *The Trained
Nurse and Hospital Review*, volume 34 (1905): 381-383.
https://books.google.com/books?id=Q8ICAAAAYAAJ&pg=PA381
&dq=erysipelas+nineteenth+century&hl=en&newbks=1&newbks_r
edir=0&sa=X&ved=2ahUKEwiYk_TPp6foAhXemHIEHa50ADgQ
6AEwAXoECAAQAg#v=onepage&q=erysipelas&f=false.

102   and Lewis did so the next day: "Trial of Abigail Gardner for the
Murder of her Husband." *Weekly Messenger* [Boston, MA],
September 9, 1857.

102   *meet you at the earliest date*: MA Historical Society, Boston – John
H. Clifford papers, 1696-1967, Ms. #N-2158, Box 34, Legal:
Commonwealth v. Gardner, 1857.

103   *as I am at your command*: Ibid.

103   to meet Keith at his Boston office: MA Historical Society, Boston –
John H. Clifford papers, 1696-1967, Ms. #N-2158; John H. Clifford
Diaries, August 22, 1857 entry.

106   *will meet us at the Samoset House*: MA Historical Society, Boston –
John H. Clifford papers, 1696-1967, Ms. #N-2158, Box 34, Legal:
Commonwealth v. Gardner, 1857.

107   "…prepared for him by his wife:" "Death of an Important Witness
in the Gardner Murder Case." *Hingham Journal and South Shore
Advertiser*, August 28, 1857.

107   laid to rest beside her beloved husband, Hosea, at Hingham Centre
Cemetery: "Rumored Death of Mrs. Gardner, of Hingham, from
Poison." *Boston Traveler*, August 27, 1857. See also, Massachusetts
Vital Records, Massachusetts State Archives, Deaths, Hingham,
1857, volume 112, page 292.

108   "…worst woman I have ever had to deal with:" "Letter from
Plymouth; Trial of Mrs. Abigail Gardner for the Murder of her
Husband by Poison; Interview with the Alleged Murderess in Jail,
etc." *Boston Herald*, September 1, 1857.

108   "…a well-directed blow over one of her eyes:" "The Trial of Mrs.
Abigail Gardner for the Murder of her Husband, Hosea J. Gardner,

by Poison, on the 28th January, 1857; Supreme Judicial Court-Special Session for Plymouth County; Before Justices Metcalf, Merrick, and Bigelow." *Boston Herald*, September 2, 1857 (First Edition).

109   "...a verdict of murder against the suspected woman:" "Letter from Plymouth; Trial of Mrs. Gardner." *Boston Traveler*, September 1, 1857.

Chapter 6

122   Boston train bound for Braintree: "South Shore Railroad – Winter Arrangement." *Hingham Journal and South Shore Advertiser*, January 27, 1854.

122   ...bright, balmy day with light breezes: "City and Suburbs; Meteorological." *Boston Traveler*, September 1, 1857.

123   6:35 a.m. for its twelve-mile, half-hour journey to Braintree: "Railroads." *Boston Traveler*, August 25, 1857. Charles Eben Fisher. *The Story of the Old Colony Railroad* (Taunton, MA: C. A. Hack & Son, 1919), 451.

123   double breasted frock coat and straight visor cap: Ibid., 62.

123   passengers might see themselves "as others saw them:" Ibid., 105.

123   steam engine with its bright yellow cars: Ibid., 63, 146.

124   bands of their hoopskirts for comfort: Ibid., 32-33.

124   "...for the past quarter of a century:" "The Trial of Mrs. Gardner for the Murder of her Husband by Poison." *Boston Traveler*, September 1, 1857. This newspaper quote is in error. Hanover resident Seth Perry was tried for murder at the Plymouth County Courthouse in 1845.

126   "...cursing, both loud and deep, [was] accomplished:" "Letter from Plymouth." *New York Evening Mirror*, September 4, 1857.

127   opened the proceedings with a prayer: "Letter from Plymouth; Trial of Mrs. Abigail Gardner for the Murder of her Husband by Poison; Interview with the Alleged Murderess in Jail, etc." *Boston Herald*, September 1, 1857.

127   "...as you have good cause for challenging": Alan Rogers. *Murder and the Death Penalty in Massachusetts* (Amherst and Boston, MA: University of Massachusetts Press, 2008), 297. A peremptory challenge, which is a challenge based on no more than "sudden impressions and unaccountable prejudices the defense was apt to conceive upon the bare looks and gestures of another," guaranteed Abigail a randomly selected and impartial jury. The law also permitted Abigail challenges for cause to identify and exclude those

who might hold biases against her, the prosecution, or the case. The prosecution was denied the use of peremptory challenges, but was allowed challenges for cause. The law also required trial judges to challenge a potential juror for cause to determine if the person had "conscientious scruples or such opinion on the subject of capital punishment as to preclude him from finding a defendant guilty." These challenges allowed the court to empanel a "death qualified jury."

128   Thomas Loring of Plymouth as jury foreman: "The Case of Mrs. Gardner." *Hingham Journal and South Shore Advertiser*, September 18, 1857. Besides Loring, the jury included Timothy French of Kingston; Daniel L. Hayward of Bridgewater; Horatio Howard of West Bridgewater; Thomas C. Standish, Jr., of Plympton; Abiel W. Southworth of Lakeville; William S. White of Plympton; Roland F. Copeland of East Bridgewater; Thomas Ellis, Rochester; Matthew Cushing, Middleboro; Spencer Leonard, Jr., Bridgewater; and Samuel C. Stetson of Marshfield.154 The jurors were between thirty-two and fifty-two years of age. All were farmers with the exception of Loring, a trader; French, a peddler; and White, a shoemaker.

128   "...hearken to your evidence:" George Bemis, Esq. *Report of the Case of John W. Webster, Indicted for the Murder of George Parkman, before the Supreme Judicial Court of Massachusetts* (Boston: Charles C. Little and James Brown, 1850), 5-9.

130   "...in the progress of the trial:" "The Hingham Poisoning Case; Trial of Mrs. Gardner for the Murder of her Husband; Testimony of Dr. Jackson and Others; Conclusion of First Day's Proceedings." *Boston Traveler*, September 2, 1857.

131   to show it was caused by the prisoner: "The Trial of Mrs. Abigail Gardner for the Murder of Her Husband, etc." *Plymouth Rock*, September 10, 1857.

132   "...before anything was deposited:" Ibid.

132   could not have the same effect as arsenic: Ibid.

134   "...poison by arsenic," said Jackson: "Trial of Mrs. Gardner, at Plymouth, for the Murder of her Husband, Hosea J. Gardner, on the 28th of January 1857, etc.; Conclusion of Tuesday's Proceedings." *Boston Post*, September 3, 1857.

134   "...no one but me:" Ibid.

135   "...mercury in calomel is not poisonous," Jackson asserted: "The Trial of Mrs. Abigail Gardner for the Murder of Her Husband, etc." *Plymouth Rock*, September 10, 1857.

135   as the examination neared an end: "Trial of Mrs. Abigail Gardner for the Murder of her Husband, Hosea J. Gardner, by Poison, on the 28th of January 1857." *Boston Herald*, Third Edition, September 2, 1857.

135   "...no decomposition has occurred:" "The Trial of Mrs. Abigail Gardner for the Murder of Her Husband, etc." *Plymouth Rock*, September 10, 1857.

136   "...It contains 100 grains:" "Trial of Mrs. Gardner, at Plymouth, for the Murder of her Husband, Hosea J. Gardner, on the 28th of January 1857." *Boston Post*, September 3, 1857.

136   "...who lived at the cove:" "The Trial of Mrs. Abigail Gardner for the Murder of Her Husband, etc." *Plymouth Rock*, September 10, 1857.

137   "...on the day Mr. Gardner died:" Ibid.

137   not for her but a Paddy woman: Ibid.

139   "...twittering like a flock of bluebirds:" "Trial of Mrs. Abigail Gardner, for the Murder of her Husband, Hosea J. Gardner, by Poison, on the 28th of January 1857." *Boston Herald*, September 3, 1857.

140   ...the court sustained it: "Trial of Mrs. Gardner, at Plymouth, for the Murder of her Husband, Hosea J. Gardner, on the 28th of January 1857, etc.; Conclusion of Tuesday's Proceedings." *Boston Post*, September 3, 1857.

143   "...unless they went in with me:" Ibid.

144   "...specified upon this plan:" Ibid.

Chapter 7

146   "...anything for Mr. Gardner, except us:" "Trial of Mrs. Gardner, at Plymouth, for the Murder of her Husband, Hosea J. Gardner, on the 28th of January 1857, etc.; Conclusion of Tuesday's Proceedings." *Boston Post*, September 3, 1857.

148   "...to a prejudice against Mrs. Gardner:" Ibid.

151   "...her position the warmest sympathy:" Ibid.

153   "...present when your father died? Yes," Abby said: Ibid.

153   "...by my father during his illness:" "Trial of Abigail Gardner for the Murder of her Husband, Hosea J. Gardner, Before the Supreme Court at Plymouth; Wednesday-Second Day." *Boston Daily Bee*, September 3, 1857.

154   introduced them to their patients: "The Electro-Chemical Bath." *Boston Courier*, November 22, 1855; See also, John R. Chapin, *The Historical Picture Gallery or, Scene and Incidents in American*

History, a Collection of Interesting and Thrilling Narratives from the Written and Unwritten, Legendary and Traditionary, History of the United States; Volume 5 (Boston: D. Bigelow & Co., 1856), page 121.

155 "...went to the grave with sorrow soon after:" "Trial of Mrs. Gardner for the Murder of her Husband." *Weekly Messenger* [Boston, MA], September 9, 1857.

155 freely down her face: The Hingham Poisoning Case; Trial of Mrs. Gardner for the Murder of her Husband; Conclusion of Government's Testimony." *Boston Traveler*, September 3, 1857.

155 "...when court resumes at two-thirty:" "Trial of Mrs. Gardner, at Plymouth, for the Murder of her Husband, Hosea J. Gardner, on the 28th of January 1857, etc.; Conclusion of Tuesday's Proceedings." *Boston Post*, September 3, 1857.

160 "...by the swallowing of arsenic:" Ibid. See also, "The Hingham Murder; Interesting Testimony; Dr. Jackson Testifies to Finding a Large Quantity of Arsenic in the Intestines of the Deceased; Mrs. Gardner, the Accused, Fully Committed to Trial; Her Appearance, etc. etc." *Boston Herald*, February 12, 1857.

Chapter 8

162 crochet and knitting work with them: "Trial of Mrs. Gardner at Plymouth for the Murder of her Husband, Hosea J. Gardner, on the 28th of January 1857, etc.; Conclusion of Wednesday's Proceedings." *Boston Post*, September 4, 1857.

163 "...and with great pleasure:" "The Trial of Mrs. Abigail Gardner for the Murder of her Husband, Hosea J. Gardner, by Poison, on the 28th of January 1857." *Boston Herald*, Evening Edition, September 3, 1857.

166 "...Mrs. Gardner was not insane:" Ibid.

166 "...I cannot swear there was any," the physician replied: Ibid.

167 "...but I am not confident:" "The Hingham Poisoning Case; Trial of Mrs. Gardner for the Murder of her Husband; Conclusion of Government's Testimony." *Boston Traveler*, September 3, 1857.

168 "...rest alone on its merits:" "Trial of Mrs. Gardner at Plymouth for the Murder of her Husband, Hosea J. Gardner, on the 28th of January 1857, etc.; Conclusion of Wednesday's Proceedings." *Boston Post*, September 4, 1857.

169 "...of which she now stands charged:" "The Arguments, etc., in the Gardner Murder Case." *Hingham Journal and South Shore Advertiser*, September 11, 1857.

170   Society of the Abolition of Capital Punishment: Alan Rogers, *Murder and the Death Penalty in Massachusetts* (Amherst, MA: University of Massachusetts Press, 2008), 102.

171   with her handkerchief and fan: "Trial of Mrs. Gardner at Plymouth for the Murder of her Husband, Hosea J. Gardner, on the 28th of January 1857, etc.; Conclusion of Wednesday's Proceedings." *Boston Post*, September 4, 1857.

171   "…might so argue before the jury:" "The Hingham Poisoning Case; Trial of Mrs. Gardner for the Murder of her Husband; Conclusion of Government Testimony; Third Day." *Boston Traveler*, September 4, 1857.

173   "…to poison her husband in a week:" "Trial of Mrs. Gardner at Plymouth for the Murder of her Husband, Hosea J. Gardner, on the 28th of January 1857, etc.; Conclusion of Wednesday's Proceedings." *Boston Post*, September 4, 1857.

173   "…would not have made such a confession:" "Trial of Abigail Gardner for the Murder of Her Husband." *Boston Daily Advertiser*, September 4, 1857.

174   "…probably never have been known:" "The Arguments, etc., in the Gardner Murder Case." *Hingham Journal and South Shore Advertiser*, September 11, 1857.

174   "…who is now dead: "Trial of Mrs. Gardner at Plymouth for the Murder of her Husband, Hosea J. Gardner, on the 28th of January 1857, etc.; Conclusion of Wednesday's Proceedings." *Boston Post*, September 4, 1857.

175   "…by sending the boy: Ibid.

175   "…secret places nearby?:" "Trial of Abigail Gardner for the Murder of her Husband." *Weekly Messenger* [Boston, MA], September 9, 1857.

175   windows overlooking Plymouth harbor: "City and Suburbs; Meteorological." *Boston Traveler*, September 4, 1857.

176   "…for God's sake, say so:" "Trial of Abigail Gardner for the Murder of her Husband." *Weekly Messenger* [Boston, MA], September 9, 1857.

179   "…I will let it pass:" "The Arguments, etc., in the Gardner Murder Case." *Hingham Journal and South Shore Advertiser*, September 11, 1857.

179   had spoken for nearly three hours: "Trial of Abigail Gardner for the Murder of her Husband, Hosea J. Gardner, before the Supreme Court at Plymouth." *Boston Daily Bee*, September 4, 1847.

180   "…before court resumes in the morning:" "The Hingham Poisoning Case; Trial of Mrs. Gardner for the Murder of her Husband;

Conclusion of Government Testimony; Third Day." *Boston Traveler*, September 4, 1857.

182   "...not knowing what you do:" "Trial of Mrs. Gardner for Murder." *Evening Standard* [New Bedford, MA], September 4, 1857.

182   more comfortable accommodations at Davis Hall: "The Gardner Trial." *Plymouth Rock*, May 20, 1858.

182   Built in 1854 by Charles Davis, Abigail's defense attorney: *Representative Men and Old Families of Southeastern Massachusetts: Containing Historical Sketches of Prominent and Representative Citizens and Genealogical Records of Many of the Old Families, Volume II* (Chicago: J.H. Beers & Co., 1912), 564.

182   two spacious halls: William T. Hollis, *Old Plymouth: a Guide to its Localities and Objects of Interest* (Plymouth, MA: Avery & Doten, 1881), 85.

182   all fitted with gas lighting: "Davis's Assembly Rooms." *Plymouth Rock*, February 8, 1855.

Chapter 9

183   six for conviction, six for acquittal: "The Trial of Mrs. Gardner; Disagreement of the Jury." *Boston Post*, September 7, 1857.

183   "...they should have no sleeping facilities:" "Trial of Abigail Gardner for the Murder of her Husband." *Weekly Messenger* [Boston, MA], September 9, 1857.

184   The jurors had remained firm: "The Case of Mrs. Gardner." *Hingham Journal and South Shore Advertiser*, September 18, 1857.

185   to try the case again: "The Hingham Poisoning Case; Trial of Mrs. Gardner for the Murder of her Husband; Disagreement of the Jury." *Boston Traveler*, September 5, 1857.

187   "...increase in murder, I don't agree:" Alan Rogers, *Murder and the Death Penalty in Massachusetts* (Amherst, MA: University of Massachusetts Press, 2008), 112-113.

187   "...our most important link in the chain:" "The Hingham Poisoning Case." *Weekly Messenger* [Boston, MA], September 9, 1857.

190   "...in the trial that has passed:" "Trial of Mrs. Gardner; Disagreement of the Jury." *Plymouth Rock*, September 10, 1857.

193   "...*impaired in the least degree*:" "The Gardner Trial." *Plymouth Rock*, September 24, 1857.

194   publicly hanged on August 30, 1850: "The Execution of Prof. John White Webster for the Murder of Dr. George Parkman in the Medical College in Boston on the 23rd of November 1849." *Boston Evening Transcript*, August 30, 1850.

"…against the prisoner on that ground:" "The Case of Mrs. Gardner." *Hingham Journal and South Shore Advertiser*, October 16, 1857.

196 *in case the charge is not sustained*: "The Case of Mrs. Gardner." *Hingham Journal and South Shore Advertiser*, October 23, 1857.

198 *…from Judas Iscariot to Mrs. Gardner*: "The Case of Mrs. Gardner." *Hingham Journal and South Shore Advertiser*, October 30, 1857.

198 left the jail in the guard's charge: "Mrs. Gardner." *Boston Traveler*, January 14, 1858.

200 "…*give all to know, to see, and to praise Thee*:" "The Messenger." *Banner of Light* [Boston, MA], September 10, 1857, page 7. http://www.iapsop.com/archive/materials/banner_of_light/banner_o f_light_v1_n23_10_september_1857.pdf, accessed September 29, 2019.

200 deciding the degree of murder upon the jury: Alan Rogers. *Murder and the Death Penalty in Massachusetts* (Amherst and Boston: University of Massachusetts Press, 2008), 112-113. See also, "The Legislature." *The Congregationalist* [Boston, MA], April 2, 1858.

201 appointed her as Hingham Postmistress: Record of Appointment of Postmasters, 1832-1971. National Archives and Records Administration; Microfilm Publication, M841, 145 rolls; Records of the Post Office Department; Record Group Number 28; Washington, D.C; volume 27, 1857-1876.

202 Sunday school teacher at the Baptist church: "Funeral of Mr. Levi Hersey." *Hingham Journal and South Shore Advertiser*, April 13, 1900.

202 Piano Company on Harrison Avenue in Boston: Boston City Directory, 1869, page 306.

203 approved the petition after a brief hearing: Ancestry.com; Massachusetts Wills and Probate Records, 1635-1991; Plymouth County, Probate File 8418, Guardian's Bond, book 11, page 108, 1858.

Chapter 10

203 established the position as an elective office: Louis Adams Frothingham. *A Brief History of the Constitution and Government of Massachusetts with a Chapter on Legislative Procedure* (Cambridge, MA: Harvard University, 1916), 53-54.

203 in the general election: "The New State Administration." *Boston Evening Transcript*, November 4, 1857.

203 Boston Police officer Ezekiel W. Hodsdon: "The East Boston Murder; Arraignment of the Murderer." *Boston Herald*, January 27, 1858.

205 mostly cloudy Wednesday: "City Matters; Meteorological." *Boston Traveler*, May 19, 1858.

205 and her complexion was sallow: "Second Trial of Abigail Gardner for the Murder of Her Husband." *Boston Traveler*, May 19, 1858.

205 guilty of murder in the first or second degree: "Second Trial of Abigail Gardner for the Murder of Her Husband." *Boston Herald*, Wednesday, May 19, 1858.

205 Twelve men were empaneled: "Trial of Mrs. Abigail Gardner for the Murder of Her Husband." *Plymouth Rock*, May 20, 1858. The jurors were Oliver Cobb, Marion; Nathaniel Damon, Pembroke; Edson Ellis, Plympton; James Foster, Kingston; William B. Gibbs, Middleboro; George P. Harden, Bridgewater; Lewis Holmes, Middleboro; John F. Holmes, Kingston; Charles A. Keith, West Bridgewater; Isaac Morton, Plymouth; Charles H. Paine, Halifax; Charles T. Reynolds, North Bridgewater.

205 James Foster, a sixty-four-year-old farmer, as jury foreman: "Second Trial of Abigail Gardner for the Murder of Her Husband." *Boston Traveler*, May 19, 1858.

206 to determine and confirm the presence of arsenic: Ibid.

206 cold, dreary Thursday: "City Matters; Meteorological." *Boston Traveler*, May 22, 1858.

216 the spot on the plan: "Second Trial of Mrs. Gardner of Hingham for the Murder of Her Husband – Second Day." *Boston Traveler*, May 20, 1858.

215 "...ever put before a jury: "The Gardner Trial." *Plymouth Rock*, May 20, 1858.

218 "...it will bear the tests of this rule:" "Trial of Mrs. Gardner; Third Day; Defense." *Plymouth Rock*, May 27, 1858.

218 Dr. Augustus Hayes, an eminent Boston consulting chemist and state assayer: "Augustus Allen Hayes." *Proceedings of the American Academy of Arts and Sciences* 18 (1882): 422-27. Accessed May 1, 2020. www.jstor.org/stable/25138705.

221 "...the cause of Mr. Gardner's death:" "The Hingham Murder Trial." *Boston Herald*, May 21, 1858.

222 "...will present its closing argument:" Ibid.

222 "...victim for punishment and death:" "Second Trial of Mrs. Gardner of Hingham, for the Murder of her Husband; Closing Plea." *Boston Traveler*, May 22, 1858.

225 "...with you I leave it:" Ibid.

Chapter 11

226 "...more than any of you here:" "Trial of Mrs. Gardner; Third Day; Defense." *Plymouth Rock*, May 27, 1858.

227 "...murder is to be found by the jury:" Ibid.

227 "...I commit the case to you:" Charles G. Davis. *Report of the Trial of Samuel M. Andrews, Indicted for the Murder of Cornelius Holmes, before the Supreme Judicial Court of Massachusetts* (New York: Hurd and Houghton, 1869), 260.

228 the jurors replied in unison: "Trial of Mrs. Gardner; Third Day; Defense." *Plymouth Rock*, May 27, 1858.

228 first in Massachusetts under the new law: "Cases conducted and argued by the Attorney-General from January 1, 1858, to January 1, 1859." Stephen H. Phillips. *Annual Report of the Attorney-General to the [MA] Legislature, February 1859*: House, No. 90, (Boston: William White, Printer to the State, 1859), 14-35. Besides Abigail's murder trial, the attorney general prosecuted two others: Commonwealth v. Francis E. Heath and Miriam Y. Heath, Middlesex County, June 1-3 (page 20); Commonwealth v. William McNulty, Suffolk County, December 14-18 and December 21-24 (page 34). The defendants in each trial were found guilty of murder in the second degree.

229 "...appearance and beginnings of evil:" "Mrs. Gardner's Trial." *Hingham Journal and South Shore Advertiser*, May 28, 1858.

229 "...crime will be much more certain:" "Hanging Abolished." *Plymouth Rock*, June 3, 1858

231 *...before the jury retired*: Commonwealth v. Abigail Gardner; Supreme Judicial Court Archives and Records, Boston, MA. See also, "Mrs. Gardner's Trial." *Hingham Journal and South Shore Advertiser*, May 28, 1858.

231 vials in the jury room during deliberation: "Mrs. Gardner's Trial." *Hingham Journal and South Shore Advertiser*, May 28, 1858.

231 "...to await the decision of the court:" Ibid.

231 "...forgive her for what she has done to Father:" "Confessed her Crime; Abigail Gardner on Death Bed Tells of a Deed of Murder." *Boston Daily Globe*, June 22, 1885.

232 had resigned to enter private practice: "Executive Appointments." *Boston Herald*, June 30, 1858.

232 in session at Taunton, Massachusetts: "Mrs. Gardner." *Plymouth Rock*, November 4, 1858.

232 on November third for sentencing: *Commonwealth vs. Abigail Gardner*; 11 Gray 438, 77 Mass. 438, October 1858.

233 her children had stayed away: "Mrs. Gardner." *Boston Traveler*, January 14, 1858.

233 committed her to the Plymouth House of Correction: *The General Statutes of the Commonwealth of Massachusetts* (Boston: Wright and Potter, 1860), 845-846. Chapter 174, Section 14 – When sentence of confinement at hard labor for any term of time is awarded against a female convict of whatever age, the court shall order such sentence to be executed either in the house of correction or jail, and not in the state prison.

233 "...suffering the merited penalty:" "Sentence of Mrs. Gardner." *Hingham Journal and South Shore Advertiser*, November 5, 1858.

234 Master of the House of Correction: "Political; Plymouth County Convention." *Weekly Messenger* [Boston, MA], October 19, 1859.

234 for his use at county expense:" "James Bates." *The Old Colony Memorial* [Plymouth, MA], October 12, 1876. Often referred to as "Major" Bates, a military title he had earned during his service with the Abington Artillery Company, he was described by the *Old Colony Memorial* as "a man of commanding physique and fine personal appearance, with very cordial and genial presence. He was generous, frank and kind, and any appeal for charity or aid found a ready response from his heart and hand."

234 serving a life sentence for murder: 1860 United States Federal Census: Plymouth, Plymouth, Massachusetts; Roll: M653_518; Page: 22.

234 "...if Mother was freed:" "Expiated Her Crime; Death after Imprisonment of Twenty-Seven Years; the Crime of Which Abigail Gardner Was Convicted; Confession of an Offense Committed in Jail." *The Daily Mercury* [New Bedford, MA], June 22, 1885.

234 fallen overboard and had drowned: "Melancholy Case of Drowning." *Hingham Journal*, October 18, 1861. See also, Massachusetts Vital Records, Massachusetts State Archives, Deaths, Hingham, 1861, volume 148, page 320; also, "Massachusetts, Town Clerk, Vital and Town Records, 1626-2001," database with images, FamilySearch (https://familysearch.org/ark:/61903/3:1:3QS 7-9979-QF8L?cc=2061550&wc=Q4DW-GPV%3A353350201%2C353451301%2C353456501 : 20 May 2014), Plymouth > Hingham > Births, marriages, deaths 1845-1880 > image 277 of 453; citing Massachusetts Secretary of the Commonwealth, Boston. This record indicates the place of death as

Kingston Harbor, New Brunswick, Canada, and place of burial as Hingham Centre Cemetery.

234　off the coast of Nova Scotia: "Resolutions on the Death of Marcus H. Gardner." *Hingham Journal and South Shore Advertiser*, October 25, 1861.

235　the Sons will see to a proper burial: Sons of Temperance of North America. *Constitutions of the Order of the Sons of Temperance of North America* (Philadelphia: Craig and Young, Printers, 1849), 14.

236　a proclamation in the *Hingham Journal*: "Resolutions on the Death of Marcus H. Gardner." *Hingham Journal and South Shore Advertiser*, October 25, 1861.

236　His first wife, Caroline Gates Whitmarsh: Massachusetts Vital and Town Records, Marriages, Boston, 1847, volume 1, page 453. The couple married on March 21, 1847.

237　at age two of cholera infantum: Massachusetts Vital Records, Massachusetts State Archives, Deaths, Hingham, 1848, volume 41, page 89.

237　Mortification (gangrene) took the life of thirty-one-year-old Caroline: Massachusetts Vital and Town Records, Boston, 1855, volume 95, page 31.

237　married Caroline's younger sister, Mary: Massachusetts Vital and Town Records, Intentions of Marriage Entered, Town of Hingham, 1858, #27.

237　Ira Grover Hersey was born in 1860: Massachusetts Vital Records, Massachusetts State Archives, Births, Hingham, 1860, volume 133, page 378.

237　Ira's birth of physical and mental exhaustion: Massachusetts Vital Records, Massachusetts State Archives, Deaths, Hingham, 1860, volume 139, page 175.

237　filed their intention to marry: Massachusetts Vital and Town Records, Hingham, Marriages Intended, 1863.

237　at the First Baptist Church: Massachusetts Vital Records, Massachusetts State Archives, Marriages, Hingham, 1863, volume 163, page 245.

237　Abby made her home: Massachusetts State Census, Hingham, Plymouth County, house #25, May 1, 1865.

237　resigned from her position as postmistress: Record of Appointment of Postmasters, 1832-1971. NARA; Microfilm Publication, M841, 145 rolls; Records of the Post Office Department, Record Group Number 28; Washington, D.C.: National Archives; volume 27 - 1857-1876; Plymouth County; page 91.

237 to the newly constructed Lincoln Building on South Street: Bouvé, et al. *History of the Town of Hingham, Massachusetts, in Three Volumes; Volume 1, Part 2, Historical* (Hingham, MA: Published by the town; printed by University Press, John Wilson and Sons, 1893), 383-384.

237 Levi's late wives: Massachusetts Vital Records, Massachusetts State Archives, Births, Hingham, 1864, volume 169, page 345.

237 died the next day: Massachusetts Vital Records, Massachusetts State Archives, Deaths, Hingham, 1868, volume 212, page 310.

237 Annie Ives, born in 1871: Massachusetts Vital Records, Massachusetts State Archives, Births, Hingham, 1871, volume 233, page 447. Annie was born on May 14, 1871.

237 Alice Bradford, born in 1874: Massachusetts Vital Records, Massachusetts State Archives, Births, Hingham, 1874, volume 260, page 350. Alice was born on July 6, 1874.

237 assigned her to domestic duties: Massachusetts State Census, 1865, Plymouth, 16 Jun 1865, dwelling house 578. Massachusetts. 1855–1865 Massachusetts State Censuses: New England Historic Genealogical Society, Boston.

237 to the Bristol County House of Correction at New Bedford: Massachusetts State Archives, Boston, MA; Bristol County House of Correction Records; New Bedford House of Correction calendar, 1829-1976; Return Concerning Prisoners Confined in the House of Correction at New Bedford in the County of Bristol for the Month ending September 30, 1871; reference CY2.03/2705x. https://www.sec.state.ma.us/arc/arcpdf/collection-guides/FA_CY.pdf.

238 inmate expenses to the receiving institution: Documents printed by order of the House of Representatives of the Commonwealth of Massachusetts during the session of the General Court, 1872; House Number 30: First Annual Report of the Commissioners of Prisons, January 1872 (Boston: Wright and Potter, Printers, 1872), 4-7.

238 to offset the institution's expenses: Documents printed by order of the House of Representatives of the Commonwealth of Massachusetts during the session of the General Court, 1872; House Number 30: First Annual Report of the Commissioners of Prisons, January 1872; New Bedford Jail and House of Correction, Charles D. Burt, Keeper and Master (Boston: Wright and Potter, Printers, 1872), 14.

238 assigned her prisoner number 3357: Massachusetts State Archives, Boston, MA; New Bedford House of Correction calendar, 1871-1873; September 30, 1871; Reference CY2.03/2705x.

239 secluded from the rest of the prison's population: Massachusetts State Archives, Boston, MA; New Bedford House of Correction records of conduct, 1856-1937; 1871-1872, page 6; Reference CY2.03/2626x; Abigail was confined on September 6, 1871 for creating a disturbance; https://www.sec.state.ma.us/arc/arcpdf/collection-guides/FA_CY.pdf.

239 stockings, boots, skirt hoops, and a shawl: Massachusetts State Archives, Boston, MA; New Bedford House of Correction Female Department Records, 1858-1956, page 87; Reference CY2.03/2713x. https://www.sec.state.ma.us/arc/arcpdf/collection-guides/FA_CY.pdf.

239 cash in an account under Abigail's name in a local bank: "Thirty Years in Prison; Mrs. Gardner Confesses the Murder of Her Husband; A Case of Poisoning in the Town of Hingham; The Old Lady Acknowledges another Crime." *Boston Herald*, March 6, 1885.

239 "...rebellious fits and half-relentings:" "Thirty Years in Prison; Mrs. Gardner Confesses the Murder of Her Husband; A Case of Poisoning in the Town of Hingham; The Old Lady Acknowledges Another Crime." *Boston Herald*, March 6, 1885.

239 a day without privileges: Massachusetts State Archives, Boston, MA; Bristol County House of Correction Records; Punishment Books, 1842-1973; Bristol County House of Correction 1871, pages 23 and 40; Reference CY2.03/ 2624x. https://www.sec.state.ma.us/arc/arcpdf/collection-guides/FA_CY.pdf. She was confined on July 5, 1872, for talking in her cell.

240 in the top story of the women's building: "Expiated Her Crime; Death after Imprisonment of Twenty-Seven Years; the Crime of Which Abigail Gardner Was Convicted; Confession of an Offense Committed in Jail." *The Daily Mercury* [New Bedford, MA], June 22, 1885.

240 death was imminent: "Thirty Years in Prison; Mrs. Gardner Confesses the Murder of Her Husband; A Case of Poisoning in the Town of Hingham; The Old Lady Acknowledges another Crime." *Boston Herald*, March 6, 1885.

241 hope the good Lord will forgive me: "Confessed an Unknown Crime; A Life Prisoner at New Bedford Accuses herself of an Old Theft." *Boston Daily Globe*, March 6, 1885.

242 the money was stolen proved fruitless: "Thirty Years in Prison; Mrs. Gardner Confesses the Murder of Her Husband; A Case of

Poisoning in the Town of Hingham; The Old Lady Acknowledges another Crime." *Boston Herald*, March 6, 1885.

242 died of uterine cancer: Massachusetts Vital Records, Massachusetts State Archives, Deaths, New Bedford, volume 364, page 137, #388. See also, Massachusetts State Archives, Boston, MA; New Bedford House of Correction Female Department Records, 1858-1956; Box 1, Calendar; Reference CY2.03/2713x, , 1885, page 85.

243 by express to Abby's husband, Levi: Massachusetts State Archives, Boston, MA; New Bedford House of Correction Female Department Records, 1858-1956; Box 1, Calendar; Reference CY2.03/2713x, , 1885, page 85.

243 Abigail's family was present: "Confessed Her Crime; Abigail Gardner on Her Death Bed Tells of a Deed of Murder." *Boston Daily Globe*, June 22, 1885.

243 in the ignominy of a solitary, unmarked grave: Massachusetts, Town Clerk, Vital and Town Records, 1626-2001; Bristol; New Bedford; Deaths 1883-1889; vol. 5; image 44 of 128; citing Massachusetts Secretary of the Commonwealth, Boston. https://www.familysearch.org/ark:/61903/3:1:3QS7-99Q1-SSV7?i=43&wc=Q4DS-N3V%3A353350701%2C353461901%2C353470601&cc=2061550 ; Massachusetts State Archives, Deaths, New Bedford, 1885, volume 5, page 39, #388.

Bibliography

Books

Barnum, P. T. The Humbugs of the World: An Account of Humbugs, Delusions, Impositions, Quackeries, Deceits and Deceivers Generally, in all Ages (New York: Carleton Publisher, 1866)

Baughman, Shima Baradaran. The Bail Book – A Comprehensive Look at Bail in America's Criminal Justice System (Cambridge, England: Cambridge University Press, 2018)

Beers, J. H. & Co. *Representative Men and Old Families of Southeastern Massachusetts: Containing Historical Sketches of Prominent and Representative Citizens and Genealogical Records of Many of the Old Families, Volume II* (Chicago: J.H. Beers & Co., 1912)

Bell, Suzanne. *Drugs, Poisons, and Chemistry* (New York: Facts on File, 2009)

Bemis, George, Esq. *Report of the Case of John W. Webster, Indicted for the Murder of George Parkman, before the Supreme Judicial Court of Massachusetts* (Boston: Charles C. Little and James Brown, 1850)

Bigelow, E. Victor. *A Narrative History of the Town of Cohasset, Massachusetts* (Cohasset, MA: The Committee on Town History, 1898)

Blum, Deborah. *The Poisoner's Handbook: Murder and the Birth of Forensic Medicine in Jazz Age New York* (New York: Penguin Group USA, 2010)

Bouvé, Thomas Tracy; Bouvé, Edward Tracy; Long, John Davis; Bouvé, Walter Lincoln; Lincoln, Francis Henry; Lincoln, George; Hersey, Edmund ; Burr, Fearing; Seymour, Charles Winfield Scott. *History of the Town of Hingham, Massachusetts, in Three Volumes* (Hingham, MA: Published by the town; printed by University Press, John Wilson and Sons, 1893)

Bradford, Adam C. *Communities of Death: Whitman, Poe, and the American Culture of Mourning* (Columbia, MO: University of Missouri Press, 2014)

Breiger, Carl H. *Medical America in the Nineteenth Century: Readings from the Literature* (Baltimore: The Johns Hopkins University Press, 2009)

Breslaw, Elaine G. *Lotions, Potions, Pills, and Magic: Health Care in Early America* (New York and London: New York University Press, 2012)

Britten, Emma Hardinge. *Modern American Spiritualism: A Twenty Years'*

Record of the Communion between Earth and the World of Spirits (New York: By the Author, 1872)

Bryant, Clifton D. *Handbook of Death and Dying*, Volume 1-The Presence of Death (Thousand Oaks, CA: Sage Publications, 2003)

Carlisle, Sir Anthony, F. R. S., *Practical Observations on the Preservation of Health and the Prevention of Diseases; Comprising the Author's Experience on the Disorders of Childhood and Old Age, on Scrofula, and on the Efficacy of Cathartic Medicines* (London: John Church, 1838)

Chapin, John R. *The Historical Picture Gallery or, Scene and Incidents in American History, a Collection of Interesting and Thrilling Narratives from the Written and Unwritten, Legendary and Traditionary, History of the United States*; Volume 5 (Boston: D. Bigelow & Co., 1856)

Coffin, Margaret M. *Death in Early America: The History and Folklore of Customs and Superstitions of Early Medicine, Funerals, Burials, and Mourning* (Nashville, New York: Thomas Nelson, Inc., 1976)

Collins, Paul. *Blood & Ivy: The 1849 Murder that Scandalized Harvard* (New York: W. W. Norton, Inc., 2019).

Crissman, James K. *Death and Dying in Central Appalachia: Changing Attitudes and Practices* (Urbana and Chicago: University of Illinois Press, 1994)

Daughters of the American Revolution-Old Colony Chapter. *Hingham: A Story of its Early Settlement and Life, Its Ancient Landmarks, its Historic Sites and Buildings* (Hingham, MA: Old Colony Chapter, Daughters of the American Revolution, 1911)

Davis, Charles G. *Report of the Trial of Samuel M. Andrews, Indicted for the Murder of Cornelius Holmes, before the Supreme Judicial Court of Massachusetts* (New York: Hurd and Houghton, 1869)

Day, J. W., Parker, T., Harry Houdini Collection (Library of Congress). (1873). *Biography of Mrs. J.H. Conant, the world's medium of the nineteenth century: being a history of her mediumship from childhood to the present time, together with extracts from the diary of her physician, selections from letters received verifying spirit communications given through her organism at the Banner of light free circles: specimen messages, essays, and invocations from various intelligences in the other life, etc., etc., etc..* (Boston: William White and Co., 1873)

Emsley, John. *The Elements of Murder: A History of Poison* (New York: Oxford University Press, Inc., 2005)

Farrow, John Pendleton. *History of Islesborough, Maine* (Bangor, ME: Thomas Burr, Printer, 1893)

Fisher, Charles Eben. *The Story of the Old Colony Railroad* (Taunton, MA: C. A. Hack & Son, 1919)

Foley, Mason A. and Stetson, George W. *Hingham: Old and New* (Hingham, MA: The Tercentenary Committee for the Town of Hingham, 1935)

Forbes, John, M.D., F.R.S., F.G.S. *Temperance and Teetotalism: An Inquiry into the Effects of Alcoholic Drinks on the Human System in Health and Disease* (London: John Church, Prince Street, SoHo, 1847), 30

Frothingham, Louis Adams. *A Brief History of the Constitution and Government of Massachusetts with a Chapter on Legislative Procedure* (Cambridge, MA: Harvard University, 1916)

Gallagher John F. *A History of Homicide in Hanover: Murder on Broadway* (Whitman, MA: Riverhaven Books, 2015)

Gore, Henry Watson. *The Independent Corps of Cadets of Boston, Mass., at Fort Warren, Boston Harbor, in 1862* (Boston: Press of Rockwell and Churchill, 1888)

Hager, Louis P. and Handy, Albert D. *A Complete History of the Old Colony Railroad from 1844 to the Present Time in Two Parts* (Boston, MA: Hager and Handy Publishers, 1893)

Hardinge, Emma. *Modern American Spiritualism: A Twenty Years' Record of the Communion between Earth and the World of Spirits* (New York: by the author, 1870)

Harrington, Thomas Francis. *The Harvard Medical School; A History, Narrative and Documentary, Volume 2* (New York: Lewis Publishing Company, 1905)

Harris, Mark. *Grave Matters: A Journey through the Modern Funeral Industry to a Natural Way of Burial* (New York: Scribner, 2007)

Hart, Lorena Laing and Hart, Francis Russell. *Not All Is Changed: A Life History of Hingham* (Hingham, MA: The Hingham Historical Commission, 1993)

Henkin, David M. *The Postal Age: The Emergence of Modern Communications in Nineteenth Century America* (Chicago: The University of Chicago Press, 2006)

Hollis, William T. *Old Plymouth: a Guide to its Localities and Objects of Interest* (Plymouth, MA: Avery & Doten, 1881)

Hurd, D. Hamilton. *History of Plymouth County, Massachusetts, with Biographical Sketches of Many of its Pioneers and Prominent Men* (Philadelphia: J. W. Lewis & Co., 1884)

John, Richard R. *The American Postal System from Franklin to Morse* (Cambridge: Harvard University Press, 1995)

Laderman, Gary. *The Sacred Remains: American Attitudes toward Death, 1799-1883* (New Haven, London: Yale University Press, 1996)

Leech, D. D. T. *Post Office Directory or Business Man's Guide to the Post Offices in the United States* (New York: J. H. Colton & Co., 1856)

Lightfoot, D. Tulla. *The Culture and Art of Death in 19th Century America* (Jefferson, NC: McFarland and Company, 2019)

Lund, Orland. *The Order of the Sons of Temperance: Its Origin, Its History, Its Secrets, Its Objects, Its Designs, Its Influence* (New York: Barns, Smith and Cooper, 1848)

McKelway, John Irvine, M.D., "Erysipelas," *The Trained Nurse and Hospital Review*, volume 34 (New York: The Lakeside Publishing Co., 1905)

Meeks. Carroll L. V. *The Railroad Station: An Architectural History* (New York: Dover Publications, 1995)

Members of the Faculty of the Yale Law School. *Two Centuries' Growth of American Law* (New York: Charles Scribner's Sons, 1901)

New England Historic Genealogical Society. *Memorial Biographies of the New England Historic Genealogical Society, Vol. IX, 1890-1897* (Boston: New England Historic Genealogical Society, 1908)

Nunnamaker, Albert John, A. B., and Dhonau, Charles Otto. *Anatomy and Embalming: A Treatise on the Science and Art of Embalming, the Latest and Most Successful Methods of Treatment and the General Anatomy Relating to This Subject* (Cincinnati: The Embalming Book Company, 1913)

Pierotti, James. *Hingham* (Charleston, SC: Arcadia Publishing, 2005)

Prescott, Joshua, Esq. *A Digest of the Probate Laws of Massachusetts, Relative to the Power and Duty of Executors, Administrators, Guardians, Heirs, Legatees, and Creditors* (Boston: True and Greene, 1824)

Putnam, Allen. *Flashes of Light from the Spirit-Land through the Mediumship of Mrs. J. H. Conant* (Boston: William White and Co., 1872)

Rand, John C. *One of a Thousand: a Series of Biographical Sketches of One Thousand Representative Men Resident In the Commonwealth of Massachusetts, A.D. 1888-89* (Boston: First National Publishing Company, 1890)

Reno, Conrad, LL.B. *Memoirs of the Judiciary and Bar of New England for the Nineteenth Century with a History of the Judicial System of New England*, Volume III (Boston: The Century Memorial Publishing Company, 1901)

Rogers, Alan. *Murder and the Death Penalty in Massachusetts* (Amherst and Boston, MA: University of Massachusetts Press, 2008)

Smith, Thomas, F.R.C.S, and Walsham, William J., F.R.C.S. *A Manual of Operative Surgery on the Dead Body*, Second Edition (London: Longmans, Green, and Co., 1876

Sweeney, Kate. *American Afterlife: Encounters in the Customs of Mourning*

(Athens, GA: University of Georgia Press, 2014)

Tarbell, Ida Minerva. *Abraham Lincoln and His Ancestors* (Lincoln, NE: University of Nebraska Press, 1997, copyright 1924)

Taylor, Alfred S., F.R.S. *On Poisons, in Relation to Medical Jurisprudence and Medicine* (Philadelphia: Lea and Blanchard, 1848)

Taylor, C. F., M.D., Ed. *The Medical World*, Volume 3 (Philadelphia: The Medical World, 1885)

Vernor, E. R. *The Book of the Dead: Death and Mourning through the Ages* (Ft. Wayne, IN: Dark Moon Press, 2016)

Volo, James M. and Volo, Dorothy Denneen. *The Antebellum Period* (Westport, CT: Greenwood Press, 2004)

Wells, S. R., Ed. *The Phrenological Journal and Life Illustrated*, Volumes 54-55 (New York: Samuel R. Wells, 1872)

Whorton, James C. *The Arsenic Century: How Victorian Britain was Poisoned at Home, Work, and Play* (New York: Oxford University Press, 2010)

Wolfe, Richard J., Patterson, Richard. *Charles Thomas Jackson: The Head behind the Hands* (Novato, CA: Historyofscience.com, 2007)

Newspapers and Periodicals

Banner of Light [Boston, MA], 1857
Boston Courier, 1855
Boston Daily Advertiser, 1857
Boston Daily Atlas, 1856
Boston Daily Bee, 1857
Boston Evening Transcript, 1850, 1857
Boston Globe
Boston Herald
Boston Post, 1857
Boston Traveler 1857, 1858
Connecticut Courant [Hartford, CT], 1857
Daily Mercury [New Bedford, MA], 1885
Evening Standard [New Bedford, MA], 1857
Hingham Journal and South Shore Advertiser, 1854
Hingham Patriot, 1846, 1847, 1848
Lowell Daily Citizen and News, 1857
National Police Gazette [New York, NY], 1857
New Bedford Mercury, 1857
New York Herald
New York Evening Mirror
Old Colony Memorial [Plymouth, MA], 1857, 1876
Plymouth Rock, 1857
Republican Journal [Belfast, ME], 1857
Weekly Messenger [Boston, MA], 1857

Characters

Victim:
Hosea James Gardner, Hingham Postmaster (1810-1857)

Accused:
Abigail Marshall Gardner, Hosea's wife (1805-1885)

Family:
Abigail (Abby) Williams Gardner (1836-1909), Hosea's daughter; Abby raised her three daughters until they all married. She suffered a stroke and died in Elyria, Ohio, while visiting her daughter, Mary Campbell. Her body is interred at Hingham Cemetery alongside her husband, Levi Hersey.

Marcus Henry Gardner (1844-1861), Hosea's son

Sophia (Cole) Gardner (1791-1857), Hosea's mother

Reuben Reed (1809-1878), Hosea's brother-in-law; Reuben died at his Leavitt Street home of pulmonary consumption. His wife, Sophia Alice (Gardner) Reed, died of diabetes mellitus in 1895. Both are buried in Hingham Centre Cemetery.

Family Friends:
Edwin Wilder, II (1829-1906), house painter and glazier; Edwin died of cystitis at his 688 Main Street home and is buried in Hingham's High Street Cemetery.

Otis Hersey (1818-1883), silk and tassel maker; Otis died at his home in South Scituate (Norwell) of gangrene. He is buried in Norwell's First Parish Cemetery.

Lucinda Lincoln (1817-1902), lived in the house adjoining the Gardner home; Lucinda died at the State Lunatic Hospital in Taunton, MA, of senile insanity. She is buried in Hingham Cemetery.

Levi Hersey (1822-1900), guardian to Marcus Henry Gardner; husband of Abigail (Abby) Williams Gardner; Levi died at his home on South Street of pneumonia. He is buried in Hingham Cemetery with Abby.

285

Inquest:

James Stockbridge Lewis (1798-1889), Justice of the Peace and Coroner; James died of heart disease at his home on Pleasant Street. He is buried with his wife, Abigail Briggs Lewis, in Hingham Centre Cemetery.

Inquest Jury:

David Fearing (1789-1876), grocer, Hingham Centre; David died at eighty-seven of "old age;" buried in Hingham Centre Cemetery.

Martin Fearing (1785-1868), trader, Hingham Centre; Martin died of paralysis and "old age;" buried in Hingham Centre Cemetery.

Peter Sprague (1773-1868), shoemaker, Hingham Centre; Peter died of apoplexy; buried in Hingham Centre Cemetery.

Joseph Sprague (1822-1888), shoemaker, Hingham Centre; Joseph died of heart disease; buried in Hingham Centre Cemetery.

George Bayley (1828-1907), carpenter, Hingham Centre; George died of chronic bronchitis; he is buried in Hingham Centre Cemetery.

Demerick Marble (1819-1898), carriage maker, Hingham Centre; he died of cancer and is interred at Hingham Centre Cemetery.

Defense:

Henry Edson Hersey (1830-1863), attorney, Hingham; consumption claimed the life of Henry at age thirty-two; he is buried in Hingham Cemetery.

Judges (First and Second Trial):

Theron Metcalf (1784-1875), Associate Justice, MA Supreme Judicial Court, appointed 1848; Justice Metcalf died of cerebral apoplexy in Boston at age ninety-one. He is interred at Forest Hills Cemetery, Jamaica Plain, MA.

Pliny Merrick, (1794-1867), Associate Justice, MA Supreme Judicial Court, appointed 1843; Justice Merrick died from the effects of paralysis; he is buried in Worcester Rural Cemetery, Worcester, MA.

George Tyler Bigelow (1810-1878), Associate Justice, MA Supreme Judicial Court, appointed 1850; elevated to Chief Justice in 1860; Bigelow died of gout and nephritis; he is buried with his wife, Anna, in Quincy, MA.

Prosecution:

John Henry Clifford (1809-1876), Attorney General of Massachusetts (1849-1858); Clifford died in New Bedford of heart disease. He is buried at Rural Cemetery in New Bedford, MA.

Stephen Henry Phillips (1823-1897) Attorney General of Massachusetts (1858-1861); Phillips later served as Attorney General and Foreign Minister of Hawaii; he died of jaundice at his home in Salem, MA; he is buried in Harmony Grove Cemetery, Salem.

James Monroe Keith (1819-1894), District Attorney for the Southeastern District of Massachusetts (Plymouth and Norfolk Counties) (1855-1858). Keith died in Boston of heart disease and is buried in Forest Hills Cemetery, Jamaica Plain, MA.

Defense:

Attorney Charles Gideon Davis (1820-1903), Plymouth; Davis died in Plymouth of "old age." He is buried in Vine Hills Cemetery in Plymouth, MA.

Attorney Benjamin Winslow Harris (1823-1907), East Bridgewater; Harris died of hemiplegia at his home in East Bridgewater and is buried in Central Cemetery.

Jury (first trial):

Thomas Loring (1813-1895), (Foreman), Plymouth, merchant; died in Newton, MA, of heart disease; buried in Congregational Church Cemetery, Plympton, MA.

Timothy French (1791-1877), Kingston, farmer; died in Kingston of "old age;" buried in Kingston, MA.

Daniel L. Hayward (1804-1871), Bridgewater, farmer; his cause of death was kidney disease; he is buried in the Vernon Street Cemetery, Bridgewater, MA.

Horatio Howard (1819-1900), West Bridgewater, farmer; influenza took Horatio's life; he is buried in West Bridgewater.

Thomas C. Standish, Jr. (1822-1884), Plympton, farmer; Thomas died in Plympton of consumption. He is buried in Plympton at Congregational Church Cemetery.

Abiel W. Southworth (1798-1868), Lakeville, farmer; Pneumonia claimed his life; he is buried in Ward Cemetery, Lakeville, MA.

William S. White (1818-1897), Plympton, shoemaker; he died of spinal sclerosis in Brockton, MA; he is buried in Plympton, MA

Roland F. Copeland (1815-1903), East Bridgewater, farmer; he died of cystitis and senile insanity in Taunton Insane Asylum; he is buried in Fern Hill Cemetery, Hanson, MA.

Thomas Ellis (1812-1894), Rochester, farmer; Thomas died of "old age" and debility; he is buried with his wife, Amy, in Center Cemetery, Rochester, MA.

Matthew Cushing (1804-1884), Middleboro, farmer; Matthew died at his home in Middleboro of Bright's disease; he is buried in South Middleboro Cemetery.

Spencer Leonard, Jr. (1814-1898), Bridgewater, farmer; he died of paralysis; buried in Pratt Town Cemetery, Bridgewater, MA.

Samuel C. Stetson (1823-1905), Marshfield, bootmaker; a cerebral hemorrhage took the life of Samuel; he is buried in Cedar Grove Cemetery, Marshfield, MA.

Jury (second trial):

Oliver Cobb (1828-1918), Marion, carpenter; a Civil War veteran, Oliver died of heart disease; he is buried with his wife, Lucy, in Old Landing Cemetery, Marion, MA.

Nathaniel Damon (1799-1862), Pembroke, farmer; Nathaniel died of heart disease and is buried with his wife, Mary, in Mount Pleasant Cemetery, Pembroke, MA.

Edson Ellis (1808-1893), Plympton, carpenter; Edson died of senile debility; he is buried in Congregational Church Cemetery, Plympton, MA.

James Foster (1793-1878), (Foreman), Kingston, farmer; a church deacon, James died of "old age" and is buried with his wife, Sarah, in Evergreen Cemetery, Kingston, MA.

William B. Gibbs (1808-1875), Middleboro, farmer; he died of typhoid fever in Carver, MA, where he is buried in Union Cemetery.

George P. Harden (1830-1912), Bridgewater, peddler; a cerebral hemorrhage took George's life; he is buried in Walnut Street Cemetery, Bridgewater, MA.

Lewis Holmes (1811-1865), Middleboro, farmer; dysentery caused his death; he is buried in Rock Cemetery, Middleboro, MA.

John F. Holmes (1830-1896), Kingston, farmer; John died of

apoplexy; he is buried in Evergreen Cemetery, Kingston, MA.

Charles A. Keith (1821-1882), West Bridgewater, farmer; pneumonia claimed his life; he is buried in Pine Hill Cemetery, West Bridgewater, MA.

Isaac Morton (1803-1869), Plymouth, thimble maker; bowel disease caused his death; he is buried with his wife, Betsey, in Chiltonville Cemetery, Plymouth, MA

Charles H. Paine (1820-1899), Halifax, bootmaker; he died of heart disease; he is buried with his wife, Cordelia, in Tomson Cemetery, Halifax, MA.

Charles T. Reynolds (1818-1898), North Bridgewater, shoemaker; Charles died of heart disease; he is buried with his wife, Sarah, in Melrose Cemetery, Brockton, MA.

Physicians:

Dr. Ezra Stephenson (1805-1874), Hosea's primary physician; Ezra continued to practice in Hingham until his death at age sixty-eight of pneumonia.

Dr. Calvin Ellis (1826-1883), Boston physician, performed Hosea's autopsy; Dr. Ellis died of peritonitis in Boston; he is buried in Dedham, MA.

Dr. Robert T. P. Fiske (1799-1866), Hingham physician, assisted Hosea's autopsy; Dr. Fiske died of apoplexy; he is buried in Hingham Cemetery with his wife, Mary.

Dr. Charles Jackson (1805-1880), Boston physician, state assayer; analyzed Hosea's viscera; he was under treatment for insanity at McLean Asylum when he died there at seventy-five years of age; he is buried at Mount Auburn Cemetery, Cambridge, MA.

Dr. Don Pedro Wilson (1821-1863), Hingham dentist, office at Union Hotel; saw Abigail bury slops and later recovered them with John Stephenson and Reuben Reed; the United States government drafted Dr. Wilson during the Civil War. He served in the MA 16th Infantry Regiment, Company A, as a private. He never returned from the war and he was presumed dead when efforts to locate his body failed. His wife, Caroline (Humphrey) Wilson, died of consumption five months before Dr. Wilson was drafted and is buried in Hingham Cemetery. They had no children.

Dr. Walter Channing (1786-1876), witness for the defense; Dr.

Channing died at age ninety of "old age" in Brookline, MA; he is buried in Mount Auburn Cemetery, Cambridge, MA.

Dr. Augustus Allen Hayes (1806-1882), chemist, witness for the defense; Dr. Hayes suffered an aneurysm and died in Brookline, MA; he is buried in Mount Auburn Cemetery, Cambridge, MA.

Religious:

Rev. John Cargill (1823-1883), pastor, First Universalist Church, Hingham; Cargill moved to Woodstock, VT, with his family about 1858; he served as a chaplain during the Civil War with the 5th Regiment, Vermont Infantry; he died in 1883 at a Universalist convention in Brewton, Alabama.

Rev. Jonathan Tilson (1818-1908), pastor, First Baptist Church, Hingham; Tilson remained pastor in Hingham for twenty-five years. He had served as a Baptist minister for fifty-seven years before he died of heart disease at age ninety in Weymouth, MA; he is buried at Forest Hills Cemetery, Jamaica Plain, MA.

Rev. Isaac Coe (1819-1911), pastor, Bonney Street Christian church, New Bedford; chaplain, New Bedford Jail and House of Correction; Rev. Coe died of apoplexy and is buried in Rural Cemetery, New Bedford, MA.

Undertakers:

Joseph Newhall (1822-1912), Hingham carpenter, part-owner, Newhall and Ripley Co.; provided coffin and undertaking services for Hosea; Joseph was three days short of his ninetieth birthday when he fell down a stairway at home and suffered a concussion to the brain; he is buried at Fort Hill Cemetery in Hingham.

Edward Wilson (1837-1919), New Bedford, proprietor, E. T. Wilson Funeral Home; provided coffin and undertaking services for Abigail. Wilson died of arteriosclerosis and is buried in Oak Grove Cemetery, New Bedford. His funeral business is still active as the Wilson Funeral Chapel.

Local Police:

Daniel Phillips (1799-1863) Sheriff, Plymouth County (1857-1860); received Abigail at Plymouth Jail; died of consumption; burial place unknown.

Gridley F. Hersey (1809-1882), Hingham constable and housewright;

arrested Abigail; Gridley died of consumption. He was living with his son, Edwin, at the time of his death; burial place unknown.

County Jail and House of Correction:

Francis J. Goddard (1816-1895), Jailer Keeper and Master, Plymouth County House of Correction; died of heart disease; buried in Plymouth.

James Bates (1810-1876), Jail Keeper and Master, Plymouth County House of Correction, Plymouth; death caused by hemiplegia; he is buried in Colebrook Cemetery, Whitman, MA.

Charles Burt (1821-1895), Jail Keeper and Master, Bristol County House of Correction, New Bedford; died of chronic Bright's disease; buried in New Bedford.

Other Witnesses:

John Todd (1813-1902), Hingham tailor, assisted Hosea after his fall on Broad Bridge; John died at eighty-nine of apoplexy; he reposes at Hingham Cemetery.

James L. Hunt (1807-1884) Hingham druggist, sold arsenic to Charles Dodge; James died of hemiplegia, a condition caused by damage to the brain or spinal cord; he is buried in Hingham Cemetery.

Henry Miller (1841-1864), Hingham boy lived across the street from the Gardners; Henry was shot and killed at the Battle of Laurel Hill, VA, during the Civil War.

Charles Augustus Dodge (1846-?), ran the errand to purchase arsenic for Abigail from James Hunt; Charles moved to Braintree with the Miller family, married a local woman, and had a daughter by this marriage; his whereabouts after 1880 is unknown.

John Stephenson (1808-1906), Hingham weight and balance maker; brother of Dr. Ezra Stephenson; recovered the slops in the Gardner backyard; John died at ninety-six of "old age" and cystitis; he is buried at Hingham Centre Cemetery.

Locations

Gardner Home – The Gardner family lived in an extended section of the Lincoln home at 123 North Street, next to the Hingham Bank at 115 North Street. The Lincoln house was moved to Chatham, Massachusetts, in 1941, and still exists.

Hingham Railroad Depot – The depot was razed in 1949.

Union Hotel – This hotel was also named Drew's Hotel and Cushing House. It was demolished in 1949. It is now the site of the Hingham Post Office.

Hingham Post Office – The 1857 post office was located where the current Winston Flowers stands.

Levi Hersey House – Noah Hersey sold this house to his son, Levi, in 1861. Levi and his wife, Abby (Gardner) Hersey lived there until their deaths. The house still exists and is located at 247 South Street.

John Todd's Tailor Shop – Todd's shop was located in the row of buildings on the eastern side of Main Street, just before the old railroad tracks. Winston Flowers is about where Todd's shop stood.

Hingham Centre Cemetery – The west entrance is located to the right of the J. F. Orr & Sons cabinetmaker shop, 8 Short Street. The gravestones and burial places of Hosea Gardner, Sr. and Sophia Gardner are twenty-five yards beyond the entrance, fifth row, twenty-five feet from the path on the right. No records exist to identify the burial places of Hosea and his son, Marcus, although death records indicate they were interred at Centre Cemetery. They are likely buried near Hosea, Sr. and Sophia.

Hingham Centre Cemetery Receiving Tomb – The tomb where Hosea was placed pending his burial is on the right, about 100 yards from the Short Street entrance.

Thaxter Mansion – Built in 1675 by Captain John Thaxter, the mansion was razed in 1864. St. Paul Catholic Church was erected on the site at 147 North Street in 1872.

Hingham Town Hall – Located at Main Street near Pleasant Street, the building no longer exists. A private dwelling is on the site.

The present town hall was built on Central Street in 1928.

Plymouth County Courthouse – The courthouse was built in 1820. Renovations made to the building in 1857 included the addition of two wings with two separate entrances. The building came into disuse when a new courthouse was built on Obery Street in Plymouth and opened in 2005. The original 1820 building was remodeled once again in 2017 and now serves the community as its Town Hall.

Captain Joseph Woodward House – The house where Abigail was employed as a live-in domestic servant was built in 1820 and still exists at 44 Spring Street in Hingham Centre.

Coroner James Stockbridge Lewis's House – The house was built in 1811 by Captain Adna Cushing and is located at 63 Pleasant Street.

Dr. Ezra Stephenson House – Stephenson built his house in 1851. It is located at 244 Main Street.

Edwin Wilder 2nd House – Edwin's father, Edward, built the Wilder house in 1805. Edwin acquired the house, located at 688 Main Street, near Glad Tidings Rock, in 1853. He conducted his paint and glazier business from the home.

Newhall & Ripley Carpentry Shop – The old shop no longer exists but was located on South Street at Hobart's Bridge.

Charles Seymour House – The architect who drew up the plans used as an exhibit at the Gardner trial built his home in 1850. It is located at 8 Water Street.

First Universalist Church – Built in 1829; no longer a church but a private residence; located at 196 North Street.

First Baptist Church – 89 Main Street, corner of Elm Street; built in 1829.

Praise for *Passion, Poison, and Pretense*

I was gripped by this account of the 1857 Gardner murder—a detailed, absorbing, and compelling page-turner. John Gallagher has given historical fiction fans another richly satisfying, complicated, and well-researched story. Bravo!

~Annie Hartnett, author of *Rabbit Cake*

Passion, Poison, and Pretense: The Murder of Hingham's Postmaster is the type of local history story I have been craving for some time - a concise, engaging, true story of one of the earliest and most well documented murder cases in Massachusetts, right here in our backyard. Filled with wonderful detail, John's book touches not only on this fascinating piece of Hingham history but also how it fits into the broader history of the development of the judicial system in the fledgling United States. I couldn't put it down!

~Michael Achille, Collections Manager,
Hingham Historical Society

About the Author:

John F. Gallagher served in the Boston Police Department for thirty years and rose to the rank of superintendent and chief of detectives before he retired in 2008. His interest in history and genealogy and his background in criminal investigation motivated him to write his first true crime story, *Murder on Broadway*, about three distinct, century-old murders in Hanover, Massachusetts. *Passion, Poison, and Pretense* is his fourth book. John lives in Hanover, Massachusetts, with his wife, Jeanne.

Riverhaven Books

www.RiverhavenBooks.com

$16.95 SET

ISBN 978-1-951854-14-0

9 781951 854140